WOMEN AND IMAGES OF MEN IN CINEMA

WOMEN AND IMAGES OF MEN IN CINEMA

Gender Construction in LA BELLE ET LA BÊTE by Jean Cocteau

Edited by
Andreas Hamburger

Routledge
Taylor & Francis Group
LONDON AND NEW YORK

Originally published in Germany as *Frauen- und Männerbilder im Kino: Genderkonstruktionen in* La Belle et la Bête *von Jean Cocteau* © Psychosozial-Verlag, Giessen, www.psychosozial-verlag.de.

First published 2015 by Karnac Books Ltd.

Published 2018 by Routledge
2 Park Square, Milton Park, Abingdon, Oxon OX14 4RN
711 Third Avenue, New York, NY 10017, USA

Routledge is an imprint of the Taylor & Francis Group, an informa business

British Library Cataloguing in Publication Data

A C.I.P. for this book is available from the British Library

ISBN-13: 9781782202905 (pbk)

Typeset by V Publishing Solutions Pvt Ltd., Chennai, India

CONTENTS

ABOUT THE EDITOR AND CONTRIBUTORS vii

PART I: BEAUTIES AND BEASTS IN FILM PSYCHOANALYSIS

CHAPTER ONE
Women and images of men in cinema 3
Andreas Hamburger

CHAPTER TWO
Psychoanalytical film interpretation—possibilities and limitations 15
Wolfgang Mertens

CHAPTER THREE
Beautiful beasts—motif tradition and film psychoanalysis in Jean Cocteau's LA BELLE ET LA BÊTE (F 1946) 43
Andreas Hamburger

PART II: THE BEAUTIES

CHAPTER FOUR
La Belle, la Bête, et la rose 101
Andrea Sabbadini

CHAPTER FIVE
"You can't say no to the Beauty and the Beast …" Or: an ending and no beautiful beast 111
Christine Kirchhoff

PART III: THE BEASTS

CHAPTER SIX
Once upon a time—Beauty and the Beast—a surrealistic survival attempt in the year 1946? 131
Marianne Leuzinger-Bohleber

CHAPTER SEVEN
Coming over to the wild side: women's yearning for beastly encounters in the course of film history 145
Andreas Rost

INDEX 173

ABOUT THE EDITOR AND CONTRIBUTORS

Andreas Hamburger is professor of psychology at the International Psychoanalytic University, Berlin and psychoanalyst (DPG, DGPT, Akademie für Psychoanalyse und Psychotherapie, Munich), writes on literature, film, and psychoanalysis, among other topics. He is a member of the Munich Work Group on Film and Psychoanalysis.

Christine Kirchhoff is junior professor of psychoanalytic cultural studies at the International Psychoanalytic University, Berlin, and trainee at the BPI, Karl Abraham Institute, Berlin.

Marianne Leuzinger-Bohleber is professor of psychoanalysis in Kassel, director of the Sigmund Freud Institute in Frankfurt, and co-chair of the IPA Research Committee. In addition to her extensive research work, she publishes regularly on topics in film and literary psychoanalysis.

Wolfgang Mertens is professor emeritus of clinical psychology at the Ludwig Maximilian University, Munich, and author of numerous standard works on psychoanalysis.

Andreas Rost, an art historian and film scholar, has taught at the University of Television and Film, Munich, and the Ludwig Maximilian University, Munich and worked as the film specialist for the Cultural Department of the City Administration of Munich.

Andrea Sabbadini, psychoanalyst (IPA), was the editor of the film section of the *International Journal of Psychoanalysis*. In 2001, he founded the European Psychoanalytic Film Festival held every two years in London, which he directs.

Past and current programmes and publications of the Munich Work Group on Film and Psychoanalysis can be retrieved at: www.psychoanalyse-film.eu.

The editor and authors express their gratitude to Prof. Christa Rohde-Dachser and the Stiftung zur Förderung der universitären Psychoanalyse [Foundation to Promote University Psychoanalysis], Berlin, for funding the translation of this book into English.

PART I

BEAUTIES AND BEASTS IN FILM PSYCHOANALYSIS

CHAPTER ONE

Women and images of men in cinema

*Andreas Hamburger**

In one of her most frequently cited texts, "Visual Pleasure and Narrative Cinema" (1975), Laura Mulvey demonstrates that women (in Hollywood films) are a construct of the male gaze. This diagnosis applies to mainstream Hollywood films, not international art house productions—a caveat largely ignored despite repeated clarifications by the author (Mulvey, 1981, 1989, 1996, 2001). Instead, Mulvey's theory has been generalised in the popular assumption that women are defined by the male perspective. And yet in her "Afterthoughts" (1981), taking King Vidor's Duel in the Sun as an example (USA 1946, with Jennifer Jones, Joseph Cotten, and Gregory Peck), the author shows that woman can indeed (in secret?) enjoy sharing the male perspective and that as protagonists they are not restricted to roles as objects. It is even more often overlooked that, in film, the woman's gaze is also cast upon the male body, and that men's roles are designed to appeal to a mixed audience.

Freeing women from imprisoning images was an important emancipatory step. But it was precisely due to this that their captivity was

---

* Translated by Shivaun Conroy & Susan Jones.

prolonged: since then, the female gaze has barely merited discussion (and it was a long time before women began appearing not only in front of, but also behind the camera). Media critique emanating from post-structuralism and feminist film theory based upon it treat the gaze as constitutive in only one direction; when attention does turn to the female cinematic gaze, it is then usually to decipher it as a gesture of gratification or resistance, still trapped in an object status. In their special issue of *Camera Obscura* entitled *The Spectatrix* (1989), J. Bergstrom and M. A. Doane address the theoretical uncertainty that the concept of the "female spectator" has given rise to in feminist film theory. What is a female spectator when understood as a social and textual construct? Is the cultural asymmetry identified by Laura Mulvey also relevant to women in the role of the observer: is their own gaze so strongly determined by patriarchal influences that they remain the object? "For the female spectator there is a certain overpresence of the image—she *is* the image" (Doane, 1982, p. 22). The special issue proposed to give an overview of specifically female approaches to viewing film. Four film theorists from Italy, Canada, Australia, and Great Britain were invited to give a detailed commentary on their positions and more than sixty female film critics were asked for short statements on this controversial question, the intent being to compile their viewpoints historically and set a benchmark (cf. Dressler, 1993 for a trenchant assessment). The outcome reads less like an inquiry into women's film experience and more like a survey among feminist film critics. Marcelline Block refers more accurately to the "feminist gaze" (2010). The question is whether this conception in its delimitation from classical feminist film discourse, focused on the constitution of the female image by the male gaze, can adequately reflect the diversity of real female cinematic perspectives (Dressler, ibid.).

A very personal reflection on this can be found in an essay by Franziska Lamott (1993) on Michael Powell's scandalous film PEEPING TOM (GB 1960). In it, the focus-puller Mark Lewis, who is obsessed with capturing mortal fear on film, to this end stabs women with the sharpened end of a camera tripod, filming them all the while. He comes up against his gently insistent flatmate Helen who is determined, together with her blind mother, to save him from himself. This puts them in danger themselves. As if in an analysis, we learn that he was traumatised by his sadistic father's psychological experiments—but the remedy does not lead to a cure. Mark is killed by his own apparatus. Lamott wonders how the voyeuristic position so dramatically conveyed in the film works for the female spectator. Does she identify with the gaze of the male protagonist? Lamott answers by pointing out the analogy to the empathetic figure of Helen, who appropriates the protagonist's camera, removing the tool on which his filmic distance from actual events depends. It is Helen who notices: this is not so much the male gaze; it is a child's gaze. Indeed Mark, the murderous cinematographer, is surrounded by the insignia of childhood: we see him in films from childhood; the only drink he can offer his guests is milk; his relationship to women is obviously asexual; in his duffle coat, he looks like a nice schoolboy. Lamott's self-inquiry as a spectator extends beyond the gender dichotomy and opens the horizon onto a wider range of female cinema gazes. Widening the horizon of inquiry in this way is consonant with Judith Butler's (1990) challenge that we overcome the gender dichotomy. Accordingly, other critical questions of feminist film theory have come under debate, for instance the concentration on "sex and gender", stemming from the psychoanalytic origin of the discourse, and whether it might overshadow other constitutive parameters of perception such as social status and skin colour (Gaines, 1991). The question of how men in cinema (also) are constructed by the female gaze has been given much less attention (cf. Cohan & Hark, 1993).

Gentle women, tough guys—the (literary) archaeology of a motif

It hasn't always been the case that women were objects, and today they are not exclusively so either. Throughout the history of literature, women have been actively involved in creating images—not necessarily as authors, but definitely as readers (Bollmann, 2013; Brandes, 1994; Schön, 1990), inasmuch as the creation of images is not equated just with the enumeration of heroic deeds, but rather with the construction of experiential worlds, as well. The understanding of literature as a force that shapes subjectivity by giving form to a protagonist perspective sets in with the *Minnesang* (the German mediaeval song and poetry tradition where the addressee was female) at the latest, achieving prominence with the turn to interiority in the eighteenth century. A significant intermediate stage is the Baroque novel, that exquisite literary form directed at women and negotiating conceptions of masculinity and femininity.

Admittedly, the construction of masculine identity is older than the *Minnesang* and the Baroque novel. In almost all pre-literate societies, there were *Rites de Passage* (Van Gennep, 1909), initiation rites usually differing greatly for boys and girls. Male youths are symbolically expelled from society's protective care and, having been tested for their ability to bear loneliness and pain, are accepted back as men. The main purpose of male initiation is, as ethnologists agree, to cut the apron strings and disengage from the mother (Gilmore, 1990; von Schnurrbein, 1997). Since its discovery by classicists and pedagogues around the turn of the twentieth century (see Brunotte, 2000), the initiation of young males has been a major topic of cultural research and theory, with frequent and far-reaching interpretations in the context of homosexuality (for instance through the work of Hans Blüher, 1918).

The situation with girls is different. The emphasis is rather on individual transformation than on a cultural change of status based on a frightening group experience: usually, the menarche serves as the signal for their integration into the social community and the ascription of a social and spiritual role. In the assessment shared by many initiation researchers, both sexes are faced with the task which Victor Turner refers to as "liminality" (1967, 1969, 1982): crossing the border to the sexual body. During adolescence, both boys and girls must learn to "cope with reciprocal sexual anxiety and the envy it generates between the sexes" (Bettelheim, 1954, p. 25). The significant difference: girls do not need to be driven away from their mothers' side, but rather are to become mothers themselves. The goal of their initiation is a psychosocial given. To quote Dieter Schwanitz's witty book *Men*: "Only masculinity is a cultural fiction" (2001, p. 77). Male identity, as culturally defined, is grounded in its differentiation from femininity. Psychoanalysts tend to explain this by a psychosocial asymmetry: boys are different from their mothers and therefore must begin by constructing themselves (cf. Mertens, 1992).

What has been understood as gender identity in various epochs does, however, deserve careful scrutiny. Societies renegotiate their conceptions of gender roles at certain junctures, such as the threshold to literacy—as classical Athens illustrates well. The consolidation of the polis had stimulated discourse on issues of identity: Greek tragedy, and comedy even more so, put inner worlds on display. What role did the female gaze play here? The authors, actors, and choreutai were men; women spectators sat in the back rows. But the chorus, that basso continuo of Greek theatre speaking onstage for the audience, was often exclusively female[1] in its role personality. Here again, the (male) subject is constituted in the mirror of female response.

The masculine ideal that LA BELLE ET LA BÊTE sets out to deconstruct (my hypothesis, see Chapter Three, this volume) is neither as primordial or as old as one might think. It developed in a meandering fashion in the course of Western cultural history. The guiding principle of "hegemonic masculinity" (Connell, 1995) is a late outcome of historically long and lively interchanges. Many times, a process of questioning and re-codifying conceptions of femininity and masculinity was set into motion by situations that put men under pressure to modernise. They were compelled to reflect on their own self-definition in normative terms. A case in point: the "New Adam" of the Renaissance was a reaction to the practice of hypergamous marriage "in which the socially superior woman has the say" (Otis-Cour, 2000, p. 49; quoted from Schmale, 2003, p. 28). It inspired a wave of texts vindicating misogyny and led to a new staging of the male (ibid., pp. 47 f.). It is in this time of increased need for stark distinctions that Boccaccio (1350–1492) rediscovered Apuleius' *The Golden Ass* and one of its stories *Psyche et Cupido* (Amor and Psyche), initiating a veritable flood of depictions of love and ultimately becoming the blueprint for LA BELLE ET LA BÊTE (see Chapter Three, this volume). Renaissance masculinity is, however, by no means so normative as to pre-empt all manner of transgressive playfulness (Schmale, 2003, p. 61 and passim). No link had yet been drawn from anatomical characteristics to male and female behavioural patterns; science assumed that their bodily constitution was essentially alike (ibid., p. 67). Not until the seventeenth century did anatomical studies bring about the transformation from a single to a dual gender model (ibid., p. 69). A specific "gender identity" did not yet exist. The principle that man is made in the image of God unquestioningly equated "man" and "human", without this being grounded in the body (cf. ibid., p. 107).

The great reversal sets in with the Enlightenment and the development of an organised state in French absolutism, as Elias points out in his *Process of Civilisation* (1939). The absolute monarch embodies the man as "hero", not only due to his likeness with God, as had been the case for the "New Adam", but now also as an individual localised within his body and distinguished by specific characteristics (cf. Schmale, 2003, pp. 120 ff.). Momentum builds in the discourse on civilising the male that had begun during the Renaissance in such works as *The Pig King* (Straparola, 1556)—a fairy tale whose motifs feed into LA BELLE ET LA BÊTE, as do those of later (girly) variations on *Cupid and Psyche* (cf. Chapter Three, this volume). The readership of these literary productions was predominantly female. It was women who wanted insight into the inner life and the messages of the "heart" (see Grimminger, 1980)—including those of their husbands. The model of masculinity conveyed by this literature tended to override class distinctions and to be linked to performance features as well as the body now precisely described by science. Under the reign of absolutism with its disciplinary societal framework, a new gender dualism took root that simultaneously commended individuality and conforming to the norm. This found expression in the French Revolution: "The 'New Human Being' [of the French Revolution] was primarily a 'New Man'. [His] emotional characteristics [...] were to be derived from the physical composition of the male body, steeled by the educational techniques of the Enlightenment" (Schmale, 2003, p. 188).

The ultimate "hegemonic masculinity", which completely excluded women from the realm of performance and from participation in solely male-defined social spheres, did not prevail on a broad scale until the bourgeois era. To establish an effective ideology of militarisation and a de-emotionalisation of manhood that would take hold of people from within and expunge anything "unmanly" from the hero image—especially, any emotional factors (cf. Szczepaniak, 2005)—it was necessary to have media resonance and a societal environment favouring individual statements of identity. Therefore, it wasn't until the 1860s that "hegemonic masculinity" could begin its march through the institutions as the mandatory (and apparently nature-given) self-image of the species; male and female social spheres were strictly separated (Schmale, 2003, pp. 152 f., pp. 195 ff.; for conceptual critique cf. Dinges, 2005; Meuser & Scholz, 2005).

Since the invention of cinema, these social construction processes took on a new dimension. Due to the specific nature of the visual medium (see Hamburger, 2014), stereotypes could be transported more immediately and, at the same time, be delivered to new audience groups.

Cinema constructs

But here we are speaking of cinema and are concerned with the interdisciplinary analysis of a film. Summarising the historical findings that both men and women are culturally defined and that societal conditions ultimately determine what prevails, we can postulate: both men and women are constructs of the cinematic gaze, and it is cast by women as well as men.

The spectatorship debate is clearly coloured by the feminist analyses from which it derives and their well-justified concentration on the asymmetry of discourse about gender distinctions. However, this focus on heteronomy does not capture the wider picture: that women can indeed enjoy lustful observation of men—and of other women. The volume at hand is a contribution towards balancing out this gender construction. Hence the deliberate inversion in the title, *Women and Images of Men in Cinema*.

The construction of gender roles, of femininity as well as masculinity, is a public act; although undertaken by individuals, from all their many attempts at self-definition it filters out those that are societally relevant, in an evolutionary process of reception. A short aside on the origins of the tango in Argentina in the early twentieth century can illustrate how this functions: the social situation in Argentina, a country of immigration, was marked by a massive surplus of men. From a local tradition, the world-famous dance took shape, with the men taking a dominant and central role—but only for the purpose of excelling in their competition for the scarce women. It was, after all, the latter who had the choice, and it was from their selection criteria that the prototype of the macho arose—a female fantasy in dance form.

If the debate on female spectatorship can be criticised for concentrating too narrowly on the "feminist gaze" and neglecting real women in cinema, it is hoped that the contributions in this volume may help to alleviate this with their perspectives from film studies and clinical psychoanalysis. The psychoanalysts, male and female, who reflect upon their experience of LA BELLE ET LA BÊTE are all in clinical practice. They extrapolate their views from their own impressions as spectators, the analysis of film aesthetics in the relevant discourse (see Mertens, Chapter Two, this volume), and their own experience with patients (cf. Hamburger, 2013).

In his chapter on the methods of film analysis, Wolfgang Mertens sets the stage for our studies in this volume, providing a critical overview of the state of the art in film psychoanalysis. Andreas Hamburger then initiates the investigation of the film, principally by providing the literary and art history backdrop against which Cocteau's staging of the motif can be read as a deconstruction of hegemonic masculinity.

Following these introductory texts, the volume is arranged into two thematic areas: "Beauties" and "Beasts".

In the first section addressing the construction of femininity in LA BELLE ET LA BÊTE, Andrea Sabbadini takes up the leitmotif of the rose to discuss the cinematic mise en scène of female identity, illustrating this with a psychoanalytical case vignette. In so doing, he also considers the filmic construction of male identity. The cultural theorist Christine Kirchhoff responds with an investigation of the representation of sexuality in LA BELLE ET LA BÊTE, beginning with a very personal account and systematic psychoanalytical interpretation of her experience as a "female spectator".

In the second section, "Beasts", the psychoanalyst Marianne Leuzinger-Bohleber integrates current research while looking into aspects of male adolescence in LA BELLE ET LA BÊTE. In terms of cultural analysis, she reads the film as a reaction to the catastrophe of civilisation in the Holocaust. The film scholar Andreas Rost replies with a critical film history of male monsters, covering the ongoing development of the motif in post-war cinema and into the present with its characteristic dissolution of classical conceptions of masculinity—pointing out, with due reserve as a male critic but on a sound historical basis, that the filmic characteristics of male monsters might also be indebted to the fantasies of female spectators (Chapter Seven, this volume), or to sum up his contribution, that (fortunately) women in the movie theatre do indeed conjure up their own images of men.

Note

1. For instance, the gruesome chorus of the Maenads in *The Bacchae* (Euripides, 405 BC) or the worried chorus of Corinthian women in *Medea* (Euripides, 431 BC), the foreign women from Chalcis in *Iphigenia in Aulis* (Euripides, 406 BC), the women of Mycenae in *Antigone* (Sophocles, 413 BC), the daughters of Oceanus in *Prometheus Bound* (Aeschylus [questionable] approx. 420 BC)—but also in Greek comedies, as in *Lysistrata* (Aristophanes, 411 BC) with its quarrelling choruses of men and women, and in Aristophanes' other comedies on women.

References

Aeschylus (questionable) (c. 420 BC). *Prometheus Bound*. J. Sculley & C. J. Herington (Trans.). New York: Oxford University Press, 1975.

Aristophanes (411 BC). *Lysistrata.* S. Ruden (Trans.). Indianapolis, IN: Hackett, 2003.

Bergstrom, J., & Doane M. A. (1989). The female spectator: Contexts and directions. *Camera Obscura. A Journal of Feminism and Film Theory, 20–21,* May–September (=Special Issue *The Spectatrix*).

Bettelheim, B. (1954). *Symbolic Wounds.* Glencoe, IL: Free Press.

Block, M. (2010). *Situating the Feminist Gaze and Spectatorship in Postwar Cinema.* Cambridge: Cambridge Scholars Publishing.

Blüher, H. (1918). *Familie und Männerbund.* Leipzig, Germany: 1918.

Bollmann, S. (2013). *Frauen und Bücher: Eine Leidenschaft mit Folgen.* Stuttgart, Germany: Deutsche Verlagsanstalt.

Brandes, H. (1994). Die Entstehung eines weiblichen Lesepublikums im 18. Jahrhundert. Von den Frauenzimmerbibliotheken zu den literarischen Damengesellschaften. In: P. Goetsch (Ed.), *Lesen und Schreiben im 17. und 18. Jahrhundert* (pp. 125–133). Tübingen, Germany: Narr.

Brunotte, U. (2000). Ritual und Erlebnis. Theorien der Initiation und ihre Aktualität in der Moderne. *Zeitschrift für Religions- und Geistesgeschichte, 52*(4): 349–367.

Butler, J. (1990). *Gender Trouble: Feminism and the Subversion of Identity.* New York: Routledge.

Cohan, S., & Hark, I. R. (Ed.) (1993). *Screening the Male. Exploring Masculinities in Hollywood Cinema.* London: Routledge.

Connell, R. (1995). *Masculinities.* Cambridge: Polity Press.

Dinges, M. (2005). "Hegemoniale Männlichkeiten"—Ein Konzept auf dem Prüfstand. In: M. Dinges (Ed.), *Männer—Macht—Körper. Hegemoniale Männlichkeiten vom Mittelalter bis heute* (pp. 7–36). Frankfurt, Germany: Campus.

Doane, M. A. (1982). Film and the masquerade. Theorising the female spectator. *Screen* 23 (3–4): 74–87. Reprinted in: Th. Schatz (Ed.) (2004), *Hollywood: Cultural Dimensions. Ideology, Identity and Cultural Industry Studies* (pp. 95–110). London: Taylor & Francis.

Dressler, M. C. (1993). *Unmasking the Female Spectator: Sighting Feminist Strategies in Chopin, Glasgow, and Larsen.* [PhD dissertation, Rice University, Houston, TX.] https://scholarship.rice.edu/bitstream/handle/1911/16617/9408614.PDF?sequence=1 (1.8.2012).

Elias, N. (1939). *The Civilizing Process. Sociogenetic and Psychogenetic Investigations. Revised edition.* Oxford: Blackwell, 2000.

Euripides (405 BC). *The Bacchae.* R. Robertson (Trans.). New York: Harper Collins, 2014.

Euripides (406 BC). *Iphigenia at Aulis.* D. Taylor (Trans.). London: Methuen, 2004.

Euripides (431 BC). *Medea.* J. Harrison (Trans.). Cambridge: Cambridge University Press, 2000.

Gaines, J. (1991). White privilege and looking relations: Race and gender in feminist film theory. In: P. Erens (Ed.), *Issues in Feminist Film Criticism* (pp. 197–215). Bloomington, IN: Indiana University Press.

Gennep, A. v. (1909). *The Rites of Passage*. Chicago, IL: University of Chicago Press, 1960.

Gilmore, D. D. (1990). *Manhood in the Making: Cultural Concepts of Masculinity*. New Haven, CT: Yale University Press.

Grimminger, R. (1980). Aufklärung, Absolutismus und bürgerliche Individuen. Über den notwendigen Zusammenhang von Literatur, Gesellschaft und Staat in der Geschichte des 18. Jahrhunderts. In: R. Grimminger (Ed.), *Deutsche Aufklärung bis zur Französischen Revolution 1680–1789. Hansers Sozialgeschichte der deutschen Literatur vom 16. Jahrhundert bis zur Gegenwart (Vol. 3)* (pp. 15–102). Munich, Germany: Hanser.

Hamburger, A. (2013). Arbeit in der Tiefe. Vorüberlegungen zu einer skeptischen Kulturanalyse. In: H. Hierdeis (Ed.), *Psychoanalytische Skepsis* (pp. 123–183). Göttingen, Germany: Vandenhoeck & Ruprecht.

Hamburger, A. (2014). Kinometaphern. Eine psychoanalytische Perspektive. *Psychosozial, 137*(3).

Lamott, F. (1993). Monsterbilder-Spiegelbilder—oder wie aus Monstren Menschen werden. *Manuskripte. Zeitschrift für Literatur, 33*(2): 27–37.

Mertens, W. (1992). *Entwicklung der Psychosexualität und der Geschlechtsidentität, (Vol. 1)*, Stuttgart, Germany: Kohlhammer.

Meuser, M., & Scholz, S. (2005). Hegemoniale Männlichkeit. Versuch einer Begriffsklärung aus soziologischer Perspektive. In: M. Dinges (Ed.), *Männer—Macht—Körper. Hegemoniale Männlichkeiten vom Mittelalter bis heute* (pp. 211–228). Frankfurt, Germany: Campus.

Mulvey, L. (1975). Visual pleasure and narrative cinema. *Screen, 16*(3): 6–18. Reprinted in: C. Penley (Ed.) (1988), *Feminism and Film Theory* (pp. 57–68). New York: Routledge.

Mulvey, L. (1981). Afterthoughts on "Visual pleasure and narrative cinema" inspired by *Duel in the Sun*. *Framework, 15/16/17*: 12–15. Reprinted in: C. Penley (Ed.) (1988), *Feminism and Film Theory* (pp. 69–79). New York: Routledge.

Mulvey, L. (1989). *Visual and Other Pleasures*. Bloomington, IN: Indiana University Press.

Mulvey, L. (1996). *Fetishism and Curiosity*. Bloomington, IN: Indiana University Press.

Mulvey, L. (2001). Unmasking the gaze. Some thoughts on new feminist film theory and history. *Lectora, 7*: 5–14.

Otis-Cour, L. (2000). *Lust und Liebe. Geschichte der Paarbeziehungen im Mittelalter*. Frankfurt, Germany: Fischer.

Schmale, W. (2003). *Geschichte der Männlichkeit in Europa (1450–2000)*. Vienna: Böhlau.

Schnurrbein, S. von (1997). Mütterkult und Männerbund. Über geschlechtsspezifische Religionsentwürfe. In: R. Faber & S. Lanwerd (Eds.), *Kybele—Prophetin—Hexe. Religiöse Frauenbilder und Weiblichkeitskonzeptionen* (pp. 249–270). Würzburg, Germany: Königshausen u. Neumann.

Schön, E. (1990). Weibliches Lesen: Romanleserinnen im späten 18. Jh. In: H. Gallas & M. Heuser (Eds.), *Untersuchungen zum Roman von Frauen um 1800* (pp. 20–40). Tübingen, Germany: de Gruyter.

Schwanitz, D. (2001). *Männer. Eine Spezies wird besichtigt (3rd edition)*. Munich, Germany: Goldmann, 2003.

Sophocles (413 BC). *Antigone*. J. E. Thomas (Trans.). Clayton, DE: Prestwick House, 2005.

Straparola, G. F. (1556). *Le piacevoli notti*. Venice, Italy: Comin da Trino.

Szczepaniak, M. (2005). Gewalt in Blau. Zum Gewaltdiskurs in Blaubart-Texten des 20. Jahrhunderts aus der Sicht der Männlichkeitsforschung. In: M. Dinges (Ed.), *Männer—Macht—Körper. Hegemoniale Männlichkeiten vom Mittelalter bis heute* (pp. 192–207). Frankfurt, Germany: Campus.

Turner, V. (1967). Betwixt and between: The liminal period in rites de passage. In: V. Turner, *The Forest of Symbol: Aspects of Ndembu Ritual* (pp. 93–111). Ithaca, NY: Cornell University Press.

Turner, V. (1969). *The Ritual Process: Structure and Antistructure*. Chicago, IL: Aldine.

Turner, V. (1982). *From Ritual to Theatre. The Human Seriousness of Play*. New York: PAJ.

CHAPTER TWO

Psychoanalytical film interpretation—possibilities and limitations*

Wolfgang Mertens†

"In the lives of most people in the 20th century, cinema plays an essential role. But it is hardly ever a topic of psychoanalytical study," as Mechthild Zeul concluded (1997, p. 27) on the basis of her research at that time. She suggested that this disdain for cinema might result from the predominantly middle-class bourgeois socialisation of analysts, who have far more esteem for literature with its traditional system of symbols than for the purportedly lower genre of film. In fact, until the middle of the 1990s, the German language periodical *Psyche—Zeitschrift für Psychoanalyse und ihre Anwendungen* (Journal for Psychoanalysis and its Applications) had not published more than a handful of psychoanalytical film interpretations, among them Janine Chasseguet-Smirgel's (1970) programmatic study of Alain Resnais' LAST YEAR AT MARIENBAD or Peter Dettmering's (1989) treatment on the

*Revised and extended version of Chapter 7, "Anwendungen der Psychoanalyse [Applications of Psychoanalysis]", W. Mertens (2005). *Psychoanalyse. Grundlagen, Behandlungstechnik und Anwendung* [Psychoanalysis—Fundamentals, Techniques of Treatment, Applications], Stuttgart, Germany: Kohlhammer.

†Translated by Susan Jones.

films of Andrej Tarkowski. In American journals of the psychoanalytical mainstream, it was a bit better: as early as 1994, the *Psychoanalytic Review* had established a rubric with psychoanalytical film interpretations, and the *International Journal of Psycho-Analysis*, one of the most well-known psychoanalytical periodicals, did so as well. In 1998, *Psychoanalytic Inquiry* even dedicated an issue to the topic "A Century of Film and Psychoanalysis" in recognition of the fact that in the year 1895, with the Freud/Breuer publication of *Studies on Hysteria* and the presentation of the first moving pictures by the Lumière brothers in Paris, both psychoanalysis and cinema were born (cf. Diamond & Wrye, 1998a, 1998b).

In recent years, astounding changes have taken place: in Germany alone, initiatives in more than twenty cities have formed to discuss psychoanalytical interpretation of films. In Munich, for example, the Akademie für Psychoanalyse und Psychotherapie e.V. (Academy for Psychoanalysis and Psychotherapy) has cooperated with the Film Museum Munich to establish a forum in which, on a regular basis, films grouped according to their directors or genres are presented and commented upon by psychoanalysts (more detail below). The number of publications on the topic of psychoanalysis and film has increased exponentially (e.g., Laszig & Schneider, 2008; Piegler, 2009; Wohlrab, 2006; Zeul, 2007; Zwiebel & Mahler-Bungers, 2007). And the British Psychoanalytical Society now hosts a psychoanalytical film festival every two years (Sabbadini, 2003). In the interim, there has been much conjecture about the reasons for such neglect over decades, but a stringent explanation has not been forthcoming. And the first exercise has been to admit to this tremendous lapse in application and to take account of the fact that, conversely, film directors have long been concerned with the professional activity of psychoanalysts. The earliest films about psychoanalysts certainly worked with clichés, but this has now changed entirely, and the audience seems quite interested in the outcome. Since the broadcast of the Israeli-American series BETIPUL/IN TREATMENT, psychoanalysts and psychotherapists in Israel have seen their clientèle double in number.

It is certainly satisfying for psychoanalysts to know that their discipline—an essential aspect of culture in the twentieth century but not necessarily congruent with today's zeitgeist, which rather tends away from holistic interpretations that integrate deeper aspects of personal history—still figures in the public imagination, as least in the cinema.

In some contemporary films there are powerful and impressive references to the process of psychoanalytic treatment, and in terms of artistic import they are surely more viable and accessible than a depiction of daily therapeutic work would ever be. For example when Hana, the French-Canadian nurse in Anthony Minghella's THE ENGLISH PATIENT (USA/UK 1996), retreats to an abandoned Italian cloister with Almasy and enables him to direct his attention to emotions buried deep inside himself, she is offering him therapeutic resonance and containment. As she ascribes significance to his fragmented memories and unspeakable feelings, a coherent history begins to take shape—co-constructed and co-narrated in a therapeutic dialogue, as modern psychoanalytic terminology would put it. The positivistic postulate that there is one truth to be detected within the patient, to be extracted as if in an archaeological excavation, has lost its sway and yielded to a dialogical and narrative understanding of how truths can be uncovered. This does not imply that transference from previously experienced relationships are without bearing; but they are intermingled at times almost inextricably with new perceptions gleaned in the present dialogue. The English patient reconstructs his relationship to his former companion Katherine not only as a means of regaining his identity, but also because of his wish to be acknowledged by Hana. And Hana attempts to assign meaning to these memory fragments, all the while dealing with the background of her own painful losses—of her fiancé, her father, and her best friend. For her, too, this shared memory work has aspects of healing and restoring identity. And in like manner, their analytical insight derives from the longing of both participants to attain a new understanding of themselves and the other. This is supported by tight film editing that closely juxtaposes the biographical perspectives of the English patient and Hana.

The dialogues between the imprisoned psychotic psychiatrist Hannibal Lecter and the young female FBI commissioner Clarice Starling in the film THE SILENCE OF THE LAMBS (USA 1991) can be read, at least in part, as a filmic realisation of analytic sessions. Hannibal Lecter, from whom the FBI hopes to glean information on a serial killer they are hunting, will only agree to talk to Clarice Starling if she gives him personal details about her own life; he is particularly interested in her most painful childhood memories. And although Lecter does not in any way represent an ideal of psychoanalytical sensitivity, but rather an image of schizoid empathy—baiting her and tormenting her with his knowledge—he nevertheless provides her with certain insights into herself and her childhood relationship to her parents, which ultimately enable Clarice to develop a more conciliatory perspective on the past (cf. Benton, 1992). It is hardly an exaggeration to say that this film and others unnoticeably explain psychoanalytical procedure to the viewer.

Similarly, the mysterious, eerie, damp, and steamy forest in Jane Campion's film THE PIANO (AU/NZ/F 1993), with its swampy sinking ground triggering fears of closeness or of being swallowed up for some viewers, can been seen as the expression of a semiotic treatment of the sensual and voluptuous state within the mother's womb: as a preverbal sensory matrix originating in the amniotic fluid and continuing in the exchange of milk and saliva via the mouth, in the skin's response to touch, in tears, mucous, and excrement. No wonder that for Freud, oriented as he was towards predominantly Oedipal symbols, the realm of female psychosexuality remained a dark continent (cf. Rohde-Dachser, 1991), and quite the same applies to Lacan with his orientation towards language and the "law of the father". Analytic sessions may not be comparable with the forests of New Zealand, but bodily evoked memories can indeed call up imprintations from the early interaction between mother and child.

In film productions, just as in literature, major psychological themes can be addressed and reposited. And as a result, films can serve as an excellent resource for differentiated study of the individual, collective, and societal unconscious in its diverse manifestations and derivations. Films consolidate different levels of significance and, just as dreams, in doing so can mask meanings that trigger anxieties. On the one hand, they can lead the viewer to believe that regressive wishes for unbroken harmony and wholeness are fulfillable, or that an identity free of conflicts is possible. But films also contain subtext that is concealed beneath captivating and poignant images and nonetheless appeals subtly to the unconscious of the viewer. Films with scenes full of manifest violence, for example, can be interpreted as a defence against other needs that are not permitted to come to consciousness in collective experience due to shame anxiety.

Cinema is not only a fertile terrain for ideological and critical study of cultural and historical content; in many respects, it is also comparable with the cathartic function of Greek tragedy, in which healing and psycho-educative effects are achieved through identification with human fates and through vicarious experience of gripping scenes (cf. Gabbard, 1997). On occasion, films bear eminent significance for the viewer, and the effect of certain film themes may last for many years. Sometimes one even has the impression that unconscious identification with film protagonists and their relationships can actually have therapeutic effects. Unlike literature, films are not digested in an individual imaginative process that can extend over many hours, but rather affect the viewer directly due to the power of their images and of the cinema aesthetic principles that go into their making. The effect of films can sometimes remain vivid for much longer than the identification with literary figures absorbed more slowly through thought and comparison with one's own understanding of self. Film productions—comparable to dreams in this respect—have a stronger internal dynamic and generate a stronger regressive undertow to let oneself go and simply follow the action rather than taking it in cognitively. This may have been one reason why Freud had some reservations about this medium. The "prohibition against making an image of God" that is to be found "among the precepts of the Mosaic religion" (Freud, 1939a, p. 111) implies not only a limitation of sensory perception, but also a requirement to forego instinctive impulses.

Relatively speaking, psychoanalysts' abstemiousness with regard to the medium of film in the twentieth century did not deter scholars in other disciplines, film theorists, or film critics from drawing on psychoanalytical concepts. Largely unnoticed by mainstream clinical psychoanalysis, feminist film theorists of the 1970s were already discussing various topics of socio-political import, such as the cinema's exclusion of female subjectivity or the genre of women's film in the historical context. In this process, as Renate Lippert (1999) has pointed out, a well-defined space was assigned to psychoanalysis as a social institution and as a theory of the unconscious. The only problem was that many psychoanalysts hardly took notice of this appropriation, nor did they comment on it. In recent years this has changed radically.

Images of women created by male film directors are, needless to say, a particularly fruitful topic for psychoanalytical interpretation, to be treated extensively in this book. In the following, I would like to lay out some thoughts on methodical aspects and unresolved issues of psychoanalytical film interpretation.

Some methodological deliberations on psychoanalytical film interpretation

What does the psychoanalytical perspective really have to offer towards understanding a film? In what respect does it differ from other interpretations that we read about or share in everyday conversations? Does psychoanalytical film interpretation go beyond the rendition of manifest content or conjecture about the director's intent in shaping the film or in ending it as he did? For example, towards comprehending the mise en scène of one or more unconscious themes through the specific technical and aesthetic options that film offers? Towards perceiving a stratum of meaning that can hardly be verified by the facticity of words or by objective measurements of human experience, but that rather becomes accessible through empathetic involvement in the sequence of scenes and through inexplicit elements? Towards comprehending the semiosis of rhythmical and prosodic patterns that are preverbal, ontogenetically related to mother-child interaction, and not confinable to syntactic limits?

Where is there a starting point for psychoanalytical interpretation in the absence of clues from the analysand that vitalise the clinical situation—the things that are skipped over or disjoint in the narrative, the contradictions between explicit semantic expression and what can only be grasped in-between the lines or through gestures and body language? Can understanding of the mutual re-enactment scene even take place without recourse to the tangible "enactment" occurring between two persons in which, subtly and to a great extent unconsciously, implicit experience of relationships and roles is proposed, denied, and negotiated? How can psychoanalytical film interpretation be possible as an application of psychoanalytical method without access to the classical setting, in which this method comes to bear in pure form through free association and evenly suspended attention, thematisation of resistance, and understanding of the mutual re-enactment?

About setting

Not only due to the fact that the cinema and Freud's analysis of dreams entered the culture at almost the same time, but also because they actually share a number of characteristics, it is unsurprising that a number of authors have called attention to the similarity of dreams and films. Baudry (1975), for example, compared the film viewer's experiential situation with dream consciousness. Sitting motionless in the cinema, in a dark room, relaxed and shielded from impressions of everyday reality, fully concentrated on visual and acoustic perceptions, we follow the sequence of images and scenes parading across an enormous screen, with no means of influencing the cuts from one scene to another, just as with the involuntarily shifting scenes in a dream. Not only in the reception of films, but also in their creation, dreaming seems to be at play: Ingmar Bergman, Federico Fellini, and Akira Kurosawa repeatedly emphasised the dream-like nature of their film work. Bergman, for instance, related that he discovered one day that all his images were generated by dreams. Fellini is quoted as saying, "Dreams are the only reality." And Bernardo Bertolucci once remarked that he wove his films as if on a dream loom. Beyond such autobiographical testimony, systematic studies also demonstrate that filmmakers are inspired by their dreams. In comparison with the general population, they more often recall their dreams, they relate them to others more frequently, they experience more vivid affects in dreams, and they also have more nightmares (Pagel, Kwiatkowski, & Broyles, 1999).

Although Freud's thesis—that dreaming serves to satisfy an unconscious wish that is inadmissible to waking consciousness, but in some transmuted form gains entry into dream consciousness—was already refuted during his own lifetime, and other approaches of deep psychology set drastic limits on the applicability of the wish-fulfilment theory (e.g., Deserno, 1999), his original theory of dreams has nonetheless served as a focal point for his adherents as well as his critics.

Film directors have, on occasion, commented on how many of their ideas are indebted to their own dreams and how dream elements have influenced aesthetic decisions in their films (cf. Gabbard & Gabbard, 1987). Film critics have described viewing films as a dream-like experience, corroborating the indistinctness of the boundary between these two emanations of the human spirit. Psychoanalytical film theorists have emphasised the similarities between dreams and films particularly with regard to the, at first glance, seemingly accidental nature of the mise en scène. But what may seem accidental—an apparently insignificant dialogue or a certain camera setting—emerges on closer examination as entirely deliberate and skilfully arranged, just as a dream manifestation initially appears to contain senseless and unrelated elements, until the interpretative ideas of the dreamer gradually uncover the context of meaning and unconscious intentions.

Moreover, the parallels are striking between viewing a film on the enormous screen mentioned above and our nocturnal experience of a dream screen that can present extremely impressive and artfully designed stories. Gertrude Koch (1995) has, however, pointed out that Baudry (1975) based his remarks on Bertram Lewin's (1953) *dream screen* model—which assumed that the mother's breast was the infant's first projection screen—whereas René Spitz several years later thanks to improved methodology was able to show that an infant at the mother's breast fixes its gaze on the mother's face, especially on the area of the eyes, nose, and forehead. Since then, research on infants has further differentiated the visual fixation points in relation to the infant's age.

Varying methodological approaches

> *Say that it's Oedipus, or you'll get a slap in the face!*
>
> Deleuze & Guattari (1974, p. 45)

The history of psychoanalytical film interpretation has seen a wide range of approaches: in part, this was due to the fact that a methodology for applied psychoanalysis outside the clinical context only developed over time and, as explained, the interpretation of literary works was given clear priority over the interpretation of films; secondly, the advancement of genuine psychoanalytical methods can be seen in the context of the overall progress of psychoanalysis with regard to mutual re-enactment, to the interdependency of transference and countertransference, to deep hermeneutics as a method of inquiry in social science, and much more. If applied psychoanalysis is occasionally purported to have, in the past, swallowed other disciplines by way of colonisation and without doing justice to the foreign subject or medium (see, for example, Reiche, 2000), then there is a certain truth to it, but at least in part this approach is the result of a lack of methodological differentiation. Still, one accusation is particularly weighty: that in earlier interpretations psychoanalysis had been applied as if it were a nomothetic discipline that by deductive-nomological conclusion could subsume certain aspects of the filmic narrative under existing theories that are universally acknowledged. Proceeding in this way, as we all know, will not lead to new discoveries, but merely to the satisfaction of confirming that the world reveals over and over again the same structures and principles that are—how very reassuring!—independent of time and location (cf. Körner, 1985). Not until the work of Argelander and Lorenzer was received, beginning in the 1970s, did psychoanalysts in Germany learn systematically to go beyond logical understanding and causal explanation and engage in another type of comprehension that always seems new and unaccustomed because it integrates what is excluded from rational everyday discourse—the bodily, sensual interaction between individuals occurring as an encounter, with transference and countertransference.

The following takes up the varying approaches in (so to speak) ascending order—also commenting on their possible advantages or methodical weaknesses for the purposes of psychoanalytical film interpretation.

Retelling

The interpreter is concerned with issues and topics such as: What is the plot? How does the director create suspense? How does the story end? What psychological, moral, and/or political messages does the director want to get across? Does the film contain an allegory of moral import? What "deeper" dimension might be suggested by such an allegory?

It has been disappointing at times to learn from an interview with a filmmaker that he didn't have any kind of deeper significance in mind, wasn't thinking of "hyponoia" but just of a love story. Often the distinction between "the story is nothing but the story" as opposed to "under the surface of the story, there is latent significance" serves as a criterion for assessing the artistic quality of a film and its potential psychoanalytical dimension, "because the director actually wanted to express more than is manifest in the movie itself". This already gives a cue to the next level of perspective.

Interpretation with familiar psychoanalytical topoi

Underlying the manifest plot is another text, an unconscious narrative that only emerges in the course of interpreting and relating its parts to one another.

In accord with this perspective, for example Alfred Hitchcock's REAR WINDOW (USA 1954) is not just about the photographer L. B. Jeffries, confined to a wheelchair because of a broken leg, who observes a murder, can't intervene due to his handicap, and finally is in danger of being murdered himself. It is also about his voyeuristic observation of the primal scene, which makes him feel guilty. Various psychoanalytical approaches suggest differing interpretations of the primal scene motif, for example, according to Freud, Klein, or object relations theory (see Maier, 2014).

While Jeffries experiences the primal scene as a sadistic, destructive event and is punished for his vicarious participation in it with another broken leg, in Michelangelo Antonioni's Blow-Up (GB 1966) Thomas embodies not only the successful star photographer in a superficial world of models and fashion glamour, but also the prototype of the narcissistically damaged child who actively strives to exclude and damage others in his struggle against his traumatisation due to the primal scene and against the recognition of generation boundaries. A psychoanalytical assessment of the film Blow-Up reveals—according to Arlow (1980), who assumes he can apply the same methodological criteria as would be appropriate in analysing clinical data—that the film is about how couples love one another and are disturbed by others. Consequently, the presence of the photographer interrupts the romantic idyll of the couple he finds in a park. In other scenes, Thomas also harasses a couple having sex. A rock concert that ends in the orgiastic destruction of the musical instruments is taken as an easily identified substitute for the primal scene, and the topic of intrusion into the private sphere can be traced throughout the film. People walk in and out of other people's flats. For Arlow, the conclusion is clear: that Antonioni not only wished to portray Swinging London and the pop culture of the Sixties, but also to create an aesthetically detailed rendering and a symbolic expression of a universal psychological theme, the fantasies and consequences of the primal scene.

This perspective, which grafts a psychoanalytical *topos* of interpretation onto a film narrative, may indeed have been the most frequent in the past, and it probably also led outsiders to assume that this was a specifically psychoanalytic approach. However, as Zeul (1997) illustrates, this leads to a trivialisation of familiar psychoanalytic themes. In her film interpretation of Campion's The Piano, she observes that the manifest images of castration, death, reincarnation, and learning to love through the love of a man "are misleading in terms of picture-book and cliché interpretations that take up the manifest content and, from there, infer unconscious symbolic content" (p. 109)—with the result that the specific creative and aesthetic options of film and film technique may be forgotten or entirely ignored (more on this below). That would transform the film into psychoanalytical humdrum, no different than a summary comment about an analytic session, by pigeonholing it into a standard psychoanalytic constellation—although this "standard" has such manifold variations. Even worse: not only would the medium of film be underestimated if its aesthetic and technical capabilities were sacrificed to such interpretations; in addition, the authentic psychoanalytical approach would be distorted, since it cannot be subsumed under logical patterns but rather emerges from the actual psychoanalytical dialogue, from the interaction of transference and countertransference. Therefore, Zeul argues in keeping with Janine Chasseguet-Smirgel (1970), that the formal and aesthetic structures of films (more below) must be taken seriously; that to date, psychoanalysts had mainly addressed the second interpretative level in dealing with films and in doing so had generally favoured classical perspectives oriented towards urges or self-psychology.

Integrating ethnopsychoanalysis, cultural and ideological criticism, and feminist considerations

In proceeding by this method, psychoanalytic theory in the strict sense is enhanced by fragments of theory from the social sciences and humanistic disciplines. This makes it possible, for example, to regard Antonioni's BLOW-UP as a critique on the male habit of distanced and mechanistic observation, which in the modern era has not only determined the standpoint of scholarship and technical knowledge, but also redefined gender relationships (cf. von Braun, 1988; Kirley, 1995; Rauschenbach, 1996). Objectivism—represented in the film by Thomas's camera—expresses the dominance of a distanced male perspective, which is gradually deconstructed: in the end, Thomas doesn't know whether the persons and events are real or only exist in his imagination. But BLOW-UP can also be understood as criticising the illusions of product aesthetics, in which flashy surfaces and state-of-the-art design induce consumers to ignore the actual usefulness of a particular object. Ravaged landscapes in Antonioni's *IL DESERTO ROSSO* (RED DESERT) (I 1964) visualise the effects of brutal enslavement to technology, and the scene of anal coitus without a trace of tenderness or eroticism in Bertolucci's *ULTIMO TANGO A PARIGI* (LAST TANGO IN PARIS) (I, F 1972) is an expression of the increasingly schizoid character of relationships. But again, for this type of interpretative approach, the observations from the preceding section are applicable. Core topics of cultural and ideological criticism are drawn upon as established patterns of interpretation. Critique of illusory product aesthetics, a popular *topos* in interpretations during the 1960s and 1970s, gives way to postmodern conceptions of individualisation and experiential rationality in the context of a surplus society no longer defining the value of commodities by their practical usefulness, but rather by their capacity to alleviate everyday monotony with the promise of enhanced experience and luxury (cf., for example, Schulze, 1992). Currently, the focus of cultural critique has moved on to topics of acceleration dynamics, deceleration, and withdrawal from a globalised world (e.g., Rosa, 2005).

But even in this interpretative perspective, no account is taken of the specific epistemology of psychoanalysis deriving from a holistic view of sensual impressions in a dialogical process of perception.

Integrating biographical detail—the psychobiographical method

Drawing on biographical details from the director's life and setting up equations with implicit or explicit biographical fragments from a film protagonist's life is, difficult as it is to believe, actually undertaken in some film interpretations. These parallelograms—here the supposed traumatisations and conflicts of the filmmaker, there the plot of the film—are presented as supposedly enlightening, sometimes as amazingly synchronic, and occasionally as a sign of "resentfulness". As a result, in the understanding of some who have interpreted films, an essential aspect of their psychoanalytical effort was devoted to investigations worthy of a detective and aimed at discovering similarities between the topic of the film and alleged conflicts in the director's unconscious. Hitchcock's maternal conflict is indeed visible in his films. Truffaut himself said that his own desolate childhood was clearly reflected in *Les Quatre Cents Coups* (The 400 Blows) (F 1959). Even though astounding parallels sometimes seem to emerge—for example, between the dénouement of the boy Léolo in Jean-Claude Lauzon's eponymous film Léolo (F/CDN 1992) and the fate of the director—it would be irresponsible to engage in "feral psychoanalysis" and would also play into the hands of critics who assert that psychoanalytic interpretation is just wild speculation. In the film, Léolo ends up in a psychiatric ward in a bathtub full of icy water, to the tune of Tom Waits singing "Cold, cold ground", and five years after making the film, the forty-four-year-old Lauzon died when his Cessna crashed in a storm, near an Eskimo settlement in Canada.

It is understandable that, faced with this calibre of "analysis", Federico Fellini for example tried to shield himself from invasive interpretations by declaring, "Everything and nothing in my work is autobiographical. ... I made it all up myself: a childhood, a personality, longings, dreams, memories, so that I would be able to tell the tale" (1981, p. 61).

At the latest, when Chasseguet-Smirgel introduced the distinction between endopoetic and exopoetic interpretation of literature into psychoanalytic discussion, the psychopathographic line of questioning came into a dubious light. Moreover, applying it to a film director would be tantamount to ignoring that a given film—as opposed to a work of literature—is the result of a compromise influenced by the original source material, the script, the producer, the technicians, the actors, and the financial framework (cf. Diamond & Wrye, 1998a). All in all, it is justified that applied psychoanalysis has sometimes been suspected of wanting to demonstrate superiority by classifying an artist or his creativity as psychopathic or neurotic, with the analyst who lays out this interpretation remaining at a safe distance and seeing no need to reflect upon his own motivation for judging this particular work or artist. In the past, quite a few biographies of artists have followed this pattern: proving once again that such-and-such an artist suffered under unresolved conflicts and traumatisations and therefore only composed his work as a means of compensation and sublimation.

Furthermore, if the artist's biography is the main focus of attention, why undertake a psychoanalytical study of a film? The appeal of psychoanalytical interpretation, of working through unconscious leitmotifs, lies in the potential for sudden insights, growing awareness, reorganisation of experiential input—and not in a triumphant conclusion that the director had some mental affliction (presumably like all filmmakers, and other artists as well) that is expressed in his film or work. As elsewhere, in the co-constructive interpretation of meaning or meanings conveyed through film, we adhere to the psychoanalytical tenet that when we talk about others, we are talking about ourselves, even if what we say may be tentative at first because we have touched upon some areas within ourselves that are not easily accessible to conscious reflection or that we prefer to forget. Cinematic reality, created by someone else and therefore foreign to us, can only be comprehended by way of investigation within our own sphere of life experience. Obviously, comprehension is only possible to the extent that we are capable of openness towards our own unconscious.

On film technique and aesthetics

The principles of form which, alongside content, are essential for the perceptive experience of the specific medium film, can be grouped into those that are related to editing in the broadest sense, and those that pertain to the language of film. To begin with editing technique:

Foreshadowing

This is the integration, at an early stage in the plot of a film, of some detail, clue, or key element that will later be of significance. Such advance references can include objects, special props, locations, recurring images, and hints contained in dialogue or subtext that already indicate some tendency or significance in the storyline or in the development of the characters and their relationships, and that ultimately feed into the overall message. An example of foreshadowing would be the banjo duel between a mentally handicapped boy and one of four middle-class Americans in DELIVERANCE (USA 1972) by John Boorman. Four friends want to demonstrate their prowess with a daring whitewater run down a river gorge where a dam is soon to be built. What was planned as a weekend lark becomes a nightmarish trip into the irrational and the uncivilised. Cultural imperatives break down in an appalling process of regression, opening the view onto an abyss of human destructivity and perversion amid the elemental force of the untamed river that rears up one last time, like an animal mortally wounded on the hunt, before being forced to succumb to the human hand in the form of a reservoir. And just as the boy by the river in the opening scene had won the banjo duel against the civilised city fellow, the four friends have to admit defeat in their struggle with the unpredictable forces of nature within themselves and on the river. Another example: at the beginning of Campion's THE PIANO, Ada relates that her father believed her last day of life would be the one when she decided to stop breathing. He is referring to her defiance and strength of will, but his prophecy is confirmed in the penultimate scene when Ada, being dragged to the depths of the sea together with her piano, decides she wants to live and frees herself from the rope with which she is tied to the instrument.

The voice from off-camera

"The voice you hear is not my speaking voice, but my mind's voice. I have not spoken since I was six years old. No one knows why, not even me." This is Ada, the heroine of Campion's film THE PIANO, speaking from off-camera. Ada's muteness forcibly enhances the language of signs, images, and sounds—meaning that this story can only be told with the tools of the cinema.

Frequently in film, a voice-over belongs to an impersonal narrator providing introductions and framework; it is also used to shift perspective from the present to the past. This device sets up a certain distance—sometimes constructively in the sense of triangulation, sometimes to indicate schizoid depersonalisation, and finally also as a means of achieving coherence through commentary, for example when events have piled up in images and scenes. For Léolo's psychotic world of primary processes in Lauzon's film LÉOLO, the voice from off-camera appears to fulfil all these functions. The background voice can announce a shift in perspective, elicit empathy, explain things that are otherwise incomprehensible, give rise to hope, and initiate reconciliation. But the voice-over can also allow another ego or self to speak, as if dissociated, can reveal a double conscience, can give an inkling of megalomanic fantasies that have been split off, or can represent an alter ego and an imaginary companion. It can also be understood as the voice of conscience warning the proud self to keep in touch with reality.

Cutbacks and flashbacks

Cutbacks make it possible to depict memories in film, often as black-and-white sequences or with indistinct contours. They are frequently used as a cinema aesthetic means of melding the past and the present, or of showing how attempts to recall something fail and are suppressed. Reconstruction in the memory may proceed in fragmentary form, repeatedly interrupted by comparisons or distractions in the here and now, as in real life or in a psychoanalytic session. Various editing techniques allow for non-chronological montage as well as ordered sequences. Memories of two or more film protagonists can be projected almost simultaneously, as in Alain Resnais's HIROSHIMA MON AMOUR (F/J 1959). Recurring memories can, like screen memories in psychoanalytical terms, conceal an intensive traumatisation, as was the case in Michelangelo Antonioni's film BLOW-UP, where the photographer Thomas was constantly revisited by a particular scene in the park—in which Arlow (1980) saw the unconscious effect of the primal scene. As in the flashbacks of traumatised patients where images, usually of great affective intensity, suddenly intrude into their consciousness but have no temporal markers and therefore seem nightmarishly real, since they are not identifiable as past memories in contrast to the perceptions and conceptions of the present: in the cinema it is possible to suspend the temporal sequence of events and present them in spatial proximity. Confusing for the viewer at first, this technique grants the past a spatial presence in or alongside present scenes. Similarly, in dreams, memory entries are compressed in a primary process, as Freud's classical view describes it; are overlaid, in the terms of information theory; or their different domains are linked to one another, as the metaphoric theory of cognitive linguistics would have it. The American dream researcher Ernest Hartmann (1998) calls this capacity of the dream consciousness "hyperconnective", and cinematic cutbacks and flashbacks take advantage of it to bridge the gap between different times and places, memories, fantasies, and present experience. This condensed and variegated sequence is similar to the stream of consciousness, which generally flows without any conscious focus on our part and only rarely is explicated—unless we deliberately direct metacognitive attention to it. But doing so usually alienates us from our direct experiential perception, and comparable camera work and editing could have quite the same effect of producing an almost artificial, schizoid-depersonalised sphere of perception and thought in which the essential function of consciousness—distinguishing between memories and present impressions, dreams, and reality, the self and the other—temporarily loses it operative effect.

Segments and zooms

With these cinematic tools, it is not only possible to fetch a scene and get close up to it, inside it, or to move away from it and let the impressions fade: one can also depict ambivalence conflicts very well by alternating the zoom settings, as Alfred Hitchcock did in VERTIGO (USA 1958) when Scottie is pining for Madeleine as an ideal symbiotic mother and at the same time feels an equally strong need to keep his distance. Hitchcock expresses this at several points in the film by zooming in on the characters and quickly zooming out again (cf. Gabbard, 1998).

And when the Coen brothers, in BARTON FINK (USA/GB 1991) train the camera on a sink and then slowly magnify the segment, the point is not the focus on an important detail (as the viewer may initially assume) but rather the formal-aesthetic gesture of proceeding to the level of the smallest, a means of metonymy as impressively described by metaphoric theory in the re-analysis of Freud's modes of dream interpretation (see

Mertens, 2001). Does the sink stand for the all-consuming, fantasised world of Hollywood commerce, for a doomed love relationship, or simply for a hole? The Coen brothers deliberately withhold an answer, for they want to point out the thematic polyphony inherent in filmic symbols and metaphors, and that the latter cannot, once and for all, be reduced to clearly defined meanings but rather have to be recreated again and again within the sphere of meaning available to the viewer.

Colours, music, sound effects

The cinema audience will never forget such dramaturgical colour effects as the red blouson jacket James Dean wears with a white shirt and jeans in Nicholas Ray's film REBEL WITHOUT A CAUSE (USA 1955), the intense golden brown of the desert in Minghella's THE ENGLISH PATIENT, or the pale green swamp landscape of New Zealand's jungle in Campion's THE PIANO. Nor will anyone forget the film music from HIGH NOON (USA 1952) with Gary Cooper, directed by Fred Zinnemann, the trumpet solo in FROM HERE TO ETERNITY (USA 1953) by the same director, the plaintive-melancholy rock vocal in LÉOLO by Claude Lauzon, the addictively eddying music in Hitchcock's VERTIGO (reminiscent of melodramatic Wagner operas), and many more musical underscorings and intensifications of film content—not to neglect the contrasting effects.

The ubiquity of sound creates a spatial atmosphere that either hovers in the background of attention where it can, as Siegfried Kracauer distinguishes, "logically support" the image or "comment" on it. Or it can even interfere with the events being presented visually, for example in Resnais's HIROSHIMA MON AMOUR, where loud traffic noise and the insistent ringing of a telephone unmistakably disturb the couple's rendezvous. Film theoreticians refer to "parallel" or "counterpointal" sound: in parallel, the sound is synchronised and related to the image, while in counterpoint it contains a commentary note and is not synchronised with the visual but rather somehow opposed to it. The dialogues and the music can also be in counterpoint to the visual flow of events (cf. Monaco, 1995).

Presentative symbolism, metaphor, metonymy, and prosody

In addition to spoken dialogue that draws on discursive symbols, film significantly makes use of presentational symbols (Langer, 1942), whereby emotionally laden images going back to early childhood experience are often encoded in sub-symbolic form and combined with acoustic and musical impressions, rhythmical and tonal body sensations, resulting in an integrated, emotionally cognitive experience of meaning in an environment—as opposed to more intellectually oriented forms of conceptual thought that de-emphasise the experiential dimension and rather depend on discursive symbols with conventional language equivalents and on sober, logical speech. It is this submersion in the world of images—accessible to most of us only during childhood and later giving way (at school age, under duress) to an emotionally isolated realm of knowledge—that constitutes the great attraction of cinema for many people. This makes Gertrud Koch's hypothesis seem all the more plausible: that the allure of viewing films does not derive primarily from the satisfaction of voyeuristic appetites, but may rather lie in the opportunity to submerge oneself in a pre-narrative, mother–child-like constellation, in which experience is determined, above all, by the mutual dance of interactive movements and by emotional consonance. In Campion's THE PIANO, many scenes are filmed from underneath, with a low camera position, for example the arrival on the beach or the hut of Ada's lover, Baines. Does this merely reflect the director's intent to get to bottom of things, or might it rather be the perspective of the small child experiencing the world prosodically in basic patterns of movement and affect, not yet fluent in the language of symbols? What medium could be better suited than film for the aesthetic portrayal of our primal sphere of experience, not yet scathed by discursive logic but already integral and balanced in matters of perception and emotion? The longing for encounters that are moving and for experience that is poignant—pressing as it is in our rational, scientific age so starkly alienated from mythical perceptions of the world—can be fulfilled without shame in the dream factory of cinema where attractive and enjoyable adventures await anyone emotionally able to suspend disbelief and "go with the flow" of events depicted on the screen.

On the veridicality of events in films

The similarities of films and dreams that have been discussed might suggest that the essential nature of cinematic reality could consist in breaking down the distinctions between actuality and imagination, between reality and fiction. Despite the formal characteristics common to dreams and films, there remains the expectation always directed towards a film that its story be "somehow" true, even if it happens to be science fiction. In David Fincher's FIGHT CLUB (USA/D 1999), this assumption is radically undermined: at the end of film, the viewer learns that he has been deceived systematically. It wasn't at all about social criticism, the depiction of consumerist identities and the cult of brand names, civilisational ennui, and non-compliance, no, the point was the internal, autonomous logic of the images. Was this an attempt to portray action sequences using video-clip editing techniques on a level of visual avant-garde meta-reflection meant to transcend veridicality or Hollywood stories? No answer is to be had.

Individual experience as the starting point for interpretation—the perspective of reception theory

Psychoanalysis and feminism have brought forth particularly convincing arguments against the dominant epistemological theory postulating *one* firmly definable meaning for reality that can be discovered by an objective observer free of subjective presuppositions. Once psychoanalysis gradually had been able to take leave of the archaic epistemological model and the illusion that the analyst only serves as a mirror, the traditional distinction between the perceiving subject and the object being perceived also came into question. Increasingly, the insight was accepted that the meanings we assign to reality—in the analytic situation, to the analysand's narrative—are inseparable from our theoretical assumptions, our life experience, and our own unconscious conflicts. Cognition is always situated in history and culture, which is not to say that reality doesn't exist since it only becomes perceivable through the perspective of the observer. Needless to say, reality exists independently.

In terms of its reception, every film has a self-diagnostic and self-analytic function. This shift in emphasis enables us to lay aside the belief that a film always has a single, objectively rectifiable meaning that can be discerned through thorough analysis and perhaps even set in relation to the artist's biography. On the contrary, it can be said that any film has as many meanings as it does viewers, since every person who sees it perceives and interprets aspects of the film events against the background of his or her own biography and sphere of knowledge. It follows that interpretation is not complete or has indeed not even begun when a film's supposedly deeper meaning has been "grasped" on the basis of some standard psychoanalytical theme, or via long-distance psychoanalytical diagnosis of the director. Instead, interpretation begins to develop its significance with the passage of the images and sequences through the self of the viewer, with empathetic participation in and reflection on the feelings, memories, and fantasies released by the film scenes.

It would therefore be too simple to think of a film interpretation as concluded once a few biographically intriguing symptoms of the director have been dissected—as some psychoanalytic interpretations have, in the past, seemed to suggest. A film is a complex outcome of creative forces related to content, artistic intent, technical options, cultural criticism, and also to economic considerations that only arrives at the level of interpretation it deserves when it is received and reflected upon by the viewer. Shifting the emphasis of observation to the viewer does not make biographical factors linking the director to his production (or other interpretative foils as mentioned above) entirely meaningless, but it does considerably reduce the import of such investigations. Moreover, from the perspective of reception theory, not only the subjective meanings that viewers assign to a film due to their own specific biographies or their subjective recreations of the film's content are of interest, but also whether films may even have a therapeutic effect on their viewers.

In clinical work, we approach the relationship to the analysand with the context of our own biography and transference in mind. A major element in analytical communication is therefore the comparison of perspectives, which has a good deal to do with the ambiguities of language, but naturally also with biographical constellations of meaning, which differ greatly. Applied to the interpretation of film, this insight implies that we cannot experience and describe the meaning of a film as something separate from ourselves, but rather respond to the film with our own (counter-) transference. Albeit, in real life and in analytical dialogue, the assignment of significance is met directly by the reaction of a feeling other, which in turn affects us. Not so with the reception of film. Nonetheless, the content of films can alter our consciousness by evoking inner images and scenes and allowing us to assess some of our experience in a new light.

Many fantasies and memories can be called up when viewing a film, leading to a reflection on one's own emotional impressions and the question of why one was able, for example, to identify so well with the male and/or female protagonist; why the film or certain scenes made one feel sad, repelled, or empty; why the effect of these scenes lingered for such a long time. If one takes the time to do this and can talk to others about it, the co-construction of meaning becomes even more pronounced in the process of reviewing the feelings, conflicts, and inner narratives activated by watching particular scenes. By way of example, one viewer of Hitchcock's VERTIGO might feel sorry for Scottie because of his fixation on a specific image of woman, while another viewer is incensed that Scottie would like to form a woman to the image he envisions. One person watching Campion's THE PIANO may not understand at all why the husband, Stewart, is irritated and turns away when his wife Ada finally ends a long period of erotic and sexual abstention by stroking his bottom (rather than his genitals, as he had hoped); a second person observing the same scene could sympathise with Stewart's reaction and be indignant over Ada's behaviour. What becomes directly evident here is the idiosyncratic nature of reception against the background of each person's subjective assignment of meaning and his or her unconscious conflicts and fantasies. Suppressions and denials have to be uncovered layer by layer in order to arrive at deeper levels of meaning. Underlying the fixation on an idealised mother imago, for instance, one gradually begins to sense depressive feelings, disappointment, and Scottie's fear of his own anger; and the scene with Ada and Stewart gives rise to an understanding that naïve male fantasies of control are perhaps being reversed here, with anger as the only immediate response available.

Psychoanalytical film interpretations, it becomes apparent, are well suited to reveal the richness and polyphony of potential meanings that emerge from the zeitgeist, varying directions of thought, and above all, individual perspectives on significance. Berman (1997) surveyed seventeen different authors' views on Hitchcock's VERTIGO, probably the most frequently interpreted film in the history of cinema, and more views have been added, for example by Zeul (1997). Militant feminist perspectives that consistently perceive women as victims of male chauvinism, such as Mulvey's (1975), are being supplanted by more reflected feminist positions in which both women and men are forced to forego experiential options due to rigid gender stereotypes. Once again it becomes evident that a film cannot be assigned one single veritable meaning, not even the one that (supposedly) the director was unconsciously intending. Instead, a range of meanings is derived from the transference and countertransference of those interpreting it, in an interaction with the emotional and visual-scenic spectrum of the film. It is impossible to overlook, for example, that some commentators of VERTIGO are themselves motivated by fantasies of rescue, attempting by virtue of their interpretations to free Madeleine from Scottie's fetishistic, "pygmalionesque", or narcissistic-intrumentalising impulses. As regulars know, watching the same film more than once leads on the one hand to an enhanced certainty about its interpretation, and on the other to an awareness of the unlimited abundance of options for differing interpretations and translations.

Merging and balancing the psychoanalytical view on content with specifically cinematographic creative tools

Genuine psychoanalytical film interpretation is based on one's own perspective of countertransference, a posture of evenly suspended attention and receptiveness for roles always open to new impressions that emerge from film narratives and specific aesthetic principles of form—from the analysis of the film's form. Despite criticism of a problematic interpretative perspective oriented solely towards topics and biography, it is nevertheless realistic to expect that in every process involving psychoanalytical insight, some theoretical foils will be applied: they need not rest on academic categories or abstract deductive grids, but may instead serve as triggers for one's own experience. However, if they were the exclusive means drawn upon, the likely result would be that the interpreter might apply them as a defence against being affected by the film himself and declare his unwillingness to modify the methodology specific to the psychoanalytical domain, that is to say, might refuse to look beyond the horizon of what he has already learned. In short, in interpreting a film, as elsewhere, various levels of perception need not be strictly separated from or weighed against one another. On the contrary, one's own sense impressions due to cinema aesthetic effects can well be linked with fragments of theory; and significance can indeed be gleaned from a perspective that oscillates between one's own countertransference as a response to specifically cinematographic presentation of content and more theoretical interpretative *topoi*, such as the primal scene, triangulation, objects of passage, jealousy, loyalty or identity conflicts, Oedipus, etc. But the above-mentioned reservations towards a one-sided perspective in interpretation continue to hold whenever the specific dynamic of the film medium is not sufficiently taken into account. Surely, there is some justification for the charge that applied psychoanalysis has colonised other disciplines. Freud's Leonardo study, for instance, one of the first major psychoanalytical works in the cultural area, has been criticised as tending to reduce complex phenomena to a single psychoanalytic concept and granting too little attention to historical and social circumstances. This is certainly true, but it is nevertheless striking in connection with such accusations that the affected disciplines are compelled to put up strong defences against an interpretation of unconscious meaning for the very reason that their own *raison d être* could be undermined or the singular creative achievement of a particular artist could be reduced to a trivial constellation of biography. The idea that both may be possible at the same time—a genuine artistic achievement and its evolvement from a more or less successful process of working through childhood conflicts and traumatisations—seems to be perceived as a slight and as somehow debasing to the artist in question.

On the significance and value of psychoanalytical film interpretation

Does it make sense to interpret a film psychoanalytically? Isn't it enough to watch it, feel moved, and let the sequence of images take effect? Why take the trouble to think about deeper meaning under the cinematic surface, why dissect cinema aesthetic intentions and effects, why risk talking the viewing experience to death in an intellectual debate? It is apparent that familiar psychoanalytical interpretation patterns of today or yesteryear are not what are called for as an approach to the experience of film in contemporary terms.

Psychoanalytic inquiry into a film does not simply involve intellectual analysis of the content, but also means allowing the impressions gathered during viewing to "percolate" in a rerun through one's own experience of self, whereby they are enriched and given new depth. This is particularly productive when undertaken in a group, with ideas expressed by the participants evoking further insights and defensive reactions—as might similarly be the case in a psychoanalytical therapy group.

In some respects, one could even compare psychoanalytical film interpretation to psychoanalytical dream interpretation. The rich spectrum of images and metaphors inaccessible to everyday consciousness, the rapid sequence of scenes, the hyperconnectivity that contextualises images, thoughts, and emotions: all this permits fascinating constellations to form—comparable to daydreams but far more powerful in their inspirational effect. Images, sound, editing sequences, and music generate an extremely stimulating scenario for the confrontation with one's own emotionally framed conceptions and memories. They create a kind of presentational foil for things that one may long have struggled to comprehend, or that one has somehow known but never fully realised (Bollas, 1989), by making it possible to depart temporarily from the conventional symbolisations of language and then approach these anew after some time. But close consideration of films is not only an excellent tool for understanding one's own little self: cinematic *topoi* also depict currents of the societal unconscious. With the support they provide, hidden aspects of societal life can be uncovered—for example, the longing for meaning and for some remnant of identity in the face of postmodern fragmentation and the destruction of meaningfulness.

In the search for latent levels of meaning a seminal role is played by emotional reactions, whose usual translation into the familiar concepts of countertransference, identification, and empathy is quite artificial. Seen from the point of view of reception theory, special interest is not due to the investigation of potential biographical elements relating to the director, but above all to the following questions: What conflicts within the viewer are touched upon by various characters in the film and by its narrative? Which of these conflicts are accessible to consciousness? Can preconscious conflicts be recognised on the basis of contributions and confrontations during a group discussion, and can fantasies be permitted to surface that were initially suppressed or considered irrelevant?

Hamburger and Leube-Sonnleitner (2014, pp. 85 ff.) have described in detail the approach taken by psychoanalysts in the Munich Film Group. Their procedure for "film analysis in the group" includes several steps. The members of the group suggest films that appeal to them from one of the topical areas that have been agreed upon in advance. Then the group selects a film and chooses the chairperson(s) (usually one or two members), who then present the film to the group and document the discussion that follows, either by recording it or making notes on the ideas expressed. Without any focus on specific themes, space is available for all the impressions the members voice, in analogy to the evenly suspended attention recommended by Freud for the analytic situation.

In this way, a considerable array of comments and emotional reactions is collected.

This internal discussion in the group is followed by a public showing of the film led by one member of the group, who first gives a short introduction about the film and the director and then, after the viewing, chairs the ensuing discussion. Since this public event has been preceded by his or her own confrontation with the film and the exchange within the Film Group, the psychoanalyst coordinating the discussion now has a wide background of experience and knowledge to call on while responding adequately to the audience comments, which can be very creative, but sometimes also far afield from the film. This helps to avoid a situation in which viewers might get the impression that a psychoanalytical interpretation is comparable to a brainstorming session—where every comment, no matter how abstruse, is given equal weight.

After the public showing of the film, the method could be extended in a further step. If another member of the Film Group made notes on the ideas contributed by the audience, these could later be examined in the group, and interesting comparisons could be made: Were there audience members who had no access at all to the affective events in the film? Were there some who responded to the affective messages reciprocally, for the most part, being drawn into the action without any distance or reflection? Did some establish distance by means of intellectually asserted criticism, for example by focusing on minor aspects such as editing technique or by dwelling on the behavioural level and disapproving of some trite responses the protagonists produced? And did some viewers gain insights that even surprised the members of the Film Group, insights that hadn't come up in their own previous discussion?

Of course the psychoanalytical film interpreter, or in this case the Film Group, wouldn't have the contextual advantage familiar from the clinical situation in dealing with ideas the analysand brings forth, wouldn't be able to situate the individual comments people made about the film in any kind of coherent narrative that could reveal omissions or breaches; but nevertheless there might be revealing insights to be gained from the audience comments that could supplement the condensed experience of the Film Group. Then it would also be possible, in a comparison between the Film Group and the audience, to combine subjective perspectives of reception with a more "objective" interpretation. That would make it possible to relate audience comments—perhaps tending to be somewhat defensive and more oriented towards vernacular psychology and everyday experience—to the observations of the psychoanalytical Film Group. And it might also be possible to reflect on sociocultural contradictions that are otherwise only encountered on the egosyntonic plane. In this process, psychoanalytical film interpretation could make a significant contribution to the psychoanalytical theory of culture.

References

Arlow, J. (1980). The revenge motive in the primal scene. *Journal of the American Psychoanalytic Association, 28*: 519–541.

Baudry, J. L. (1975). Le dispositif: approches métapsychologiques de l'impression de réalité. *Communications, 23*: 56–72.

Benton, R. J. (1992). The silence of the lambs: Clarice Starling's analysis? *Psychoanalytic Review, 79*: 457–461.

Berman, E. (1997). Hitchcock's Vertigo: The collapse of a rescue fantasy. *International Journal of Psychoanalysis, 78*: 975–996.

Bollas, C. (1989). *The Shadow of the Object. Psychoanalysis of the Unthought Known*. New York: Columbia University Press.

Braun, C. von (1988). *NICHTICH. Logik, Lüge, Libido*. Frankfurt, Germany: Suhrkamp.

Chasseguet-Smirgel, J. (1970). "Letztes Jahr in Marienbad"—Zur Methodologie der psychoanalytischen Erschließung des Kunstwerks. *Psyche—Zeitschrift für Psychoanalyse und ihre Anwendungen, 24*: 801–826.

Deleuze, G., & Guattari, F. (1974). *Anti-Oedipus. Capitalism and Schizophrenia*. Minneapolis, MN: University of Minnesota Press, 1983.

Deserno, H. (1999). *Das Jahrhundert der Traumdeutung*. Stuttgart, Germany: Klett-Cotta.

Dettmering, P. (1989). Kreatives Wagnis und Regression. Zu den Filmen von Andrej Tarkowski. *Psyche—Zeitschrift für Psychoanalyse und ihre Anwendungen, 43*: 445–458.

Diamond, D., & Wrye, H. (1998a). Prologue. One hundred years of film and psychoanalysis. *Psychoanalytic Inquiry, 18*: 139–146.

Diamond, D., & Wrye, H. (1998b). Epilogue. Projections of psychic reality: A centennial of film and psychoanalysis. *Psychoanalytic Inquiry, 18*: 311–334.

Fellini, F. (1981). *Aufsätze und Notizen*. Zürich: Diogenes.

Freud, S. (1939a). *Moses and Monotheism. S. E., 23*: 1–138. London: Hogarth.

Gabbard, G. O. (1997). The psychoanalysts at the movies. *International Journal of Psychoanalysis, 78*: 429–434.

Gabbard, G. O. (1998). Vertigo: Female objectification, male desire, and object loss. *Psychoanalytic Inquiry, 18*: 161–169.

Gabbard, G. O., & Gabbard, K. (1987). *Psychiatry and the Cinema*. Chicago, IL: University of Chicago Press.

Hamburger, A., & Leube-Sonnleitner, K. (2014). Wie im Kino. Zur Filmanalyse in der Gruppe—Methodologie der Psychoanalytischen Filminterpretation anhand von Lars von Triers *Melancholia*. In: R. Zwiebel & D. Blothner (Eds.), *Melancholia—Wege zur psychoanalytischen Interpretation des Films* (pp. 72–109). Göttingen, Germany: Vandenhoeck & Ruprecht.

Hartmann, E. (1998). *Dreams and Nightmares. The New Theory on the Origin and Meaning of Dreams*. New York: Plenum Trade.

Kirley, J. P. (1995). Blow up: The "I" of the camera. *Psychoanalytic Review, 82*: 443–453.

Körner, J. (1985). *Vom Erklären zum Verstehen in der Psychoanalyse*. Göttingen, Germany: Vandenhoeck & Ruprecht.

Koch, G. (1995). Nähe und Distanz: Face-to-face-Kommunikation in der Moderne. In: G. Koch (Ed.), *Auge und Affekt. Wahrnehmung und Interaktion* (pp. 272–291). Frankfurt, Germany: Fischer.

Langer, S. (1942). *Philosophy in a New Key: A Study in the Symbolism of Reason, Rite, and Art*. Boston, MA: Harvard University Press, 1997.

Laszig, P., & Schneider, G. (Eds.) (2008). *Film und Psychoanalyse. Kinofilme als kulturelle Symptome*. Giessen, Germany: Psychosozial-Verlag.

Lewin, B. D. (1953). Reconsideration of the Dream Screen. *Psychoanal Quarterly*, 22: 174–199.

Lippert, R. (1999). Buchbesprechung: Zeul, Mechthild: Carmen und Co. Weiblichkeit und Sexualität im Film (Stuttgart: Verlag Internationale Psychoanalyse, 1997). *Psyche—Zeitschrift für Psychoanalyse und ihre Anwendungen, 53*: 690–692.

Maier, C. (2014). Urszene. In: W. Mertens (Ed.), *Handbuch psychoanalytischer Grundbegriffe (4th revised and supplemented edition)* (pp. 1044–1047). Stuttgart, Germany: Kohlhammer.

Mertens, W. (2001). Was bleibt von Freuds Traumpsychologie? *Zeitschrift für psychoanalytische Theorie und* Praxis, *16*: 123–148.

Monaco, J. (1995). *How to Read a Film: Movies, Media, and Beyond*. Oxford: Oxford University Press, 2009.

Mulvey, L. (1975). Visual pleasure and narrative cinema. *Screen, 16*(3): 6–18.

Pagel, J. F., Kwiatkowski, C., & Broyles, K. E. (1999). Dream use in film making. *Dreaming, 9*: 247–255.

Piegler, T. (2009). *Mit Freud im Kino. Psychoanalytische Filminterpretationen*. Giessen, Germany: Psychosozial-Verlag.

Rauschenbach, B. (1996). Von uns selbst aber sprechen wir—Störenfried Subjektivität als Symptom und Methode unserer Zeit. In: M. Heinze & S. Priebe (Eds.), *Störenfried Subjektivität. Subjektivität und Objektivität als Begriffe des psychiatrischen Denkens* (pp. 15–42). Würzburg, Germany: Königshausen & Neumann.

Reiche, R. (2000). *Mutterseelenallein. Kunst, Form und Psychoanalyse.* Frankfurt, Germany: Stroemfeld.

Rohde-Dachser, C. (1991). *Expedition in den dunklen Kontinent. Weiblichkeit im Diskurs der Psychoanalyse.* Berlin: Springer.

Rosa, H. (2005). *Social Acceleration: A New Theory of Modernity.* New York: Columba University Press, 2013.

Sabbadini, A. (Ed.) (2003). *The Couch and the Silver Screen.* New York: Brunner-Routledge.

Schulze, G. (1992). *Erlebnisgesellschaft. Kultursoziologie der Gegenwart.* Frankfurt, Germany: Campus.

Wohlrab, L. (Ed.) (2006). *Filme auf der Couch. Psychoanalytische Interpretationen.* Giessen, Germany: Psychosozial-Verlag.

Zeul, M. (1997). *Carmen und Co. Weiblichkeit und Sexualität im Film.* Stuttgart, Germany: Verlag Internationale Psychoanalyse.

Zeul, M. (2007). *Das Höhlenhaus der Träume. Filme, Kino & Psychoanalyse.* Frankfurt, Germany: Brandes & Apsel.

Zwiebel, R., & Mahler-Bungers, A. (Eds.) (2007). *Projektion und Wirklichkeit. Die unbewusste Botschaft des Films.* Göttingen, Germany: Vandenhoeck & Ruprecht.

CHAPTER THREE

Beautiful beasts—motif tradition and film psychoanalysis in Jean Cocteau's La Belle et la Bête (F 1946)

*Andreas Hamburger**

Film psychoanalysis, seen in the tradition of cultural analysis (Lorenzer, 1986), takes the unconscious reaction of the viewer as its starting point. As members of a cinema audience, we are less like the analyst and more like the analysand. We are open to interpreting the work, we engage with it—in the knowledge that it is a work of art and not a patient (Hamburger, 2013; Hamburger & Leube, 2014; Mertens, 2015; Reiche, 2011; Schneider, 2008, 2014). Film psychoanalysis doesn't aim at psychological description of authors or characters, but rather at reflection on our own involvement by way of "mutual enactment". The unconscious that is evoked by films is the unconscious of the viewer. In a process of introspection, we can ascertain it and reflect on it, developing hypotheses on aspects that resonate with us—matters otherwise split off and kept hidden, even from our inner view. But establishing and introspectively reflecting on our own involvement in a film scene are only the beginning of the process of "working through", mediating the material in relation to ourselves. The confrontation with the work of art involves "labours in the depths" (Hamburger, 2013, p. 66, quoting

* Translated by Susan Jones.

Freud, 1914d), which can extend into a long series of explorations and analyses. We rely on the support of film and media scholars, since this is not a tête à tête: the analyst is never alone with the film, as it is directed to an audience and is part of a media-based process. Its language cannot be understood without reference to the overall cultural environment to which the film relates and in which it situates itself (cf. Chapter One, this volume). And this is by no means only the present: LA BELLE ET LA BÊTE was filmed almost seventy years ago and is received very differently today than it was at that time—as is shown at many junctures in this volume. For this reason a psychoanalytical approach to the film requires, alongside systematic reflection of our own response to it today, that we reconstruct the implicit audience (Kuhn, 2011) to which it originally appealed.

The following film-psychoanalytical introduction to LA BELLE ET LA BÊTE intends to reflect on its background in cultural and film history. This makes it necessary to go beyond the film as an individual opus. As a discipline within psychoanalysis, film psychoanalysis tends towards the perspective of text immanence, relying on careful examination of the work itself. This is to some extent a precautionary measure in reaction to some past interpretations that misrepresented the work of art as little more than a symptom. Building on methodological criticism especially in the field of literary analysis (see e.g., Hamburger, 1993, 1996, 2013; Lorenzer, 1986; Reiche, 2001) that has exposed the symptomatic approach as "pathography", today we regard the audience response in the here and now of cinematic reception as the subject and starting point of film psychoanalysis. The resulting tendency to focus entirely on the work and its integration into the overall artistic continuum—in accord with the dictum of the "death of the author" (Barthes, 1967; Foucault, 1969)—may, however, fall short of the mark, particularly in cases where the author has stylised his own person as a work of art and in doing so has himself become a part of his opus, or where for other reasons, a strictly text-immanent interpretation would be tantamount to a disavowal of the work (cf. Hamburger, 2001, for the example of Frank Wedekind). The following will therefore address not only the contextualisation of LA BELLE ET LA BÊTE within the traditions of art and literature from which it emerged, and the history of the film's reception as it affects today's viewers, but also will touch on the person of Cocteau. Only by taking his artistic persona into account can we comprehend the response of today's audience to LA BELLE ET LA BÊTE.

For the viewer today, LA BELLE ET LA BÊTE has a certain old-fashioned quaintness. It seems to be about an unhappy, hairy man who is exquisitely dressed but very ungainly in his demeanour and in dealing with his own sexual needs. Instead of exciting the lust of the girl he longs for, he sets her on a pedestal, like a queen, and provides amenities of all kinds. At moments in which this ideal of abstention can no longer be upheld and he is overcome by desire, he flees or goes hunting, and he begins to exude smoke. With its dramaturgy reminiscent of the silent movie, the film comes across like an optical rarity bathing the viewer in rich detail rather than taking hold of him. An artwork made of light, but strangely distant.

Does this only apply today? Or was the film already disconnected from the age in which it was produced? Calling to mind that LA BELLE ET LA BÊTE was made in 1946, one year after World War II and the Holocaust, today's viewer may be a bit alarmed. At that historical moment, wouldn't one expect something other than a timeless fairy tale, a costume film? But the response at the time was quite positive: the film premiered in Cannes and, the same year, won the Prix Louis Delluc, sometimes called the "Prix Goncourt for cinema"—directly after André Malraux's L'ESPOIR (E/F 1945), filmed during the Spanish Civil War.

From the opening titles on, Cocteau's film emphasises a manifold interrelation of media: out of the black, to dramatic music, the shutter opens onto a roomful of practical utensils. We see Cocteau at a blackboard writing the names "Jean Marais" (Fig. 1) and "Josette Day" that are then erased by each of the actors; he then writes his own name.

The image cross-fades to the film title, with Cocteau adding the circumflex mark. The remaining titles run through, also in Cocteau's

Figure 1. Cocteau writing "Marais" (LA BELLE ET LA BÊTE 00:00:52).

handwriting but visibly with more effort at calligraphic perfection, on the blackboard that Cocteau wipes clean several more times—with repeated cross-fades clearly directing attention to the film medium. After the titles, a camera assistant appears with a clapper board, announces the take, and is interrupted by Cocteau saying "Cut! One minute!" This is followed by a text also written in chalk but scrolled over the blackboard, accompanied by a buzzing sound. It addresses the viewer directly and ends with the magic formula used to introduce fairy tales:

> Children believe what they are told and doubt it not. [...] I am asking of you a little of this naïveté now, and, to bring us all good fortune, let me say four magic words, the veritable "open sesame" of childhood: Once upon a time ... —*Jean Cocteau*. (Cocteau, 1946, p. 75)

This voice-over, where the author and director Cocteau appears as a figure in his own film and directly addresses the viewer, is referred to in classical rhetoric as an "apostrophe". With it, the film creates a narrative situation that it simultaneously deconstructs: the formula "once upon a time" is typical to the genre of (oral) fairy tales, while the blackboard stands for classroom learning and paradigmatically for the quantum leap of civilisation, the introduction of writing. Oral tradition and the written word are intermingled here—although, as Derrida (1967) points out, they are antagonistic because the irreversibly univocal written word undermines the equivocal poetry of oral narration. Moreover, the opening titles are laced with over-explicit allusions that say "this is a film" (clapper board, camera noise), announcing the next shift of a cultural paradigm, this time to moving pictures that in turn threaten to undermine the culture of writing (cf. Hamburger, 2014). By creating this inter-media connection between the magic of personal narrative and its fixation or depletion in written text, the opening titles of LA BELLE ET LA BÊTE immediately evoke a great tradition: the history, extending back at least 1700 years, of the literary fairy tale *La Belle et la Bête*. That history is itself characterised by the reciprocal interaction of oral and written traditions.

The following considerations trace the convoluted history of this fairy-tale motif, which is closely associated with the *topos* of female gender identity and gender construction. This is not being undertaken in the sense of a metahistorical psychological view—as in the Jungian and, partly also in some Freudian perspectives (e.g., Bettelheim, 1975; Dieckmann, 1966; Neumann, 1971 among others; for critique see Bottigheimer, 1989b and Burton, 1978)—but rather in order to show how the universal demand that cultural symbolisation[1] is expected to fulfil has elicited, under differing historical circumstances, re-articulations including the new interpretation of this seemingly familiar story in Cocteau's LA BELLE ET LA BÊTE.

The contributions that follow in this volume (Chapters Four to Seven) will take up this issue in greater depth from the differing perspectives of film and cultural scholarship on the one hand, and psychoanalysis on the other. The present chapter is meant to situate the film in its historical context and thereby derive a suitable approach for film-psychoanalytic reflection on this classic after almost seventy years. Many indicators suggest the construction of masculinity as the central theme.

Beautiful girls and wild guys—on the history of a motif

LA BELLE ET LA BÊTE makes explicit reference to the eponymous literary fairy tale by Jeanne-Marie Leprince de Beaumont (1756). Before Cocteau, this was the most well-known version of the tale, based on the lesser-known precursor by Gabrielle-Suzanne Barbot Gallon de Villeneuve (1740), which takes up the ancient fairy tale theme of the animal bridegroom and modifies it in a characteristic fashion. The earliest literary documentation of the theme is Apuleius' *Amor and Psyche* from the second century (AaTh 425;[2] cf. Megas, 1977; Uther, 2004, pp. 252 f.). In this gamut of motifs,[3] a virgin is to be married off to an animal-man under some unusual circumstances. In the eighteenth century, while the combined type of fairy tale *La Belle et la Bête* is developing (AaTh 425C), another story thread is added with the vow of sacrifice, which points towards an even deeper historical layer of tradition. Both motifs, the sacrificial vow and the animal bridegroom, relate to the construction of femininity.

Primal scene I: Jephthah's daughter

The motif of the fatal vow appears early, in the Old Testament narrative on the daughter of Jephthah (Judges 11: 30–40, KJV; cf. Bauks, 2010). It served as a pattern for innumerable sagas about pacts with the devil or "bridge sacrifices" (Daxelmüller, 1987; Schnyder, 2010) that generally present a man on terrain foreign to him and faced with an impossible task, who promises some higher power (god, devil, demon) that he will sacrifice the first being he encounters upon his return home. The story takes a tragic turn: this first being is at the same time the best-loved, in the case of Jephthah his only daughter. What frequently ensues is a crafty attempt to escape from the pact that was sealed. In bridge sacrifice stories, it's usually the devil who is promised the first soul to cross the bridge; and easy to outwit as the devil is, he ends up (as in Regensburg at the Stone Bridge) with a dog. In the story of Jephthah, there is no crafty trick. It is God Himself to whom the cruel promise was given, "… whatsoever [first] cometh forth of the doors of my house to meet me […] shall surely be the Lord's, and I will offer it up for a burnt offering" (Judges 11: 31). The solution is achieved—as in LA BELLE ET LA BÊTE—through obedience:

> And it came to pass, when he saw her, that he rent his clothes, and said, Alas, my daughter! thou hast brought me very low, and thou art one of them that trouble me: for I have opened my mouth unto the Lord, and cannot go back. And she said unto him, My father, if thou hast opened thy mouth unto the Lord, do to me according to that which hath proceeded out of thy mouth; […] Let this thing be done for me: let me alone two months, that I may go up and down upon the mountains, and bewail my virginity, I and my fellows. […] And it came to pass at the end of two months, that she returned unto her father, who did with her according to his vow which he had vowed: and she knew no man. And it was a custom in Israel, that the daughters of Israel went yearly to lament the daughter of Jephthah the Gileadite four days in a year. (Judges 11: 35–40)

The end of the biblical story is devastating: Jephthah's daughter is immolated, in accordance with the vow. Like Apuleius' Psyche and La Belle, she accepts her fate, but she is not rescued, she is sacrificed. The sacrifice itself is not described in the biblical text, only her virginity and the transformation of the story into an annual religious ritual.

The motif of the sacrificial vow, like that of the animal bridegroom, is related to another gamut of motifs in which the girl is married off with some kind of delay, as in *The Girl without Hands* (AaTh 706; Grimm nr. 31; Masoni, 2010). From a psychoanalytical point of view, there is an astounding subliminal connection between these motifs: both in the biblical account of Jephthah's daughter and in *The Girl without Hands,* virginity is associated with death or disfigurement.

Primal scene II: Amor and Psyche

The core motif of the animal bridegroom (AaTh 425), to which LA BELLE ET LA BÊTE also refers, addresses the connection between virginity, attractiveness, and death. In the history of this motif, the reciprocal influence of oral and literary transmission is characteristic (cf. De Vries, 1989; Swahn, 1989). The earliest literary evidence, which is also the earliest literary fairy tale handed down, is from the key narrative "Amor [Cupid] and Psyche", which Apuleius (2nd century AD/1895), wove into his *Metamorphoses [The Golden Ass]*:

> Psyche is the youngest of three daughters of a king. She is so beautiful that she is worshipped by human beings, even overshadowing Venus. But no suitor dares approach her. In accord with an oracle, she is dressed in a bridal gown and taken to a lonely peak, where she is to marry a terrible demon. Obediently, she accepts her fate. In the meanwhile, Venus has ordered her son Amor to smite Psyche with irrepressible love for the most miserable human being. But Amor himself falls in love with her and has Zephyr carry her to a magical castle filled with riches. There, invisible hands serve her and bring the very best of foods. Amor visits her every night. He allows her sisters to visit her, under the condition that she make no attempt to find out who he is. Within three visits, the envious sisters persuade her that she has married a serpent who never appears by daylight because he is such a horrible sight, and who will devour her now that she is pregnant. Out of fear for her unborn child and herself, she follows her sisters' advice and, in the next night, awaits her husband with an oil lamp and a knife.
>
> When she casts the light on her lover, she doesn't see a monster, but rather the beautiful body of winged Amor—the description of this moment is a wonderful image both of the man's youthful beauty and of the sexual desire of the young woman. In her craving, she touches his arrow and pricks her finger. Then she makes love to him and doesn't notice that a drop of hot oil is falling onto his

> shoulder. The god awakens, realizes that he has been betrayed, and disappears swearing that he will punish the evil sisters. Psyche wants to plunge to her death. But the river god saves her, and the god of the forest, Pan, advises her to ask Amor for forgiveness. She visits her sisters and makes them think that Amor now wants to marry them: delighted, and in the assumption that Zephyr will carry them away to Amor, they leap from the same cliff—with fatal result.
>
> Due to Amor's injury, the (dis-)order of human love is also endangered; Venus, who learns what has happened and realizes that her son has disregarded her command, plans revenge. She wants to castigate Amor and she persecutes pregnant Psyche, having Mercury call out Psyche's name and even announcing a reward of her own kisses for Psyche's capture. Not even the other goddesses can help Psyche, who decides to surrender. Venus tortures and ridicules her, giving her four irresolvable tasks. At each task, she wants to plunge to her death, but natural forces and the gods allied with Amor help her to complete them. But when she reaches the last task, she is unable to withstand the temptation: she tries out Venus' cosmetic cream (Proserpina's beauty salve) and falls into a deep, death-like sleep. Amor, who by now has escaped from his mother, rescues her and gains Jupiter's permission to marry her. Psyche is given a cup of ambrosia, becomes immortal, marries Amor and gives birth to her daughter Voluptas [lust].

The late Roman literary fairy tale is based on a (lost) Greek precursor that in turn had its origin in a much older oral tradition handed down in many cultures (Hearne, 1989b, p. 10; Reinhardt, 2012, chap. 2; Uther, 2004).

Absolutism and gender order—baroque versions of La Belle et la Bête

After Apuleius' text was rediscovered by Boccaccio in about 1350, or after its first printing in 1472, the motif was reduplicated in literary versions. It entered the baroque universe of French absolutism via a short novel by Lafontaine, *Les amours de Psyché et de Cupidon* (1669), which was later adapted several times. The title *La Belle et la Bête* was used for the first time by Gabrielle-Suzanne Barbot Gallon de Villeneuve (1740); she also added the motifs of the rose and the vow, and placed the plot into a complex context involving the feudal world and magic.

Her work was followed by the better-known and dramaturgically more concise version of Jeanne-Marie Leprince de Beaumont (1756), on which Cocteau's film is directly based.

But the motif of the animal bridegroom also made its way to France independently, without such novelistic extensions—and in this line of reception, where male socialisation is more in focus than female socialisation, the animal bridegroom is quite a threatening figure. A Venetian version, the tale of a prince born in a pigskin who kills his wives, is already represented in the popular fairy tale collection *Le Piacevoli Notti* by Giovanni Francesco Straparola (1556). It was also known in France (Bottigheimer, 1989a). In 1697, Charles Perrault published a version influenced by the Enlightenment, the fairy tale "Riquet à la Houppe" (Riquet with the Shock of Hair). It presents the animal bridegroom as a disgusting dwarf, Riquet, who isn't blessed with magical powers or riches, but rather with extraordinary intelligence that the girl comes to share through love, while her beauty is transferred to him as well, as her lover.

This short glance at the history already shows how differently the fairy tale motif has been realised in varying societal contexts. This is of great significance for our attempt to interpret LA BELLE ET LA BÊTE psychoanalytically: it indicates that we must take into account the currents of historical transmission and reception. In contrast to early psychoanalysis, we don't regard fairy tales as the precipitate of an ahistorical, potentially gender-related psychic constitution, but instead as cultural artefacts. Literary psychoanalysis that addresses such texts assumes—as does film analysis—that the unconscious aspects evoked by the work are in part governed by the requirements of socialisation within a specific culture and epoch. Analytical interpretation therefore needs to integrate scholarly insights from other disciplines (cf. Hamburger, 1996, 2001, 2003, 2006, 2013; Hamburger & Leube, 2014; Lorenzer, 1986; von Hoff & Leuzinger-Bohleber, 1997). Surely, one motif threading through *Amor and Psyche*/*LA BELLE ET LA BÊTE* is adolescence, which is a phenomenon—be it a sexual or a social one—calling for symbolisation in practically all cultures. This topic is, however, treated very differently under varying societal circumstances (Baker, 1989; Bohleber, 1996; Erdheim, 1993; Hamburger, 2001; Mertens, 1996). Analogously, fairy tale motifs are reformulated in keeping with societal conditions.

What is it that has changed? In its ancient, early stages, the fairy tale motif of the animal bridegroom addresses the societal conflicts set in motion by femininity as it unfolds: fantasised rivalry with the mother (Venus) and with envious sisters, concupiscent fascination with the male sex.[4] Read in this way, the early tradition is focused on female coming-of-age and the fantasies it releases concerning male sexuality. By contrast, variations in the early modern age, such as Straparola and Perrault, direct less attention to girls and more to the sexual transformation of the boy in the familial constellation: they are concerned with identity problems of the pig-like prince or the ugly dwarf Riquet. With this, the history of the motif takes a new turn: neither Amor nor Psyche had to worry about gender identity. The fact that Straparola's animal bridegroom is perceived as threatening bespeaks the unsurmountable social distinctions and asymmetric gender economy of sixteenth-century Venice (Bottigheimer, 1989a), while the ironic final twist of the modernist Perrault tells us how the Enlightenment toyed with myth: due to her marriage with the monstrous dwarf, the simpleton princess is not only blessed with intelligence, but in a second step also falls in love with Riquet and initiates his transformation, which—and this is the joke—is subjective. In accord with the tenet that beauty is in the eye of the beholder, he becomes attractive only in her eyes (Barchilon, 1959).

What happens when the fairy tale arrives in the seventeenth century and is functionalised as a tool for bringing up girls? Very different things, as the two most important text precursors of La Belle et la Bête will show us.

Intrigue in the realm of the fairies—La Belle et la Bête by Barbot Gallon de Villeneuve (1740)

Gabrielle-Suzanne Barbot Gallon de Villeneuve, who published the material as a novel in 1740 and was the first to use the title *La Belle et la Bête*, connects it with two additional motifs. Alongside the above-mentioned motif from the story of Jephthah's daughter, the sacrificial vow, she adds the rose and with this anchors the dramaturgy for the first time to a fateful—albeit innocent—wish of the girl. Typical for this epoch is the introduction of the girl as a bourgeoise who later reveals her noble standing, so that the feudal order is maintained. The narrative of the novel will be recapitulated here as the first essential foil upon which the film La Belle et la Bête is built.

> In the 186 pages of her novel, Barbot (1740) first describes the impoverished state of Belle's family (she is the youngest of eleven

> children, the most beautiful and the kindest, envied by her sisters). After two years, the father travels to the city to save a part of his fortune. The older sisters want him to bring them jewelry and dresses, the youngest only wishes for his safe return and finally also requests a rose.

The addition of the rose motif seems to be an original contribution of Barbot's (see also Chapter 4, this volume). Since then, it has been instated as an indispensable constituent of the tale—one adaptation in 1804 even appeared under the title *Beauty and the Beast; or, The Magic Rose* (quoted from Hearne, 1989b, p. 207). Since ancient times, the rose has been established as a symbol with a wide variety of meanings; its range of connotations extends from ephemeral youth and virginity to symbolising Christ or love, particularly in the combination of longing and pain. Mintz (1970) interprets the symbol of the rose in the movie LA BELLE ET LA BÊTE as connecting the manliness of La Bête (thorns) with the femininity of La Belle (period and defloration). Sabbadini (Chapter Four, this volume) situates the rose in yet another context, understanding it above all as a communicative sign, a declaration of love, and in this sense he even sees the film itself as an "already slightly withered, hypnotically scented, black-and-white … rose" (p. 109, this volume). With regard to the history of the motif, another very specific significance of the rose is of interest in our context: it relates directly to the frame narrative of Apuleius' *The Golden Ass*. There, the rose is the antidote sought by the storyteller, who has been transformed into a donkey, throughout the entire text so that he can transform himself back into a human.

> Returning from the unsuccessful business trip after six months, in Barbot's telling the father is caught in a snowstorm, hides in a hollow tree, and the next morning looks out onto a castle in a park full of flowers and statues, spared from the snow, where an exquisite meal awaits him. He begins to take the castle for the gift of a good spirit, and packs away all the treasures he can find. Just as he is leaving and wants to pick the rose, he is suddenly threatened by a monster with a trunk and horns, who only pardons him under the condition that he bring back one of his daughters within a month. The father asks what ruse he should apply to lure her, but the fiend insists that she must come of her own will. Riding home on a magic

horse after spending a night in the castle, the father regrets his promise, but can't get the horse to turn back. At home, when he tells the whole story, the sons want to sacrifice themselves but the daughters don't: only Belle, who thinks this could all be her fault, is willing to assume the sacrificial role. Her father returns to the castle together with her. After one night the father is sent away, laden with gifts. Together with Belle he decides to take mostly money, since that will make him more independent.

After her father's departure, Belle has a dream about a handsome prince who asks her to rescue him by complying with her feelings of gratefulness and staying with him forever. In a second dream, a fairy appears and promises that all will be well, and Belle goes on dreaming for five more hours, during which she sees the prince in hundreds of situations. She also discovers paintings of him in the castle. At dinner the first evening, La Bête appears and is extremely mild-mannered, but also asks her directly whether she wants to sleep with him ["Elle lui demanda sans détour si elle vouloit la laisser coucher avec elle" (Barbot, 1740, p. 73)], which she declines. La Bête withdraws, Belle retires to bed, and again dreams of the prince, who reproaches her for refusing him. She is confused by this dream. The next day, she explores the castle and the garden. She finds the setting of her dreams and discovers a group of well-mannered and well-dressed monkeys, who serve her food and perform plays for her. The days pass by and she sees La Bête every evening at dinner, but doesn't dare to ask him about the dream prince. While further investigating the castle, she discovers a room where a theatre performance in Paris can be watched on a crystal pane—a precise premonition of cinema, in the year 1740.

Now Belle becomes pensive. She acknowledges the persistent love of La Bête, but she herself loves the nocturnal prince. To him, she explains her dilemma, and he replies: "Love the one who loves you, don't be fooled by appearances, and free me from my prison" ["Aime qui t'aime, ne te laisse point surprendre aux apparences, & tire-moi de prison" (ibid., p. 83)]. Essentially, up to this point the fable is about Belle's slow-wittedness: she simply doesn't understand what has long been perfectly clear to the reader—that the prince and La Bête are one and the same person. She spends more days in the crystal-pane theatre, taking in an opera performance and other cultural events from the capital. She has become accustomed to La Bête, both to his ugly appearance and his oafish conversation. In the evenings, she longs for the dream prince and fantasises that he could be locked up somewhere in the castle. She gets caught up in an inner crisis, from which she distracts herself by frequently switching programmes in the crystal theatre: "She had nothing to calm her disquiet but the pleasure of theatre-going. She was at the commedia dell'arte, left during the first scene to go to the opera, but left that again just as quickly" ["Elle n'avoit pour calmer ses ennuis que le plaisir des spectacles. Elle fut à la comédie italienne, d'où, dès la premiere scène, elle sortit pour aller a l'opéra, mais elle en sortit encore avec la meme promptitude" (ibid., p. 93)]. Despite all this "zapping", she feels melancholy and longs for her family; on her request, but filled with sadness, La Bête gives her leave for two months, along with gifts and a magic ring to speed her return. Confronted in a dream with the option of taking the prince back with her into her real life and in doing so hazarding the death of La Bête, she replies that she would rather take her own life than his.

Spirited away to her home by magical powers, she discovers that La Bête has also taken care of her family. She longs to go back to him (and to the nocturnal dream prince), and her father advises her to enter into a liaison with La Bête. Her sisters' suitors woo her; her father asks her to stay longer. She agrees—but then she dreams that La Bête's life is in danger. The ring takes her back to the castle, where she finds La Bête in the garden, apparently lifeless, just as she had dreamt. She fetches water and pours it onto him out of her hands (an allusion to baptism), repeating this process with the aid of her servant monkeys until he finally comes back to life. Not until now had she realised how much she loves him, and she promises to become his wife. The dream prince also advises her to do so (to her disappointment), as does the dream fairy. Belle still has not understood the connection. In another dream, the prince thanks her solemnly for saving him and his entire realm, and she sees him lying there as if dead. When she wakes up, he is there, in the flesh, lying on a couch next to her bed. Now she finally comprehends that the two are one and the same.

The hitch: the prince can't be awakened. In Barbot de Villeneuve's novel, the second and more extensive part of the plot now begins, serving to rectify the fairy-tale elements of the first part (and of the motif AaTh 425A) rationally and historically. The

> good fairy arrives with the prince's mother, who is thankful for his rescue but won't allow him to marry a bourgeoise. Generously, Belle withdraws, but then it emerges that she is actually of noble blood (she is the fairy's niece). Now, the prince tells the story of his transformation. It is related to the absence of the queen-mother, who was waging war, to the marriage proposal of the moody and ancient fairy to whom he had been entrusted, to the curse she put on him when he refused, and to the lengthy counter-intrigue spun by the good fairy. As we soon learn, the same fairies were struggling with one another in the complicated case of the little princess Belle, which finally resulted in her being slipped, unnoticeably, into the merchant family.

As we see, in the first baroque fairy tale of *La Belle et la Bête*, the challenge of love and sexuality is treated as a de-stabilisation and re-stabilisation of the feudal universe. Not so a few years later in the next version.

The merchant's daughter—La Belle et la Bête by Leprince de Beaumont (1756)

Cocteau's direct model, the version by Leprince de Beaumont published in 1756, alters essential details of the plot and, in particular, spares the reader the lengthy second section with its baroque convolutions about warring fairies. Leprince casts Belle as a bourgeois girl, and she treats money and property as leitmotifs of the literary fairy tale. "'Beauty and the Beast' [is] a fable about coming to terms with the institution of marriage and with the person of a husband" (Bottigheimer, 1989b, p. 8). In the framework plot of her *Magasin des enfants, ou dialogues entre une sage gouvernante et plusiers de ses eleves de la premiere distinction (The Young Misses Magazine, Containing Dialogues between a Governess and Several Young Ladies of Quality, Her Scholars)*, where *La belle et la Bête* is embedded as a educational tale, the narrator admonishes her listeners (and, likewise, her readers) to remember that good behaviour is always rewarded.

> In the version of Leprince (1756), the story is situated in a bourgeois family context. The merchant family consists of the father, three daughters, and three sons, significantly (again) with no mother. The story tells about the father's loss of fortune due to shipwrecks, and

> about their move to the country. When the father, who is hoping to recover his fortune, stumbles upon the castle, first he is served food by invisible powers, and he doesn't pick the rose until the next morning. The monster gives him three months to hand over his youngest daughter, and allows him to take whatever treasures he wants from the castle. Here, there is also a fairy figure who encourages Belle to persevere. There is a magic mirror, in which she sees that her father is ill. Her visit home is not extended at her father's request, but rather—as in the film—because of the theatrical tears of her envious sisters, who want Belle to fall out of La Bête's grace. After the prince is redeemed, the envious sisters are turned into statues by the fairy, and the moral of the story is proclaimed: that fortune rests on virtue.

The two baroque versions differ in many respects from the ancient source. "The story of *Cupid and Psyche* communicates unbridled passion leading to ultimate pleasure, while *Beauty and the Beast*'s language and plot tell of ethicalised hypocrisy resulting in queenship and wealth. The tales are about as similar as the togas and the embroidered bodices of their tellers" (Bottigheimer, 1989b, p. 12).

It is interesting that one reason why the Leprince version enjoyed such wide distribution was that the author, whose background was modest, after a failed marriage emigrated to England—which was better developed, economically and politically. At first she worked as a governess, then as a successful author of children's books. There, she also published her adaptation of Barbot's forerunner novel (1740) in English.

In the nineteenth century, this version was disseminated widely, especially in the English edition (cf. Erhart, 2007, pp. 25 f.). But in France as well, it was popular enough to appear in the Epinal pictorial series,[5] in radically reduced form. The story is told in ten individual frames:

> (1) A merchant has three daughters; the others are jealous of the youngest, who is the most beautiful and gracious; (2) he promises to bring her back a rose from his travels. (3) He arrives at the magic castle and finds that dinner is served; (4) when he picks the rose, a monster appears and sentences him to either die or hand over one daughter. (5) At home, he relates his adventure, and Belle decides to die in his stead. (6) La Bête is host to the merchant and

> his daughter. (7) He asks Belle for her hand in marriage. (8) Belle refuses and receives permission to visit her father for a few days. (9) On her return she finds La Bête dying of sorrow and promises to marry him, (10) whereafter La Bête is transformed into a young prince and takes her as his wife.

This is the skeleton version of the fairy tale from the perspective of the nineteenth century. The popular, abbreviated form merely contains the key concepts of envy—wish—pleasure—punishment—renunciation—reward; magical embellishments are omitted, as are the nocturnal encounters with the handsome Amor, who Barbot (1740) had already reduced to a dream apparition and Leprince (1756) had done away with altogether. In the twentieth century, the theme saw various adaptations before and after World War I (cf. Hearne, 1989b, Chap. Five), including the frivolous satire "A Fairy Tale in Two Acts" by Nozière (1909). All this notwithstanding: virginal femininity remains the core element of all the literary precursors of the film.

Static and moving pictures

The background of the film in terms of cultural history is, however, not just a matter of narrative tradition. Films are essentially formed by images, and particularly LA BELLE ET LA BÊTE draws its reference from a tradition of images that had given shape to the motif over the centuries. Iconic images of femininity and animal-like masculinity span the ages, from the frequently depicted ancient myth of Zeus and Europe, through the iconography of the unicorn,[6] and on into modern times: in representational-romanticised depictions such as *Beauty and Strength* (1894) by Angelo Graf von Courten, showing a coquettish but child-like girl with a sheath and arrows beside a gentle lion; and later Henri Rousseau's *Sleeping Gypsy* (1897), Emil Nolde's *Animal and Woman* (1931/1935) or Picasso's many treatments of the minotaur motif—to name only a few.

One of the major themes of images relating to the tension between the sexes is the myth of Amor and Psyche. Numerous ancient depictions show the couple, usually with the protagonists in harmony and rarely emphasising the drama of their story (Reinhardt, 2012, p. 122). Not until Boccaccio's above-mentioned rediscovery of Apuleius, who had been forgotten in medieval times, did images of the myth begin to appear after 1470 that called attention to the individual episodes of the couple's dramatic relationship (ibid.). One excellent example from the High Renaissance would be Raphael's frescos in the Villa Farnesina (Fig. 2).

Around 1800, the myth of Amor and Psyche is revitalised, or even reinvented (Holm, 2006). Now the focus is on the harmonious integration of love into an optimistic and enlightened order of society and gender. Particularly well known and frequently copied: the graceful sculpture by Antonio Canova (1793), in which winged Amor, tenderly touching her breast, sinks into the arms of a languishing Psyche. And although the moment captured by the sculptor portrays the Oedipal force of the myth—Psyche has fallen into a death-like sleep after applying the beauty salve Proserpina had made, solely for Venus, and is awakened by Amor—in the aestheticised treatment there is no hint of the dramatic complexities of their love story: beauty and sensuality take the day (Fig. 3).

Figure 2. Raphael: Le nozze di Amore e Psiche. Villa Farnesina (1518) (detail).

Figure 3. Antonio Canova: Psiche rianimata dal bacio di amore (1793). Musée du Louvre, Paris.

Increasing attention given to the theme of the animal bride and animal bridegroom in French courtly literature and art since the eighteenth century (cf. Shojaei Kawan, 2010, col. 556) indicates a need to redefine the role of women, first in the upper class and later in the bourgeoisie; for a wider societal spectrum in the nineteenth century, the widely distributed pictorial series from Epinal extended this tradition.

Another pictorial tradition can be seen as a side current of this normative discourse on gender: it relates to the contrast between animal nature and *civilté* that was particularly relevant in the seventeenth and eighteenth centuries. Paintings such as that of the "hairy man" by Petrus Gonsalvus from Teneriffa (Fig. 5), who suffered from hypertrichosis,

Figure 4. La Bête (La Belle et la Bête 00:22:11) (detail).

Figure 5. Petrus Gonsalvus (sixteenth century), Ambras Castle (Tirol).

were on exhibition at European courts, as were the man himself and his similarly afflicted daughter Tognina. Cocteau's make-up artist Hagop Arakelian apparently found inspiration there for La Bête's visage (Fig. 4).

In the history of film before Cocteau, the motif of the animal bridegroom was already firmly established and already enhanced by a fascination with wildness as the "Other of Reason" (Böhme & Böhme, 1983), in melodramas such as KING KONG (USA 1933) or—more ironically—in comedies such as BRINGING UP BABY (USA 1938). In the realm of human ugliness it recurs, analogous to the above-mentioned Perrault literary fairy tale *Riquet à la Houppe*, for example in William Dieterle's THE HUNCHBACK OF NOTRE DAME (USA 1939) (cf. Liptay, 2007).[7]

As its worldwide popularity shows, the basic motif of LA BELLE ET LA BÊTE corresponds to a demand for symbolisation that transcends individual cultures. Although the persistence with which new adaptations have been produced in the widest variety of genres can been regarded as proof of its timelessness, the comparison of the versions discussed here reveals how differently the motif can be realised in specific cultures or epochs.

Being a man—Cocteau's interpretation of the motif in LA BELLE ET LA BÊTE

Cocteau was influenced, as was his audience, by all these strands of tradition when he adapted the fable anew in 1946. It is worthy of note that, in his reception, there is a decisive shift of emphasis. While the educational literature of the eighteenth century had concentrated on female identity, for him the focus of dramatic transformation and the centre of aesthetic interest are changes in the male protagonist. "The Beast's twentieth century angst may reflect obsession as well as imagination on the part of modern adapters" (Hearne, 1989b, p. 137).

Before Cocteau, the tale of Amor and Psyche had unfolded within a feminine framework. As early as Apuleius' text, the narrator is an old woman who belongs to a band of robbers; her story is intended to calm down the girl they have absconded. Barbot de Villeneuve (1740) and Leprince de Beaumont (1756) also consistently pursue the moral enlightenment and fortification of girls in their framework plots and authorial intent. In numerous later adaptations (Hearne, 1989b; Erhart, 2007), alarming masculinity is regarded as animal-like, particularly from the feminine point of view.

This changes with Cocteau's version of LA BELLE ET LA BÊTE. Formerly, the power of the girl's love had been the main determinant of dramaturgy and depiction; now it was the staging of the animal. Cocteau's aestheticised version in LA BELLE ET LA BÊTE places the construction of masculinity at the centre of attention—and a very specific conception of it, as we will see. Cocteau's version is, however, contrary to his own assertions and many claims in secondary literature, not dependent on Leprince (1756). He harks back to Apuleius as well as Barbot de Villeneuve[8] and adds numerous embellishments of his own, along with an entirely new side plot. In contrast to Leprince (1756), the backstory is not told, but only implied. The film begins in the humble farmhouse of the impoverished family. The entrance of the envious sisters is given extensive space, with comical highlights provided by hot-headed male figures.

The incident that opens the film—Avenant's arrow flies into the sisters' room—already presents a symbol of male sexuality (De Nitto, 1976). Cocteau adopted the arrow, which also is decisive for the film's ending, from Apuleius as an essential erotic element.[9] Directly after this phallic exposition, there is a reference to female anatomy in the comical sequence about the drunken lackey and the sedan chairs turned into a henhouse. We will return to this scene: it is the first in which extremities appear prominently as partial objects (Fig. 6), as they will again later on in the castle (Fig. 7). As Cocteau's diary reveals, this allusion is deliberately vulgar: with the camera swinging back to Felicie, who "climbs into her chair settling herself as if she's on the lavatory" (Cocteau, 1946, appendix, p. 392) (Fig. 8).

Women are barely relevant in Cocteau's approach; they are either sexually inaccessible like Belle in her attachment to her father, or they

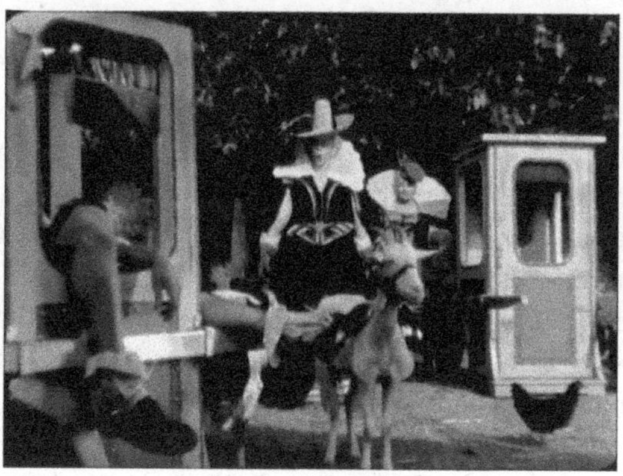

Figure 6. The sedan chair and the lackey's leg (LA BELLE ET LA BÊTE 00:05:27).

Figure 7. Autonomous extremities in the castle (LA BELLE ET LA BÊTE 00:30:40).

Figure 8. The sedan chair as a toilet (LA BELLE ET LA BÊTE 00:05:33).

are strategists like the sisters who, although declassed, rule over and exploit their male antagonists. In the dialogue that follows the opening scene, Avenant proposes to Belle and is turned down—which brings into play Cocteau's decisive addition to the traditional tale. This narrative thread is missing entirely in Leprince (1756)—quite in contrast to Apuleius: here, Psyche enjoys her lover, even though she can't see him. In Barbot (1740) female joys of the flesh are deleted—La Bête is purely revolting—but at least she introduces the dream prince representing Psyche's nocturnal lover, the invisible Amor. In Cocteau, a suitor is identifiable, her brother's friend Avenant, and that solves one of the major dramaturgical contradictions of the Leprince version:

how is it possible that Belle, who has just managed to fall in love with La Bête, can suddenly transfer her affections to the sleek prince? In Cocteau's version, she already knows the man into whom La Bête will be transformed—although she is not entirely pleased about this transformation. More on that later.

After the father departs (accompanied by hope and the diverse wishes of his daughters) we see the two young men sitting at ease in an inn, taking out a loan on the anticipated riches of the father. Immediately, in the cut to the next scene, we see the father at the bailiff's office: he has already had to pawn everything he owned. This sequence of scenes is also from Cocteau, and it's striking that the pawnbroker looks very Jewish (Fig. 9, cf. Fischlin, 1998).[10]

In the next sequence, with the father riding home humiliated and financially ruined, Cocteau sets off a thunderstorm in the forest and with it, he reverses the optics of the film. Up to this point, the images had been more like tableaus, well composed with soft contrasts and shadows: suddenly, we experience a wild scenario full of motion, with graphic contrasts verging on the abstract. Tame as the "beast" will later appear, here the screen is taken over by rawness and roughness (Fig. 10). Cocteau described filmmaking as writing "with the ink of light" (1973, p. 18). Here, he adopted the ink of shadow. At this point in the dramaturgical curve, the wildness of the light effects does not yet have a sexual connotation; instead, the affect being mirrored or cinematically illustrated is the annihilation of the father's pride, the fact

Figure 9. Avenant, Ludovic, and the Jewish moneylender (La Belle et la Bête 00:12:12).

Figure 10. Travelling through the magic forest (LA BELLE ET LA BÊTE 00:14:42).

that he is lost. Differently than in the precursor versions of the *Amor and Psyche* motif, here the staging of the loss of security begins with a male figure (albeit, this also applies to the motif of the sacrificial oath, as in the case of Jephthah's daughter: under duress, the father makes the vow, and then the daughter is killed).

The father reaches the perron of the enchanted castle,[11] enters, and finds himself in even denser darkness than in the preceding scene in the forest. Then we see "torches held by sculptured arms" (Cocteau, 1946, p. 78). The magical furnishings of the castle, now presented extensively in the film, are partly contained in precursor versions—for example, the sumptuous meal that is waiting—but the rest is an original creation of the film: the dismembered arms or the statue's eyes that move, following the action. It is interesting that Cocteau, bypassing Leprince (1756) and Barbot (1740), takes up an element from Apuleius, where Psyche in the magic castle is served by invisible hands: "nullo serviente, sed tantum spiritu quodam impulsa subministrantur" ("without trace of servants, set before her as though by a breath of air") (Apuleius, *The Golden Ass* 5.3), and interprets it as a partial object of a (male) body. The appearance of optically dismembered extremities had been foreshadowed in the lackey scene (scene 19), where a boy's naked leg is hanging out of the sedan chair (Fig. 6). It would be tempting to pursue the idea of partial objects further by linking this observation with the interpretation of Christine Kirchhoff (see Chapter 5, this volume), who views the castle as the body of the absent mother.[12]

Now the main character enters, La Bête. His appearance is different in each version. In Barbot (1740) he has horns and a trunk, in Leprince (1756) he is described as ugly and revolting—and in his own description of himself as insensitive and stupid, which (as Belle correctly replies) is neither a sign of insensitivity nor of stupidity. In Cocteau's version, La Bête is:

> … a lord in fashionable court dress, having nothing of the animal to him but the head and the hands. His head is a magnificent animal's head, a sort of lion with clear eyes. His muzzle glistens in the sun. He speaks like a human. The actor will be dubbed by a bass voice until the time that he assumes his normal voice. His hands are a man's hands, hairy and tipped with claws. His open shirt exposes a dark fleece. (1946, p. 92)

Despite this human emanation and the fact that, for the viewer, this is clearly costuming, La Bête seems rather stern when he demands the life of the merchant—even when he "commutes" this sentence upon hearing about the daughter's wish for a rose: now, as a substitute, he demands one of the three daughters who is willing to be punished in place of the father. It is striking that here, as in the fairy tale precursors, there is no sign of an inner struggle or process. La Bête simply speaks the magic words that set the events in motion. What follows, relating to the sacrificial decision, is presented in condensed form: the respite, which in Leprince was three months, is reduced to three days in LA BELLE ET LA BÊTE, and in contrast to all the precursors (Apuleius, Barbot, and Leprince), no inner development among the sisters is indicated. They are envious and scheming from the outset, even wishing that the beast will devour the father and Belle, while the latter two are in competition to take the sacrifice upon themselves. Belle sneaks out to the stable alone and rides to the castle without her father. That Belle takes the path to sacrifice by herself is a major new element in comparison to all the former versions. Both in Judges and in Apuleius, the girl to be sacrificed is accompanied by her people, and the baroque adaptations also maintain this social integration of the sacrificial motif. Belle's lonesome ride to the castle, her entry into the rite of passage, is associated with the father in terms of cinematic imagery: just as in his storm scene, her ride through the woods is characterised by graphic, spooky images in dark outlines (scenes 133 ff.).

Here again, the images become brighter and less abstract when Belle enters the inner sphere—the magic world we already have some inkling of from the first part of the film. This time, however, the first contact is cause for celebration: in a cleverly constructed series of intercuts, with Belle moving forward confidently, we see her greeting the interior and it greeting her in return, even speaking to her (scenes 135–156). The correspondence is succinctly inscribed on the mirror: "Réfléchissez pour moi—Je réfléchirai pour vous" ("Reflect for me and I will reflect for you") (scene 151; Cocteau, 1992, p. 117). But in the mirror, Belle doesn't see her own beauty or, as in Leprince, the sisters who assume they have triumphed and are rid of her: instead she sees her father, who is ill and tonelessly calls for help (ibid.). Here, the father's illness already figures at the beginning of the second act, while in Leprince it was three months before it triggered Belle's wish to return home, and became the turning point in the drama. Belle tries to flee and, in the garden, meets La Bête for the first time. She faints, and he carries her back to her boudoir. When she awakens, they avoid eye contact: "You must not look me in the eye" (Cocteau, 1946, p. 144). Again, with this dramaturgical decision, Cocteau sets a new accent unknown in earlier versions: he reinterprets the theme of mirroring, making it into an issue of contact. The motif of the mirror, magically empowered in the rococo tradition, is transmuted into an exchange of glances with the other (the father, La Bête).

The plot, now developing in parallel to the literary precursors, proceeds with La Bête's request to be allowed to watch Belle eating dinner. Eating always plays an essential role in *La Belle et la Bête*—so much so, that even in the radically truncated version of the Epinal pictorial story, an entire frame is devoted to the magically laden dinner table. In terms of social history, this is certainly indebted to the importance of securing nourishment in times when it could not be taken for granted. In a psychoanalytical reading, however, the bodily nature of this exquisite spread comes to the fore. Julia Kristeva (1980) develops her concept of abjection using the example of nourishment that is accepted and expelled; the central affect is disgust. In the traditional lore of *La Belle et la Bête*, both play a role: the envious sisters of ancient Psyche had already tried to persuade her that Amor was a serpent who would devour her and her child; and in Leprince (1756) their intention is the same, when they try to keep Belle away from La Bête. In the film, La Bête can be recognised as representing the abject side when he is overcome by his animalistic hunting instinct or by sexual greediness. In the interaction between Belle and La Bête, the core theme is disgust—just one level removed, so to speak, from the primal scene of animalistic gorging. Consequently, the canonical dinner scene stands in relation to the themes of sexuality and debased excesses of eating.

After the first evening dinner and La Bête's question—whether Belle thinks him ugly and whether she will marry him, new interactive scenes ensue: Belle goes off to explore the castle, followed by its living eyes (Fig. 11). She hides behind a well-built young man of stone, from whom a waft of smoke is rising (Fig. 12) (this is the last trace of Apuleius' graceful Cupid, who was still represented in Barbot's adaptation with the figure of the nocturnal dream prince); then she sees La Bête coming. Also giving off smoke, he goes looking for her in her bedchamber. She follows him, accosts him, and throws him out with regal aplomb.

Figure 11. Belle investigates the castle, pursued by many pairs of eyes (La Belle et la Bête 00:39:24).

Figure 12. Belle hides behind the young man made of stone (La Belle et la Bête 00:40:20).

In the next scene, however, she is looking for him again; she is bored and instead of just having him as a spectator at her evening meal, she wants to go walking in the garden with him. Distracted by a doe that arouses his hunting instinct, La Bête can hardly rein in his animal nature. Belle coaxes him over to a spring and lets him drink out of her hands. She doesn't find it disgusting. Here, abject eating and hunting are introduced into the film. Compared to older versions, the depiction is aestheticised, but not nearly as strongly downplayed as in the Disney version of 1991 (Jeffords, 1995). This prepares the stage for the core theme of the myth, sexuality. As we know, despite all attempts of ancient myth, baroque tales, or Disney to suggest "sweet nothings", Amor is not the god of tender affection, but of bodily love.

Some time later, it could be the same evening, La Bête shows up at the door of Belle's chamber highly aroused, deranged, and spattered with blood. Initially, his wildness is convincing (Fig. 13), but faced with Belle's appalled response—not to his arousal, but to the fact that he's filthy (Fig. 14)—it quickly crumbles into contriteness (Fig. 15).

Belle scolds him like a child and gives him her shawl to cover himself and clean up (Fig. 16). This gesture, at surface level the expression of civilising or maternal power: "Clean yourself up. And go to sleep" (Cocteau, 1946, p. 180), is at the same time moving in its intimacy. It doesn't seem to calm La Bête down, but rather to arouse him even more: "Close your door—quickly! Quickly!" (ibid.).

The camera now departs from the scene of the action, for the first time without the mediation of the magic mirror, and this reinstates the

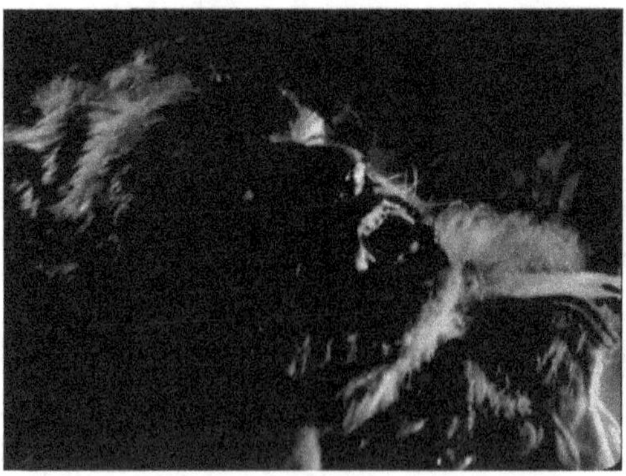

Figure 13. La Bête in his arousal (LA BELLE ET LA BÊTE 00:52:23).

Figure 14. Belle reacts with horror to his filthiness (LA BELLE ET LA BÊTE 00:53:03).

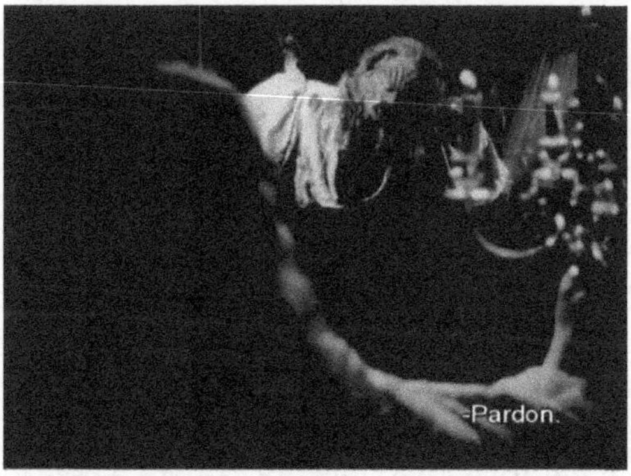

Figure 15. La Bête's arousal turns into contriteness (LA BELLE ET LA BÊTE 00:53:07).

Figure 16. Belle sees to it that he gets cleaned up (LA BELLE ET LA BÊTE 00:53:31).

omniscient narrator from the first act with insight into all the locations. We are taken to the father's house, where the parallel plot is advancing. Ludovic's loan is in default, the sick father's furnishings are being pawned. Although the table and chessboard at which they are sitting is being carried away, Avenant and Ludovic seem more amused than disturbed. The insertion of this parallel plot is another significant divergence from previous adaptations of the story: in both rococo versions, La Bête had ensured the financial security of the family when Belle was handed over.

Cut, back to the castle: Belle pleads with La Bête to be allowed to see her father and promises to return within a week. Cocteau is building up to a dramaturgical turning point, condensing what had been much lengthier in the ancient myth: at this point, Apuleius describes the sisters' visits, their crafty suggestions, the banishment, wanderings, and trials of Psyche. In the baroque versions, this interval is reduced to a short stay at home motivated by boredom, loneliness, or longing for the father (in Barbot lasting two months, in Leprince one week—the home leave keeps getting shorter). Cocteau's cinematic staging of this constitutive scene again brings male beauty into play. In the castle, Belle's plea is framed by handsome telamones, men's heads made of stone, with smoke rising from their mouths—as just a bit earlier from their master's in his arousal.[13] As the film proceeds, the shift in empathetic perspective becomes more and more evident: It is not so much Belle's inner drama that we are witnessing, but rather La Bête's. Our sympathy is with him alone, for instance when he says, "You stroke me the way you stroke an animal," and she replies coolly, "But you are an animal!" (Cocteau, 1946, p. 192). La Bête appears as the one being rejected—even more so when he, reaching out towards the Oedipal triangle, asks about Belle's suitor. The film even offers an optical view of the triangle: the couple is filmed from below, behind them the androgynous bust of a Roman man wearing a kind of toga (Fig. 17)—or is it a Roman woman?

She speaks his name, Avenant, triggering a fulminant reaction: La Bête hunches up, as if he'd been hit, and bounds off into the park in great leaps, surrounded by a cloud. Is it the name Avenant (in French, handsome, pleasing) that causes this attack? In the perception of Cocteau's contemporary audience, a contextual aspect would also come into play: that the figures of Avenant and La Bête converge, since they are both played by Marais and the contemporary viewer was fully aware of this—"Avenant" also in the sense of "the one who is arriving".[14] La

Bête's roar could thus pertain to the threat of losing his animal mask, clearly recognisable as such in the film (cf. also Chapter Seven). The audience in 1946 couldn't help but see Jean Marais, the idol, in La Bête with his opulent packaging (previously, Marais had been presented in another exclusive packaging, in the play *Œdipe Roi*, see Fig. 18). This is the moment at which the two men, the handsome and the hairy one, come together for the first time—and this opposition, this mirrored encounter is Cocteau's essential addition to the narrative of *La Belle et la Bête*.

The next scene is also to be understood in the context of this additional narrative thread. La Bête leads Belle out onto the balcony—the view over the castle grounds resembles, in cinematic terms, the abstract

Figure 17. La Bête asks Belle about the third party, Avenant (LA BELLE ET LA BÊTE 00:53:13).

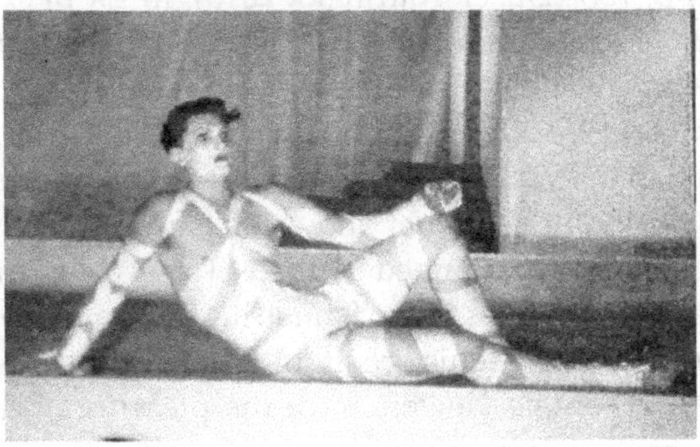

Figure 18. Jean Marais in Œdipe-roi (1937).

storm of contrasts during the passages through the forest (Cocteau, 1946, p. 240)—and shows her the mysterious temple of Diana. Why did Cocteau introduce Diana into his film narrative? What function does this additional role fulfil? An essential one, as we will see.

Inserting the figure of Diana into the myth of *Amor and Psyche*, here la Bête and la Belle, is syncretistic and not easy to comprehend. In the mythological tradition, they never appear together, not even the gods Diana/Artemis and Amor (Cupid)/Eros. According to Hesiod, Eros is one of the primordial gods; Aristophanes has him hatching from an egg laid by the Night; Apuleius says he is the son of Venus by an unknown father. Cicero's intimation that he could be a son of Hermes and Artemis (Diana) is an isolated opinion (Cicero, *De Natura Deorum* III, p. 60). And even if Cicero himself questions this variant, it was very probably familiar in France due to Voltaire's high opinion of Cicero's book. Is it possible that Cocteau saw the goddess as the mother of Amor, the mythological precursor of La Bête? That is not very likely. Nonetheless, he has his protagonist speaking lines that create the closest of connections to the virginal goddess of the hunt and the moon. La Bête claims that the secret of his existence lies in this temple:

> You see this lodge. It's called Diana's lodge. It is the only place in the estate that no one may enter, nor you, nor I. […] It is entered by means of a golden key. (Cocteau, 1946, pp. 240 f.)

The prohibition to enter the pavilion of the virgin goddess and her power, even over La Bête, could be read as references to the female body—above all, when one considers that Diana transformed Actaeon into a stag merely because he saw her naked while bathing (Ovid, *Metamorphoses* 3, pp. 138–252; cf. Katrinaki, 2010). In La Belle et la Bête, the temple of Diana represents the occult magical nexus that rules over the other five magical objects: three of them govern contact and transport to the outside world (mirror, horse, glove), and two more link the magical power to inaccessible taboo areas. The first, the rose, is the most precious possession of its owner and establishes contact to the love of the girl, which cannot be attained by force. The second, the golden key, is the tool that grants access to the female body/Diana temple, which is taboo. It is interesting that this occult interior is later shown in the film, so that male and female viewers have the pleasure of uncovering its secret: inside, as they will see, lies a mound of gold and jewels guarded by a statue of Diana armed with bow and arrow.

But let's not skip ahead, let's leave the riddle of Diana unsolved for another moment. In the succession of the film, the magic glove now has its role to play. It transports Belle to her father's sickbed; she tells him of her love for La Bête: "It is suffering, father. One side of it is struggling against the other" (Cocteau, 1946, p. 133). Out of compassion with La Bête, Belle begins to cry and her tears crystallise into diamonds—this magical moment is another addition specific to the film and also, by way of Belle's body, represents the first subtle transfer of fortune to the father: "You can live on that" (ibid., p. 135). In the precursor versions, this transfer works differently. In Barbot, La Bête provided the family with a house, income, and gifts; in Leprince it is a chest full of gold that the merchant receives immediately in exchange for his daughter, along with a trunk full of Belle's royal gowns that, however, disappears when she tries to give some to her sisters.

The scene that now follows has to integrate the side plot with Ludovic and Avenant introduced by Cocteau. At first, it plays on the comical exposition from the film's opening: the sisters hanging up laundry. Surprised and envious, they greet Belle as she returns home in magnificent clothing. Here, Cocteau quotes from the Leprince version the motif of the inalienable gift: Belle's necklace is transformed to a length of burnt rope as soon as she gives it to her sister. Now the sisters begin scheming (as in Apuleius) over how they can do what Belle has done (not without humour: "There are also other men who are hairy and wear horns" (ibid., p. 147)), or with help from the men can get their hands on La Bête's treasure (ibid.). Avenant and Ludovic sound out Belle so that they will be able to rob the treasure. This rather fuzzy planning of the group is more coherent in the precursor versions: In Leprince, the sisters—the men aren't involved—want to persuade Belle to overstep the time limit in the hope that La Bête will then devour her. In the film, the motif is less oral and more anal: with their (onion) tears, the sisters get Belle to stay longer so that they can steal the golden key. After that, they treat Belle like an inferior. In a brief intercut, we see La Bête in the castle, waiting for Belle full of anxiety and tenderly stroking her bedcover (cf. Cocteau, 1946, p. 306, footnote). Back at the father's house, the conspirators still don't know how to get to the castle, but yet another magical intervention by La Bête serves practically as an invitation: he sends the horse Magnifique, and Avenant and Ludovic finally grasp the opportunity. The magic mirror that the horse had brought along shows the sisters their true faces as a wizened hag and a monkey (ibid.,

p. 158).[15] They take the mirror to Belle and find her dressed as a princess. In the mirror, Belle sees the crying face of La Bête and immediately pulls on the glove to return to him. Arriving at the castle, she notices that the key is missing and travels back one more time, only to find that the key has disappeared. The mirror breaks into bits. This relatively complicated staging of her return (in Apuleius, stretched over long months of trials) heightens the suspense in terms of film dramaturgy, since we now have two parties racing to reach the castle: the brother and the suitor out to kill La Bête, and Belle trying to save him. Again using the glove to reach the castle, she desperately searches for La Bête and finds him dying next to the pond.

Before she can save him through her love, as in all the preceding versions, the second narrative thread approaches its climax in a parallel sequence: Avenant, together with Ludovic, has reached the pavilion of Diana and is about to unlock it when his friend holds him back: "Wait! This key may release some evil trap. We must be very careful" (ibid., p. 56). Abstruse as this fear may be, it is immediately accepted by Avenant—and resolved. Smiling, he replies: "Right. We won't go in through the door," and leads him up onto the roof where he tries to enter the temple through the skylight. If the forbidden temple of Diana, as suggested above, stands for the taboo female-maternal body, then the idea that penetrating from the front with the "golden key" might release a "treacherous mechanism" is quite a graphic expression of male sexual anxiety. And the attempt to take the back route instead is a solution that at least avoids the "treacherous" gate, the opening of the female genitals. So, while the boys are taking this detour, the rescue of La Bête proceeds. Belle takes the blame: "I'm the monster, Beast!" (ibid., p. 55), begging La Bête to stay alive. Cut back to the temple of Diana: through the skylight, we see the statue of Diana above a mound of sparkling jewels. Avenant breaks the window and begins climbing in. We see the statue move and shoot an arrow that strikes Avenant between the shoulders, whereupon before our very eyes Avenant's features turn into those of the Beast. Ludovic lets go of him, he falls to the ground (ibid., p. 58). At the same moment beside the pond, Belle backs off, startled, as a smiling prince stands up, looking exactly like Avenant, and says, "Where is the Beast?"

The film ending that follows is idiosyncratic and is regarded by many viewers as disingenuous (cf. Chapters Four, Five, and Seven, this volume). However, this effect corresponds to Cocteau's explicit intention:

"I wanted to disappoint the audience and Beauty at the same time [...] It was my intention to make the monster so human, so sympathetic, so superior to a human that his transformation into a fairy tale prince would be a bitter disappointment for Beauty. Many, many letters from women and young girls, from little girls and children have been written to me and the actor to protest, in this day and age—1947—, against this transformation and to grieve for the poor monster" (Cocteau, 1973, p. 51). The obvious inconsistency of this ending has also given rise to speculation within the discussion. De Nitto (1976, pp. 152 f.) sees a de-sensualisation in the fusion of La Bête and Avenant: the prince who takes Belle up to spiritual heights is offering her an asexual relationship. De Nitto traces this turn of events to "Cocteau's antipathy toward heterosexual contacts" and sees it as illustrating the sexual maturation of the girl. However, one needn't fall back on psychological comments about the author or—dissociating entirely from the film—focus on female development in order to postulate that in LA BELLE ET LA BÊTE the ostensible dramaturgical conclusion, the union of the loving couple, is systematically undermined. For the film itself provides us with the solution.

Belle is anything but enthusiastic about the transformation, and immediately discusses the prince's similarity with Avenant. When asked directly, she avows that she loved both Avenant and La Bête. Whether she's happy now, the redeemed prince wants to know. "I have to get accustomed to it," is her cautious reply. The prince announces that he will fly with her into his realm, where she as a great queen will be served by her sisters. To his question whether she is afraid she replies, already showing a bit more interest, "I like to be afraid—with you" (ibid., p. 171).[16] The two rise up to heaven in a cloud of fluttering cloth, iconographically speaking a rococo apotheosis.

The script goes into epic detail at this point to describe the necessary camera tricks. Nonetheless, the outcome is ostentatiously unreal: the apotheosis is about as convincing as La Bête's mask had been. It's no coincidence that this conclusion seems to be tacked on, since it diverges most decisively from all earlier adaptations of the material.

The specific peripeteia of the film drama is quite surprising—since it shifts from the love of the girl to the second narrative thread added by Cocteau, the heroic adventure of the airheads Avenant and Ludovic. Despite Belle's declarations of love and the post hoc explanation given by the prince, it is not love that brings about redemption in the film, but rather transgression—which is also why the superficial emphasis on redemption and apotheosis seems so unreal and unsatisfying. In opposition to the entire tradition of the motif, Cocteau's film does not give us a redeeming transformation brought about by the "loving gaze", in fact not even brought about by Belle: in the causal sequence running parallel, a virgin armed with an arrow shoots the rapacious suitor Avenant, who is breaking into the temple of femininity, in the back—and not until this moment is La Bête transformed into the prince. At this moment, the La Belle narrative is reduced to the status of an iconic shell, so unimportant that even Belle's promise of marriage is left out—a significant omission of the very juncture that marks the moment of redemption in all the modern precursor versions. In Cocteau, La Bête is preserved, his animal mask is merely passed on, like a curse, to the next handsome young man. The mise en scène of the fairy tale has taken the myth about the dangers of a girl coming of age sexually and has used it to create a new myth about the dangers of a boy coming of age sexually. And it suggests a solution in which, for one thing, the direction of penetration is reversed (the man is struck by the arrow), and for another, a narcissistic constitution of self occurs: he becomes a flying statue of himself by casting off all his animalistic, aggressive components.

In his interpretation of *La Belle et la Bête*, Cocteau placed the construction of masculinity at the centre of attention, both in terms of plot and cinematic realisation. The element that connects or separates the conception of adolescent femininity and the construction of masculinity in LA BELLE ET LA BÊTE is the figure of the phallic woman, Diana, who shoots Avenant and in doing so enables (more than Belle's kiss does) the transformation back into a prince.[17]

Le Beau est La Bête, or the poet as a monster

As explained in the introduction to this chapter, there are situations in which psychoanalytic inquiry into film cannot be restricted to mediating between the audience reaction and a precise analysis of the text and its intertextual environment; then we also need to consider the presentation in which the *auteur* linked himself to his work. Needless to say, the approach to the filmmaker as a person must be undertaken cautiously, since psychoanalytical film interpretation treats the work as a cultural artefact rather than a subjective product (cf. Chapter Two, this volume). To this extent, we accept the maxim of the death of the author

(Barthes, 1967; Foucault, 1969) that postulates the irreversible entry of a text into the realm of art reception, regardless of the original intention of the author in creating the work. When, however, the effect of the work is intertwined with the position of the author in a particular sphere of reception, when the effect is deliberately reliant on that position—as was the case with authors such as Goethe or Cocteau, who established a public art persona for themselves—then the validity of this dictum is not quite as universal. LA BELLE ET LA BÊTE cannot be comprehended without reference to its author Jean Cocteau and the context of his art and his life, or to the point in time when the film appeared.

Cocteau's meticulous documentation of the filming (1947) must be considered a part of the *Gesamtkunstwerk*. An audience familiar with Cocteau as an aging poet associated with various scandals is told about a film shoot afflicted by skin ailments and fickle weather. How closely Cocteau identifies the film project with himself as a person and an artist is apparent in the journal's constant attention to the triangle relationship Marais-Mila-Cocteau—with the entrance of a horse called Aramis (an anagram for Marais) ridden by Mila Parély, Marais's wife for a time and one of the evil sisters in the film, resulting in a fractured pelvis (Cocteau, 1947, p. 49 [English ed. p. 23]). Boils and skin inflammations are interconnected with the project by the artist himself, as the entry from October 18, 1945 reveals: "Je suis réveillé par les douleurs insupportable et comme je ne peux ni dormir, ni marcher de long en large, je me soulage en prenant ce cahier pour essayer de crier mon mal aux amis inconnus qui liront ces lignes. Ils existent. Je les connais sans le connaître. Je les devines dans l'ombre. Une bête féroce (la Bête) me tenaille la nuque d'une griff puissante. L'anthrax en est à cette période ou il dévelope son cratère, ou les armées de microbes ennemis le cerrnent èt me défendent" (ibid., p. 129 [p. 67]).[18] When Cocteau compares the film to the claw of a wild animal that has a hold on him and calls upon an army of enemy germs to protect him, as well as his "unknown friends", invisible readers, we see him wearing the mask of the tortured animal himself. Here, this is not to be taken biographically, but rather as a part of his film appearance. Film psychoanalysis is not concerned with the fate of those participating in the production, but rather with the audience. "The construction of gender roles, of femininity as well as masculinity, is a public act; although undertaken by individuals, from all their many attempts at self-definition it filters out those that are societally relevant" (see Chapter One, p. 9). As a text accompanying the film, the journal tells us that the film should be understood as documenting a struggle—for poetry, for love, and (as I would add) for male identity.

This is meant quite literally. Since his first appearance in the salons of Paris, the young Cocteau was a total work of art, closely interweaving his artistic production and his lifestyle. His first volumes of poetry, *Lampe d'Aladin* (1909) and *Le prince frivol* (1909), were just as self-referential as his first short film, produced fifteen years later (and lost), JEAN COCTEAU FAIT DU CINÉMA (1925). He cooperated with Diaghilev, Apollinaire, Stravinsky, and many others, also encountering rejection in various forms within the Parisian scene, which is reflected in his work. Early on, due to his ostentatious homosexuality, he attracted the enmity of the homophobic circle of surrealists surrounding André Breton. After the death of his friend Raymond Radiguet in 1923, he briefly lapsed into depression and opium addiction, but soon reinvented himself and resurfaced in 1924 with the play *Jean l'Oiseleur*—literally *Jean the Bird-catcher* and figuratively *the Cockcatcher* as "oiseau" is French slang for the penis. André Gide's Cocteau portrait as Count Passavent in *The Counterfeiters* presents him as an openly homosexual sugar daddy, in contrast to the other, secretly homosexual protagonists of the novel published in 1925. Marcel Proust gave him a somewhat friendlier, but nonetheless ironic cameo as an artist working a beach resort in *Albertine disparue* (1925). When LE SANG D'UN POETE (BLOOD OF A POET) came out in 1932, the film was denounced by the surrealists as a feeble attempt at copying Luis Buñuel's heterosexual shocker L'AGE D'OR (THE GOLDEN AGE) (Williams, 2006, p. 37).

When he released LA BELLE ET LA BÊTE in 1946, a fairy-tale film amid the wreckage of the war, Cocteau stylised himself ostentatiously as a poet—at the same time presenting yet another of his provocations and a wilful assertion of his own art. The apotheosis of poetry as an eternal fairy tale and simultaneously as a triumphant struggle (in the journal) was meant to defy the contemporaries he felt misjudged by. "Cocteau's film is about the conflict between appearance and reality […] because, due to that conflict, it is impossible for the poet's contemporaries to see beyond the 'scandal and parade' to the genuine merit of the poet's work" (Popkin, 1982, p. 108).

The contemporaries didn't fail to notice that LA BELLE ET LA BÊTE also contained a statement. By featuring his lover, Cocteau was also publicly staging the homosexual couple per se (Riou & Pouchain, 2013).

Cocteau's unfailing belief in the handsome boy, whom the press had called "the worst actor in France" after his theatre debut as *Oedipus Rex* in 1937 (Fig. 18; cf. Riou & Pouchain, 2013), in the end brought forth one of the great film beaus of our time. With Jean Dellanoy's modern adaptation of *Tristan and Isolde*, L'ÉTERNEL RETOUR (THE ETERNAL RETURN) (F 1943), for which Cocteau wrote the sceenplay, Marais had already become a male role model and, for the girls, a heart-throb. For a short while, he almost succumbed to this heterosexualisation—he was even married for two years to Mila Parély, whom we see in LA BELLE ET LA BÊTE as the evil sister Adélaïde. He, who in comparison with his intellectual lover Cocteau always described himself as "bête", that is to say, stupid (Riou & Pouchain, 2013; see also Chapter Seven, this volume, p. 147), became the ambassador of male aestheticisation: Le Beau comme La Bête. In the film, Marais functions perfectly as La Bête precisely because the packaging is so obvious, as with the German rapper Cro today appearing in a panda mask. Everyone, male and female, knows that it's Marais, whom they've already seen as Avenant at the beginning of the film.

Cocteau's urge to present a post-hegemonic masculine body ideal (see Chapter One, this volume) did, however, lead to another altercation. In his radical poetic, apolitical understanding of self, he hardly had compunctions about contact with the German occupiers: his eulogy to Hitler's favourite sculptor, published in 1942 under the title "Salute to Arno Breker" on the occasion of the latter's exhibition in occupied Paris, escalated into a political scandal. He also thought that he saw a similarity to Breker's heroes in Marais's physiognomy (Williams, 2006, p. 62).

Both elements—the outsider perspective of the homosexual and an affinity to the national socialist body cult and its implications—are unmistakably woven into the fabric of LA BELLE ET LA BÊTE—particularly in a scene that was suppressed in the published version of the film (Fischlin, 1998). When and why this sequence (takes 211–256) was cut out, will never be known; Cocteau, who otherwise reports extensively on the shooting in his journal, doesn't mention the deletion (Cocteau, 1992, p. 161 note 1, p. 175 notes 1 and 2).

In this (deleted) scene, Avenant and Ludovic pursue a transvestite game of masquerades with a textile merchant who is clearly identified as Jewish, dressing up in the gowns of the older sisters, seducing him, and finally beating him up.

In the film version that was released, all that remains of this anti-Semitic strain is the figure of the moneylender, whose features are more than distinct (scenes 196 ff.). Despite the clearly negative attributes assigned, Fischlin (1998) interprets the introduction of the Jew and of overt homosexuality as a way of marking a "queer margin", either as a deliberate provocation or in unconscious, projective self-stigmatisation: if, in reflecting psychoanalytically on the film, we take the author's self-positioning into account, including his public display of sexual preference—permissible here, given that it plays a role—then certainly not to suborn a psychoanalysis of the author. Analysis, including analysis of artists, is not possible without the clinical encounter (Berman, 2003; Hamburger, 1996; Harris & Sklar, 1998). In artists' works, we perceive only what they have inscribed there, not their personal unconscious. Because artists find forms of expression that resonate with the audience, their personal unconscious becomes a projection surface for the public reception of their work. They place it at the disposal of the audience, just as an analyst works with his or her own consciousness in order to comprehend the mutual enactments occurring in the analytical encounter and to work through them together with the patient. The psychoanalysis of art is well advised to refrain from extending its reach into the private dimension. Such encroachment, in the "pedantry of sensitive doctors" (Adorno, 1970, p. 8), reinterprets whatever is distressing in a work as a symptom of the author's and instead reads itself in the upheavals of the work (cf. Hamburger, 2013; Reiche, 2001, 2011). The topic here is not the biography, as such, of Cocteau and Marais (tempting as it might be to relate that as boys both were shaped, even modelled, to an unusual degree by their mothers). Of interest is rather the need of the audience, particularly the female audience, to possess a youthful hero, handsome and gay like Rodolfo Valentino (but who never came out, and also didn't survive the role) (cf. Studlar, 1993).

Beloved animal—on the reception of La Belle et la Bête

With his staging of masculinity in La Belle et la Bête, Cocteau set standards that have since determined the overall reception of the motif. After the self-destruction of the hero ideal, formed during the nineteenth century, in two successive, industrially engineered, annihilating wars, Cocteau made his contribution towards a new male image. La Belle et la Bête inspired literary works and has never disappeared from the silver screen. "Cocteau has done for the Beast what Bela Lugosi did for Nosferatu. He has become an attractive, suave, hero with a dark side" (Hains, 1989, p. 82).

Remakes

The literary reception of *La Belle et la Bête* after Cocteau is widely ramified, hardly possible to survey, and in general characterised by trivialisation (Hearne, 1989b, p. 91). The title alone has been replicated and varied hundreds of times: the British Library lists 201 entries, and amazon.com more than 5,000. Of course, most of these are fairy-tale editions and adaptations, usually focusing on the inner developmental process of the girl. A look at the history of the story's illustration (cf. Hearne, 1989b, pp. 90 ff.), reveals a tendency towards increasing humanisation and empathic portrayal of the beast. The genre also includes crime novels centred on a woman's murder, for instance *Beauty and the Beast* by Ed McBain (1982); erotica, such as *Hunted—A Sultry Retelling of Beauty and the Beast* by Cerys du Luis (2011), Shoshanna Evers's *Beauty and the Beast—An Erotic Re-Imagining* (2014), or Skye Warren's *Beauty Touched the Beast* (2011); not to forget the paranormal take-offs, for example the "interracial paranormal romance" *Beauty IS The Beast* by Lena Skye (2011).

Like the book market, the film industry has also taken possession of the title in the form of numerous remakes. There is a children's film remake with Joyce Taylor and Mark Damon (1962), a star-studded (Susan Sarandon, Angelica Huston, Klaus Kinski) but otherwise unimpressive slap-bang remake by Roger Vadim (USA 1983) (cf. Erhart, 2007, pp. 41 ff.) and several more, equally unoriginal fairy-tale films as well as a number of animations (ibid.). Ultimately, the Disney version of 1991 replaced the Cocteau film as a reference source. The animated film BEAUTY AND THE BEAST (USA 1991) was a project that Walt Disney had been wanting to realise since 1937, but had put off again and again because he hadn't found the form for a beast who was horrifying and likeable at the same time (Berberi & Berberi, 2013, p. 197). Apparently, Disney's major staging problem was the mise en scène of male identity. It was the same identity problem that informs Cocteau's new interpretation. When Disney finally produced a Broadway musical in 1950 and the film in 1991, in both it emerged that he was focused mainly on the staging of masculinity (Bolden, 2009). As to be expected, the Disney version turns Cocteau's tragic monster into a teddy-bear hero: La Bête, in Cocteau's film already recognisable as a costumed human, appears in Disney from the first as an attractive, leonine man. There is no longer any sense of distress over being a hegemonic, terrifying man (Zipes, 1995; see also DiPaolo, 2010).

Further literary and cinematic developments

The theme of maturing from a girl to a woman, on which the tradition of the motif is based, continues to be developed in modern responses to the material and the film. For one, Sara Henderson Hay deconstructs the tacked-on ending of the fable in her poem "Sequel" from 1963 (Hay, 1998; cf. Götzl, 2012). She describes how life continues for Beauty, with the Beast now transformed into the Prince: extensive representational duties, everyday activities, and the longing to transform the handsome Prince back into the Beast who was so in love with her—a reaction we already saw in Cocteau, when La Bête has been transformed into a Prince looking exactly like her suitor Avenant and Belle asks after La Bête, with a note of disappointment (scene 403). But the reading of the film described above, centred on a homosexually contextualised construction of masculinity, is also reflected in modern literary adaptations. The poem "Beauty and the Beast" by Olga Broumas from the volume *Beginning with O* (1977), in which traditional fairy-tale motifs are reinterpreted from a decidedly lesbian perspective, is one illustration of this. In "Beauty and the Beast" Broumas drafts the story of a girl who, after a heterosexual socialisation had coupled her hope for pleasure with a connotation of suffering pain, discovers her capacity for lesbian love as an emancipation: "stunned/by the tangible/pleasure that gripped my ribs, every time/like a caged beast, bewildered/by this late, this essential heat" (Broumas, 1977, pp. 55 f.; Götzl, 2012). With her sexual transformation, the girl can accept the "beast" within herself and integrate it. What previously, in the wildness of male sexuality, was experienced and suffered as coming from without, now becomes something from within. It belongs to herself as an integral part ("essential heat"), can be felt in the cage that is her breast ("pleasure that gripped my ribs"). In this transformation—the particular achievement of this adaptation—the wildness of the beast need not give way to tame courtly demeanour, but rather can be maintained as her own desire, in its own right. Cocteau's adaptation can be understood as a comparable deconstruction, inasmuch as Marais/Avenant, locked into a stuffed-animal body yet always identifiable to the audience, finally comes into his own.

Heterosexual discourse in the film tradition has been no less creative in further developing the motif (cf. Chapter Seven, this volume). Naturally, first mention goes to CREATURE FROM THE BLACK LAGOON (USA 1954)—a film whose far-reaching effect is played on in one of the most famous scenes in cinema history. In 1955, in THE SEVEN YEAR ITCH, Marilyn Monroe comes out of a movie theatre after seeing CREATURE FROM THE BLACK LAGOON and says (as empathetically as Belle would), "It just wanted to be loved"—and immediately, a sudden gust rising from a vent in the pavement blows her white, pleated skirt up into the air (which, incidentally, was no magic: it was a cleverly installed wind machine). On the manifest level, the film does not make reference to LA BELLE ET LA BÊTE, but to the American animal bridegroom tradition, with KING KONG (USA 1935); however, producer William Alland is said to have taken his inspiration for the first pitch from LA BELLE ET LA BÊTE. The material reached its greatest renaissance of all with a dramaturgical twist that further develops Cocteau's new interpretation of the motif as a drama of male development: in Spielberg's E.T. THE EXTRA-TERRESTRIAL (USA 1982), the unhappy alien stands in for La Bête, and the little boy Elliott takes the place of Belle. A story among men. But Elliott is also able to redeem E.T. through his love, and the film's compassionate impetus, supported by the boy's empathy, is directed towards the stranger, as in LA BELLE ET LA BÊTE. Spielberg deftly dodges the issue of the ending, which had already been a problem in Cocteau: The alien does not need to be transformed by love, instead love makes it possible that he return home. The worlds remain unconnected. In EDWARD SCISSORHANDS (USA 1990), Johnny Depp plays the monster, who is saved by the love of Kim (Winona Ryder). In this tragicomedy, Edward is not afflicted by a curse, but rather (in keeping with the times) represents a kind of beta version of the artificial human being. The conflict and the rescue have nothing to do with transformation through love: Kim has to protect Edward from a mob, which she does by telling a lie. The happy ending consists merely in the fact that they both survive and they never see one another again. Summing up these two films one could say that, towards the end of the century, the identity problem is entirely on the beast's side and the solution is that he gets to retain his identity.

The composer Philip Glass created a minimal music opera in 1995 that is synchronised to Cocteau's original as an "opera to the film", an attempt to counteract what I call its "disneyfication" and restore the deep significance of LA BELLE ET LA BÊTE. And it is no coincidence that he chose Cocteau's film as a trustworthy carrier for this effort towards liberating male identity—this time not from a hegemonic uniform, but from the clutches of consumerist kitsch.

In a broader sense, the reception history of the material used in LA BELLE ET LA BÊTE also includes the type of love film, occurring in the form of romantic comedy or melodrama, in which an uncivilised, hardened, or egoistic man changes because he is loved by a woman (cf. Krützen, 2007). An example would be PRETTY WOMAN (USA 1990, cf. Hamburger & Pramataroff-Hamburger, 2014), with a self-assured call girl bringing a finance investor, who is incapable of affection, to experience feelings—a Disney-like variation on Jonathan Demme's SOMETHING WILD (USA 1986), whose plot is similar but has a more radical ending: instead of aspiring to high moral goals like education and a fair economy, as in PRETTY WOMAN, the couple in SOMETHING WILD with its unresolved, ironic ending seems to prefer a career in hustling. Blake Edwards's comedy SWITCH (USA 1991) also tells the story of a macho trapped in his masculinity. After being murdered by three of his ex-girlfriends, he is turned down in heaven as well—at least until he succeeds in getting one person to like him well enough to say "I love you". The complication: he is sent back to earth in the body of a woman. His customary macho behaviour gives more cause for rejection than for affection; as if in a game of reversals, mirrored characteristics of the "other" come to light. The motif of the uncouth, "wild" man is cleverly intertwined with that of bodily transformation: civilising his male behaviour involves a change of gender. Once the hero (as heroine) has managed to earn the love of a lesbian woman and has also slept with his best friend, he returns (pregnant) to heaven and is given the choice of entering as a female or male angel. Each option, as a heavenly voice explains to him (her), has its advantages.

It would of course be rash to try to discern an effect of LA BELLE ET LA BÊTE on every film in which the power of feminine compassion redeems a hardened man—or doesn't, as in Godard's A BOUT DE SOUFFLE (BREATHLESS) (F 1960). We might have to quote half of the films ever made. LA BELLE ET LA BÊTE is an eddy in the current of motif traditions going back thousands of years. In most cases, whether redeemed or not, the beasts somehow tend to be more interesting—as Cocteau was well aware. In retrospect he admitted that he wanted the happy ending to be perceived as a let-down (Cocteau, 1973, p. 51).

What is Cocteau up to, after two world wars have sealed the fate of the "hegemonic masculinity" that had taken hold in the nineteenth century, when he gives us an animal in hairy armour moulting into a gentle, handsome fellow—and at the same time deconstructs heterosexual expectations of a resolution (which he has been undermining all the while) by having the fellow killed, penetrated by a woman? When he, in the year one after the historical abyss of the Holocaust, presents a poetic film that claims in the apostrophe at the very outset to be a "pure" poetic fairy tale—and at the same time demonstrates an affinity to Nazi aesthetics, which he stood accused of, by adding in the figure of a moneylender who could have come straight off the set of Veit Harlan's Nazi propaganda film JUD SÜSS (JEW SÜSS) (D 1940)? Cocteau is doing what he always did: creating a provocation, skewed and shrill, even though it's packaged as an (implausible) fairy tale. In the final chapter of her influential study *Gender Trouble* (1990), Judith Butler suggests subversive, parodic acts as an exit route out of the heteronormative constitution of femininity, as a means of breaking the dominance of gender constructions. LA BELLE ET LA BÊTE and its presentation of masculinity could be regarded as such an act.

Notes

1. Marianne Leuzinger-Bohleber explicates the aspect of embodiment underlying the ubiquitousness of these demands for symbolisation—also in the view of modern psychoanalytical research (Chapter Six, this volume).
2. The *Aarne-Thompson tale type index* AaTh identifies recurring plot patterns in the narrative structures of traditional folktales; updated version: Uther, 2004.
3. The motif also occurs in Grimms' fairy tales under the title *The Singing, Springing Lark* (nr. 88).
4. It is interesting that this fairy tale motif represents a reversal of an even earlier one, the beloved animal. We encounter it in Genesis (Adam's seduction by Eve/the snake) and also in stories of liaisons with elementary creatures, for example in the sagas of Melusine or Undine (cf. Frenzel, 2008, p. 761; Schulz, 2004).

5. My thanks to Klaus Roth (Ludwig Maximilian University of Munich) for calling my attention to this. An example of this highly condensed paraliterary tradition can be found in *La Belle et la Bête—Le chat botté* (1848).
6. A motif documented in China as well as in Greek mythology; its entry into Christian tradition resulted from a mistake in translation of the Hebrew bible into Greek, whereby it was taken to signify the Redeemer. In Christian iconography, the unicorn was later often associated with the Madonna or the virginal martyr Justina. The blatantly obvious connection to sexuality finally was noticed by the Council of Trent, which in the sixteenth century forbade the use of the unicorn as a symbol for Christ because in some tales (they mentioned Leonardo's *Bestiario*) it occurred as a symbol of lust (Mercatante & Dow, 2009, p. 982).
7. Additional examples of films are discussed by Rost (Chapter Seven, this volume) and by Erhart (2007).
8. The connections are so clear that Cocteau's later comment almost seems disingenuous: "When Madame Leprince de Beaumont published *La Belle et la Bête*, she was a poor governess in England, and I assume that the story is of Scottish origin" (Cocteau, 1973, p. 51).
9. Apuleius (1895) calls Cupid's arrows, which Psyche examines with curiosity, "*propitia tela*", "inclined weapons".
10. We will return later to this element of anti-Semitism. It is corroborated by a later scene that was deleted for mysterious reasons (see p. 81, this volume).
11. It is worth mention that in the script (cf. Cocteau, 1992, p. 80) while explaining this scene, Cocteau takes specific reference to the Perrault fairy tale *Peau d'Ane* (Donkey's Skin) illustrated by Gustave Doré—in which a daughter uses an animal pelt to escape an incestuous encounter with her father.
12. The absence of the mother is characteristic throughout the tradition of *La Belle et la Bête*; but only in the new film production from 2014 is the theme directly addressed (see Chapter Seven, this volume).
13. Cf. the contribution by Christine Kirchhoff (Chapter Five, this volume). She points out the sexual connotation of exuding smoke and considers Cocteau's own interpretation of the smoke as a sign of aggression a "distortion".
14. I am indebted to Andreas Rost for this insight (in personal communication).
15. The monkey, as Sabbadini (see Chapter Four, this volume) points out, is an animal that imitated humans, as is the parrot they also wished for. This reference also quotes the Barbot version (1740), in which Belle is served by monkeys at the castle.

16. The subtitling in the German version creates a curious lapse here, translating "I'm not afraid—with you" which practically means the opposite, even further reducing the last sensual reference in this erotically rather meagre finale.
17. Such figures occur in many Cocteau films: the whip-cracking queen in L'AIGLE À DEUX TÊTES (F 1947), the statuary Léo in LES PARENTS TERRIBLES (F 1948), the cruel princess in ORPHÉE (F 1950), and Minerva with the Gorgon's head in LE TESTAMENT D'ORPHÉE (F 1960).
18. "Woke up with unbearable pain. As I can neither sleep nor walk up and down, I calm myself by picking up this notebook and trying to shout my pain to the unknown friends who will read these lines. They exist. I know them without knowing them. I make them out in the darkness. A ferocious beast (the Beast) has got its paw on the nape of my neck and is torturing me. The carbuncle is just getting a root and legions of enemy germs encircle it, to protect me." Of course, it's uncertain whether "anthrax" here refers literally to splenic fever—Cocteau also mentions other diagnoses. But Swiderski (2004, p. 70) does actually explain the lesions afflicting the actors by exposure to anthrax bacteria due to the animal hair used for the La Bête costume.

References

Adorno, T. W. (1970). *Aesthetic Theory*. G. Adorno & R. Tiedemann (Eds.). Newly translated, edited, and with a translator's introduction by Robert Hullot-Kentor. London: Continuum, 1997.

Apuleius (1895): Apvlei Psyche et Cvpido, recensvit et emendavit Otto Iahn. Lipsiae, formis et impensis, Breitkopfii et Haertelii. http://www.thelatinlibrary.com/apuleius/apuleius.cupid.shtml (13.10.2013).

Baker, R. L. (1989). Xenophobia in "Beauty and the Beast" and other animal/monster-groom tales. *Midwestern Folklore*, *15*(2): 71–77.

Barbot Gallon de Villeneuve, G. -S. (1740). La belle et la bête. In: *Le Cabinet des fées, ou collection choisie des contes des fées, et autres contes merveilleux* (pp. 27–214). Geneva: Slatkine Reprint, 1978.

Barchilon, J. (1959). Beauty and the Beast: From myth to fairy tale. *Psychoanalytic Review*, *46*: 19–29.

Barthes, R. (1967). Death of the author. In: Bartes, R., *Image Music Text*. Essays selected and translated by Stephen Heath (pp. 142–148). London: Fontana, 1977.

Bauks, M. (2010). *Jephtas Tochter. Traditions-, religions- und rezeptionsgeschichtliche Studien zu Richter*, *11*: 29–40. Tübingen, Germany: Mohr Siebeck.

Berberi, T., & Berberi, V. (2013). A seat at the table: On being human in the Beauty and the Beast tradition. In: J. Cheu (Ed.), *Diversity in Disney*

Films: Critical Essays on Race, Ethnicity, Gender, Sexuality and Disability (pp. 195–207). Jefferson, NC: Mcfarland.

Berman, E. (2003). Reader and story, viewer and film: On transference and interpretation. *International Journal of Psychoanalysis, 84*: 119–129.

Bettelheim, B. (1975). *The Uses of Enchantment: The Meaning and Importance of Fairy Tales.* New York: Vintage, 1989.

Bohleber, W. (Ed.) (1996). *Adoleszenz und Identität.* Stuttgart, Germany: Klett-Cotta.

Böhme, H. & Böhme, G. (1983): *Das Andere der Vernunft: Zur Entwicklung von Rationalitätsstrukturen am Beispiel Kants.* Frankfurt: Suhrkamp, 1985.

Bolden, J. (2009). *The Metamorphosis of Masculinity in Disney's Broadway Musical Beauty and the Beast.* [MA Thesis, California State University, Sacramento, CA.] http://www.gobookee.org/ebook/the-metamorphosis-of-masculinity-in-disney-s-broadway-wtisb/ (31.3.2014).

Bottigheimer, R. B. (1989a). "Beauty and the Beast": Marriage and money—motif and motivation. *Midwestern Folklore, 15*(2): 79–88.

Bottigheimer, R. B. (1989b). Cupid and Psyche vs. Beauty and the Beast: the Milesian and the modern. *Merveilles & Contes, 3*(1): 4–14.

Broumas, O. (1977). *Beginning with O.* New Haven, CT: Yale University Press.

Burton, A. (1978). Beauty and the Beast: A critique of psychoanalytic approaches to the fairy tale. *Psychocultural Review: Interpretations in the Psychology of Art, Literature and Society, 2*: 241–258.

Butler, J. (1990). *Gender Trouble: Feminism and the Subversion of Identity.* London: Routledge.

Cicero, M. T. (45 BC) *De natura deorum. Liber III.* http://www.thelatinlibrary.com/cicero/nd3.shtml (1.8.2013).

Cocteau, J. (1946). *Beauty and the Beast.* French and English edition. Scenario and Dialogs by Jean Cocteau. R. M. Hammond (Ed.). New York: New York University Press, 1970.

Cocteau, J. (1947). *La Belle et la Bête. Journal d'un Film.* Paris: Editions du Rocher, 1999. (English edition: *Beauty and the Beast. Diary of a Film.* New York: Dover, 1972.)

Cocteau, J. (1973). *Kino und Poesie.* Munich, Germany: Hanser, 1979.

Cocteau, J. (1992). *La Belle et la Bête.* Photographies et commentaires d'Henri Alekan, Texte établi et annoté par Robert Hammond, Préface de Jean Marais, Postface de Mila Parely. Paris: Editions du Collectionner.

Daxelmüller, C. (1987). Gelübde. In: K. Ranke (Ed.), *Enzyklopädie des Märchens. Handwörterbuch zur historischen und vergleichenden Erzählforschung, Vol. 5* (columns 976–982). Berlin: de Gruyter.

De Nitto, D. (1976). Jean Cocteau's Beauty and the Beast. *American Imago, 33*: 123–154.

De Vries, L. (1989). Literary beauties and folk beasts. Folktale issues in Beauty and the Beast. In: B. G. Hearne, *Beauty and the Beast: Visions and Revisions of an Old Tale* (pp. 155–188). Chicago, IL: University of Chicago Press.

Derrida, J. (1967). *Writing and Difference*. Translated, with an introduction and additional notes, by Alan Bass. London: Routledge, 1978.

Dieckmann, H. (1966). Die symbolische Sprache des Märchens. In: W. Laiblin (Ed.), *Märchenforschung und Tiefenpsychologie* (pp. 442–470). Darmstadt, Germany: Wissenschaftliche Buchgesellschaft, 1969.

DiPaolo, M. (2010). Mass-marketing beauty: How a feminist heroine became an insipid Disney princess. In: P. Frus & C. Williams (Eds.), *Beyond Adaptation: Essays on Radical Transformations of Original Works* (pp. 168–180). Jefferson, NC: MacFarland.

Erdheim, M. (1993). Psychoanalyse, Adoleszenz und Nachträglichkeit. In: W. Bohleber (Ed.), *Adoleszenz und Identität* (pp. 83–102). Stuttgart, Germany: Klett-Cotta, 1996.

Erhart, R. (2007). *Die Schöne und das Biest: ... von der Erzählung zum Film*. Frankfurt, Germany: Lang.

Fischlin, D. (1998). Queer Margins: Cocteau, *La Belle et la bête*, and the Jewish differend. *Textual Practice, 12*(1): 69–88. Reprinted in: D. Boyarin, D. Itzkovitz, & A. Pellegrini (jEds.) (2003), *Queer Theory and the Jewish Question* (pp. 365–394). New York: Columbia University Press.

Foucault, M. (1969). What is an author? In: *Aesthetics, Method, and Epistemology* (pp. 205–222). J. Faubion (Ed.); R. Hurley et al. (Trans.). New York: New Press, 1998.

Frenzel, E. (2008). *Motive der Weltliteratur*. Stuttgart, Germany: Kröner.

Freud, S. (1914d). On the history of the psycho-analytic movement. *S. E., 14*: 1–66. London: Hogarth.

Gide, A. (1925). *The Counterfeiters*. New York: Alfred A. Knopf, 1927.

Götzl, S. F. (2012). *Feminist Fairy-Tale Poetry: Sara Henderson Hay, Anne Sexton and Olga Broumas*. [Diplomarbeit Anglistik und Amerikanistik, University of Vienna.] http://othes.univie.ac.at/20114/1/2012-05-02_0204616.pdf (1.3.2014).

Hains, M. (1989). Beauty and the Beast: 20th century romance? *Merveilles & Contes, 3*(1): 75–83.

Hamburger, A. (1993). Psychoanalyse und Literatur. In: W. Mertens (Ed.), *Schlüsselbegriffe der Psychoanalyse* (pp. 391–400). Stuttgart, Germany: Verlag Internationale Psychoanalyse.

Hamburger, A. (1996). Goldne Träume kommt ihr wieder. Bericht über eine Lektüre. In: J. Cremerius, G. Fischer, O. Gutjahr, W. Mauser, & C. Pietzcker (Eds.), *Methoden in der Diskussion* (Freiburger

Literaturpsychologische Gespräche, Vol. 15) (pp. 47–81). Würzburg, Germany: Königshausen & Neumann.

Hamburger, A. (2001). Zur Konstruktion der Pubertät in Wedekinds *Frühlings Erwachen*. In: O. Gutjahr (Ed.), *Frank Wedekind* (pp. 55–92). Würzburg, Germany: Königshausen & Neumann.

Hamburger, A. (2003). Erinnerter Abschied. Zur psychoanalytischen Interpretation des Trakl-Epitaphs von Else Lasker-Schüler nebst Anmerkungen zum Übertragungsangebot der Lyrik. In: W. Mauser & J. Pfeiffer (Eds.), *Trauer* (pp. 185–226). Würzburg, Germany: Königshausen & Neumann.

Hamburger, A. (2006). Traum und Zeit. Traumerzählungen als Elemente der Spannungsdramaturgie. *Forum der Psychoanalyse, 22*: 23–43.

Hamburger, A. (2013). Arbeit in der Tiefe. Vorüberlegungen zu einer skeptischen Kulturanalyse. In: H. Hierdeis (Ed.), *Psychoanalytische Skepsis* (pp. 123–183). Göttingen, Germany: Vandenhoeck & Ruprecht.

Hamburger, A. (2014). Kinometaphern. Eine psychoanalytische Perspektive. *Psychosozial, 37*(3): 65–92.

Hamburger, A. & Leube, K. (2014). Wie im Kino. Zur Filmanalyse in der Gruppe. Methodologie der psychoanalytischen Filminterpretation anhand von Lars von Triers "Melancholia". In: R. Zwiebel & D. Blothner (Eds.), *Melancholia—Wege zur psychoanalytischen Interpretation des Films* (pp. 72–109). Göttingen, Germany: Vandenhoeck & Ruprecht.

Hamburger, A. & Pramataroff-Hamburger, V. (2014). Die Hure als Heilige. Vivian Ward (Julia Roberts), Edward Lewis (Richard Gere): Pretty Woman. In: S. Doering & H. Moeller (Eds.), *Mon Amour trifft Pretty Woman. Liebespaare im Film* (pp. 437–449). Heidelberg, Germany: Springer.

Harris, A., & Sklar, R. (1998). Wild film theory, wild film analysis. *Psychoanalytic Inquiry, 18*: 222–237.

Hay, S. H. (1998). *Story Hour*. Fayetteville, AR: University of Arkansas Press.

Hearne, B. G. (1989b). *Beauty and the Beast: Visions and Revisions of an Old Tale*. Chicago, IL: University of Chicago Press.

Holm, C. (2006): Amor und Psyche. Die Erfindung eines Mythos in Kunst, Wissenschaft und Alltagskultur (1765–1840). Munich, Germany: Deutscher Kunstverlag.

Jeffords, S. (1995). The curse of masculinity: Disney's Beauty and the Beast. In: E. Bell, L. Haas, & L. Sells (Eds.), *From Mouse to Mermaid: The Politics of Film, Gender and Culture* (pp. 161–172). Bloomington, IN: Indiana University Press.

Katrinaki, M. (2010). Tierverwandlung. In: K. Ranke (Ed.), *Enzyklopädie des Märchens. Handwörterbuch zur historischen und vergleichenden Erzählforschung, Vol. 13* (columns 653–658). Berlin: de Gruyter.

Kristeva, J. (1980). *Powers of Horror: An Essay on Abjection*. New York: Columba University Press, 1984.

Krützen, M. (2007). *Väter, Engel, Kannibalen. Figuren des Hollywoodkinos*. Frankfurt, Germany: Fischer.

Kuhn, M. (2011). *Filmnarratologie: ein erzähltheoretisches Analysemodell*. Berlin: Walter de Gruyter.

La Belle et la Bête—Le Chat botté (1848). [conte] [estampe] Epinal, France: Fabrique de Pellerin, Imprimeur-Libraire. http://gallica.bnf.fr/ark:/12148/btv1b6938052w (14.3.2014).

Lafontaine, J. de (1669). *Les amours de Psyché et de Cupidon*. Paris: Editions Flammarion 1990.

Leprince de Beaumont, J. -M. (1756). La Belle et la Bête. In: *Contes moraux pour l'instruction de la jeunesse* (pp. 1–32). Paris: Barba, 1806.

Liptay, F. (2007). Der Glöckner von Notre Dame (The Hunchback of Notre Dame) (USA 1939). In: T. Koebner & J. Felix (Eds.), *Filmgenres—Melodram und Liebeskomödie* (pp. 70–74). Stuttgart, Germany: Reclam.

Lorenzer, A. (1986). *Tiefenhermeneutische Kulturanalyse*. In A. Lorenzer (ed.), Kultur-Analysen (pp. 11–98). Frankfurt/Germany: Fischer.

Masoni, L. (2010). Tochter, Töchter. In: K. Ranke (Ed.), *Enzyklopädie des Märchens. Handwörterbuch zur historischen und vergleichenden Erzählforschung, Vol. 13* (columns 689–696). Berlin: de Gruyter.

McBain, E. (1982). *Beauty and the Beast*. London: Hamish Hamilton.

Megas, G. A. (1977). Amor und Psyche. In: K. Ranke (Ed.), *Enzyklopädie des Märchens. Handwörterbuch zur historischen und vergleichenden Erzählforschung, Vol. 1* (columns 464–472). Berlin: de Gruyter.

Mercatante, A. S., & Dow, J. R. (Eds.) (2009). *The Facts On File Encyclopedia of World Mythology and Legend (3rd ed.)* New York: Facts On File.

Mertens, W. (1996). *Entwicklung der Psychosexualität und der Geschlechtsidentität, vol. 2*. Stuttgart, Germany: Kohlhammer.

Mintz, T. (1970). The meaning of the rose in "Beauty and the Beast". *Psychoanalytic Review, 56*: 615–620.

Neumann, E. (1971). *Amor and Psyche: The Psychic Development of the Feminine—A Commentary on the Tale by Apuleius*. Princeton, NJ: Princeton University Press.

Noziere, F. (1929). *Three Gallant Plays: A Byzantine Afternoon, Beauty and the Beast, The Slippers of Aphrodite*. C. Stratton (Trans.). New York: William Edwin Rudge.

Ovid (Publius Ovidius Naso) (1 AC). *Metamorphoseum libri*. http://www.thelatinlibrary.com/ovid/ovid.met3.shtml (1.8.2013).

Perrault, C. (1697). Riquet à la houppe. In: *Histoires ou Contes du temps passé*. Paris: Édition Claude Barbin. http://fr.wikisource.org/wiki/

Histoires_ou_Contes_du_temps_pass%C3%A9_%281697%29/Riquet_%C3%A0_la_houppe (11.9.2013).

Popkin, M. (1982). Cocteau's Beauty and the Beast: The poet as monster. *Literature/Film Quarterly, 10*(2): 100–109.

Proust, M. (1925). *The Captive.* C. K. Scott Moncrieff (Trans.). New York: Vintage, 1970.

Reiche, R. (2001). *Mutterseelenallein. Kunst, Form und Psychoanalyse.* Frankfurt, Germany: Stroemfeld.

Reiche, R. (2011). *Mutterseelenallein 2. Das Tabu der Schönheit in Kunst und Psychoanalyse.* Frankfurt, Germany: Stroemfeld.

Reinhardt, U. (2012). *Mythen—Sagen—Märchen. Eine Einführung mit exemplarischen Motivreihen.* Freiburg, Germany: Rombach.

Riou, Y., & Pouchain, P. (2013). *Cocteau Marais—Ein mythisches Paar.* TV documentary, ARTE. October 13, 2013, *21*: 45.

Schneider, G. (2008). Filmpsychoanalyse—Zugangswege zur psychoanalytischen Interpretation von Filmen. In: P. Laszig & G. Schneider (Eds.), *Film und Psychoanalyse. Kinofilme als kulturelle Symptome* (pp. 19–38). Giessen, Germany: Psychosozial-Verlag.

Schneider, G. (2014). Das Container-Contained-Modell als Zugang zu Lars von Triers Melancholia. In: R. Zwiebel & D. Blothner (Eds.), *Melancholia—Wege zur psychoanalytischen Interpretation des Films* (pp. 44–71). Göttingen, Germany: Vandenhoeck & Ruprecht.

Schnyder, A. (2010). Teufelspakt. In: K. Ranke (Ed.), *Enzyklopädie des Märchens. Handwörterbuch zur historischen und vergleichenden Erzählforschung, Vol. 13* (columns 447–455). Berlin: de Gruyter.

Schulz, A. (2004). Spaltungsphantasmen. Erzählen von der "gestörten Mahrtenehe". *Wolfram-Studien, 18*: 233–262.

Shojaei Kawan, C. (2010). Tierbraut, Tierbräutigam, Tierehe. In: K. Ranke (Ed.), *Enzyklopädie des Märchens. Handwörterbuch zur historischen und vergleichenden Erzählforschung Vol. 13* (columns 555–565). Berlin: de Gruyter.

Straparola, G. F. (1556). *Le piacevoli notti.* Venice, Italy: Comin da Trino.

Studlar, G. (1993). Valentino, "optic intoxication", and dance madness. In: S. Cohan & I. R. Hark (Eds.), *Screening the Male. Exploring Masculinities in Hollywood Cinema* (pp. 23–45). London: Routledge.

Swahn, J. -O. (1989). "Beauty and the Beast" in oral tradition. *Merveilles & Contes, 3*(1): 15–27.

Swiderski, R. M. (2004). *Anthrax: A History.* Jefferson, NC: McFarland.

Uther, H. -J. (2004). *The Types of International Folktales. A Classification and Bibliography. Based on the System of Antti Aarne and Stith Thompson. Volume 1: Animal Tales, Tales of Magic, Religious Tales, and Realistic Tales, with an introduction.* Helsinki: Suomalainen Tiedeakatemia, Academia Scientiarum Fennica.

Von Hoff, D., & Leuzinger-Bohleber, M. (1997). Versuch einer Begegnung. Psychoanalytische und textanalytische Verständigungen zu Elfriede Jelineks "Lust". *Psyche—Zeitschrift für Psychoanalyse*, *51*: 763–800.

Williams, J. S. (2006). *Jean Cocteau*. Manchester, UK: Manchester University Press.

Zipes, J. (1995). Breaking the Disney spell. In: E. Bell, L. Haas, & L. Sells (Eds.), *From Mouse to Mermaid: The Politics of Film, Gender and Culture*. Bloomington, IN: Indiana University Press.

PART II

THE BEAUTIES

The interpretations of La Belle et la Bête in this section address the film's construction of femininity in the form of a dialogue.

Andrea Sabbadini questions the concept of beauty that is suggested in the title of the film and the name of the female protagonist, and he examines the tension between medially constructed feminine "beauty" and the qualities it subliminally connotes—among them virtue, submissiveness, and mirroring—as a partial-object perception of the maternal object. With the complex McGuffin of the rose, La Belle et la Bête symbolises both unbroken attachment to an idealised father entirely divested of aggression, and the inimicable moment when passionate love is inflamed—but it also symbolises maternal sympathy, as he illustrates in a vignette taken from an analytical case. As a work of art, the film proposes poeticising the medium itself—this is particularly poignant in the implausible ending, which only a superficial reading could interpret as overcoming the Oedipal attachment.

Christine Kirchhoff responds with a reading that takes as its starting point her own experience as a contemporary viewer. She, too, relates the alienation, boredom, and defence triggered by the film to the desexualisation it presents, but also to a basal experience of being swallowed and then spewed out again. She decodes this experience as resulting from the significant omission of adult, sexual femininity in the film—seeing traces of the absent mother in the partial-object-like caretaking machinery of the magic castle, which itself is a body laced with unreal passageways, reversing the within and the without in a kind of "pre-Oedipal jumble". When a masculine expression of sexuality—indicated by the smoke recurring in the film—breaks into this eerie realm, a synthesis of Beauty and the Beast could take form as a "beautiful beast, if the transition from splitting and projection [...] to an integrated object were achieved". Instead, this is disallowed by the desexualised ending of the film.

CHAPTER FOUR

La Belle, la Bête, et la rose

Andrea Sabbadini

> *For women are as roses, whose fair flower*
> *Being once display'd, doth fall that very hour.*
>
> —Shakespeare, *Twelfth Night*, Act 2, Scene 4

In the title of the eighteenth-century fairy tale *La Belle et la Bête* by Jeanne-Marie Leprince de Beaumont (1756),[1] as well as in that of Jean Cocteau's cult movie (1946) based on it,[2] the two-letter French conjunction *et* (and its three-letter English equivalent *and*) acts as a strong connecting magnet, thus making Beauty almost inseparable from its Beast. I shall, however, attempt in this chapter to leave the Beast in the background and to engage instead more closely with the Beauty side of the equation.

It may be useful to notice here that, even in the absence of her companion the Beast, in cinema (and in life) no *femme* can afford to be just *belle*: she could also be *fatale*, that is, a cruel maneater and/or a greedy gold-digger, like in most *film noir* (a genre that emerged in the same years, the 1940s, as our movie); or *de Jour* like Buñuel's (1967) part-time prostitute Séverine (Catherine Deneuve); or dying of cancer like Jenny (Ali MacGraw) in Hiller's LOVE STORY (1970); or belle but also very, very stupid (the *bimbo* role embodied by Marilyn Monroe); or belle but also very, very poor, and perhaps even blind, like the flower girl in Chaplin's CITY LIGHTS (1936). Etcetera.

The tendency to focus on beauty (and specifically the obsession in the media, cinema included, with *female* beauty) by detaching it from such other individual characteristics as personality, intelligence, sensitivity, and past history, and furthermore by fragmenting women's bodies into their component parts, bears some resemblance to the process (normal in early childhood, but with a fetishistic quality later in life) of relating to "part objects" instead of to a whole person; the way in which, to give an example, a hungry baby relates to his mother's breast before becoming aware that there is a whole person behind it.

As well as occasionally closing in on some of Belle's individual body parts (such as her face, hands, or hair), the film follows in the fairy-tale tradition of including in its mise en scène (by production designer Christian Bérard) a number of "objects" invested with magical powers: a white horse, a glove, a mirror, a golden key, and various *unheimlich* animated features of the castle's furniture. I shall focus here on the object which, at least on the surface,[3] performs the main bridging function in this film's narrative: the *rose*. This is the flower from the Beast's garden, picked by Beauty's father for her (just when we the viewers first encounter the Beast, springing up on the screen through a curtain of leaves) and later offered to her as his gift.

Let me now make a short detour and recall an episode recounted to me in the course of a session by my analysand Anthea, a young artist. The previous day, she told me, upon leaving my consulting room in desperate tears, she was walking down my street, weeping silently, and clutching her face in her hands.

It was a warm and sunny June day, when the front gardens of many London houses are lushly blessed with the colours and scents of the most wonderful flowers. Anthea stops in front of one of them, its small wrought-iron gate open to the pavement, and picks up a pink rose, still wet with morning dew. She sits on the pavement, still sobbing to herself, hugging her knees, the flower in her hands lightly pressed against her cheek. She thinks of herself as a rosebud, already withering before having had the chance to bloom to life.

The house owner, a middle-aged lady who had observed Anthea from the sitting-room bay window, walks out into the front garden with her shears. She cuts one, five, ten roses from her bushes, the most beautiful she can find. She picks them up in a bunch and, without uttering a word, places them in Anthea's arms.

Then she goes back inside.

Gertrude Stein (1913) was right to state, if tautologically, that *"a rose is a rose is a rose is a rose"*—nothing more than what it says it is (like Freud's cigar, maybe, and unlike Magritte's *pipe*). In Cocteau's film, though, such a flower is presented as the catalyst of the drama that, in the world of celluloid fiction, unfolds and eventually finds a resolution (if anything ever does ...). Yet at the same time the rose, which in the words of a colleague of Cocteau's (the sixteenth-century poet François de Malherbe, 1598) only lives for *"l'espace d'un matin"* ("the space of a single morning"), has that quality of impermanence or transience that for Freud adds to, rather than subtracting from, the beauty of nature and our aesthetic pleasure. "Limitation in the possibility of an enjoyment raises the value of the enjoyment," Freud wrote. "A flower that blossoms only for a single night does not seem to us on that account less lovely. Nor can I understand any better why the beauty and perfection of a work of art or of an intellectual achievement should lose its worth because of its temporal limitation" (1916a, pp. 305–306).

Beauty's avaricious and manipulative sisters, modelled on those of Cinderella (or perhaps on King Lear's elder daughters), demand from their father presents with narcissistic qualities, not only "brocaded dresses" and "jewelry, fans, ostrich feathers" (Cocteau, 1946, pp. 56 f.) but also a monkey and a parrot—animals with a reputation for imitating human behaviour. The feature they share with the rose asked for by Beauty is that all three are "exotic" presents insofar as none of them exists in their land. But while those two animals can be regarded as capricious gifts for spoiled children, the rose—the veritable queen of the vegetable kingdom according to Sappho, and a Romantic symbol of pure passion—is the flower exchanged in order to express one's loving feelings. It stands, therefore, for object relationships rather than for narcissistic ones.

* * *

Being "belle" (*schön, beautiful, bella, hermosa ...*) is an aspect relative to time, space, and culture, not to mention each individual subject's personal taste and current state of mind. Beauty, it is said, is in the eye of the beholder. In other words, the Beauty of our movie (and of the first half of its title) is one whom not everyone would consider as particularly beautiful. Here I am not, or not only, referring to one's idiosyncratic aesthetic assessment of Mademoiselle Josette Day's looks, but to the fact that her very name of Beauty emphasises a *physical* quality, while what Cocteau seems to focus on throughout his film is a *moral* one. Not on Beauty's beauty, then, but on her goodness: her generosity of spirit, her affection for her father,[4] her patience with her sisters' bullying, her inability to lie and, at the dramatic core of the whole story, her loving feelings towards the Beast. If we want to use the term Beauty at all, then, we should refer to the beauty of Beauty's mind, not to that of her body. If it were not too hard to imagine a film (or fairy tale) with such a title, we could have been watching *La Bonne et la Bête*.

The association of beauty with goodness (and, conversely, of ugliness with badness) is one ingrained in our Western mythologies and iconologies. I have yet to come across a children's book where good-hearted Snow White is portrayed as physically less attractive than her nasty stepmother—even her magic talking mirror reflects such a truth. Looking glasses, incidentally, are also present in our film: in the mirror which reflects Adelaide's head as "the head of an ugly old woman with similar head-dress" (Cocteau, 1946, pp. 330 f.), Beauty at first … sees her own reflection. Then the Beast appears to her: "He has almost a human face and he weeps" (Cocteau, 1946, p. 360)—the projection, we could argue, of Belle's own latent "beastly" side is presented as coexisting with her manifest goodness.[5]

These associations, however, can be fleeting and easily undone in stories intended, as many are, to surprise or even shock us. Then, either suddenly or after living through all sorts of adventures and overcoming all manner of hurdles, the Beautiful Girl is revealed to be a Cruel Witch in disguise, trying to seduce some innocent adolescent; the Loving Prince morphs into a Sadistic Tyrant; or conversely, in the situation concerning us here, the Monstrous Beast turns out to be the almost exaggerated prototype of a Handsome Young Man (the *beau par excellence*, Jean Marais).

In a different but related context the association between moral and physical features is also related to a culturally specific construction of masculinity and femininity. Men's and women's identities—including their bodies, their sexualities, and their social functions—are represented by the media, in collusion with the public they address, in ways which either confirm or (less often, and more interestingly) challenge those gender roles already sanctioned by existing social codes. Such representations themselves play an important part in shaping those values; or, better, there is a circular and mutually reinforcing contamination between the two. For instance, many American men of the 1950s coming home from work would rush to the drinks cabinet to help themselves to a stiff whisky (or indeed had one served to them by their devoted wives, busy until a minute before with washing the dishes at the kitchen sink …) and it was this common real-life situation that Hollywood so regularly presented to its audiences; at the same time, it could be argued that many American men and women adopted such stereotypical roles through identification with the characters, and with the idealised stars whom they were admiring on the screen of their local cinemas.

We know that the literature on film spectatorship has privileged a view of cinema as being produced by men for the consumption of other men, whereas women are treated by the film industry, and portrayed on celluloid, as passive objects (sexual or otherwise) of the male gaze, for men's exclusive voyeuristic gratification. Such a view, influenced by the important feminist contributions to spectatorship film studies from the 1970s and 1980s, is now considered outdated, or at least only partially justified, insofar as it seems to ignore the fact that audiences are made up of women as well as men, that women's and men's "visual pleasures" (to refer to the title of Laura Mulvey's seminal 1975 essay in this field) have homosexual as well as heterosexual connotations, and that in any case many movies are produced, written, and directed by women. As Andreas Hamburger reminds us, "… that both men and women are culturally defined and that societal conditions ultimately determine what prevails. […] both men and women are constructs of the cinematic gaze, and it is cast by women as well as men" (this volume, p. 9).

What can we then expect the men portrayed by the (gay) duo Cocteau-Marais in our film to be like? As my main focus is on the *belles* of LA BELLE ET LA BÊTE, I will only briefly remark on its *beaux*. Those we meet are Ludovic, a moralising young man pretending to protect his sister's virginity from her feckless suitor (who happens to be his best friend); a pathetic father gone bankrupt (impotent?) and left at the mercy of the greed, or pity, of his own children; a moneylender—Dickensian Scrooge or Shakespearian Shylock lookalike—caricatured with stereotypical Jewish features ….

Of all the male characters in the film, the most "human" happens to be, ironically, the one supposed to be monstrous: the Beast itself. Even before magically turning into a Prince, he shows more clearly than the other fellows at least some credible emotional qualities, such as being torn between the exercise of ruthless authority as "king of the castle" and a kinder side stimulated by his attraction to a beautiful Beauty. On one occasion we watch the Beast struggling between the impulse to give in to his instincts when he sees a deer leaping through the bushes, and the need to contain such drives in order not to scare Beauty, his human prey. Because this is what the world described by the film is about: men (and male beasts) are "hunters" while women, especially the *belle* ones, are their prey if not entirely their victims. When, at the end of the fairy tale, the Beast and Beauty get together as man and woman (i.e., as a less transgressive couple than the one walking hand-in-paw in the castle's gardens) and are ready to fly off to heavenly carnal pleasures, an unexpected touch of masochistic perversion creeps in when our heroine admits: "I don't mind being afraid … with you!"

It seems that there are no three-dimensional women in Cocteau's film but, as Christine Kirchhoff (Chapter Five, this volume) implies, only immature girls: motherless Beauty herself and her vain sisters Felicie and Adelaide. Kirchhoff also wonders whether the Beast's transformation into a Prince is paralleled by one of young Beauty into a Woman. I would hesitate to give a positive answer to that question, and even question Marianne Leuzinger-Bohleber's belief that "Both protagonists, the Beauty and the Beast, find themselves in an individuation process, away from an infantile way of loving to a more mature capability" (Chapter Six, this volume). At the same time, I am sympathetic to Kirchhoff's interpretation of Cocteau's work as a coming-of-age film: "[A] girl with oedipal attachment to father encounters the wild beast sexuality," she writes (this volume, p. 118), and "… the film addresses Belle's attempt to leave her father and family and to find a new object" (ibid., p. 121). Like Kirchhoff, I do not believe in the outcome, according to which "On the level of character development, Belle's sexuality, which initially confronts her from without, as something foreign, could potentially become her own desire" (ibid., p. 122). Does she really? I would argue that the story as presented in the film, rather than being about Beauty's journey of growth and self-discovery, portrays her throughout in a submissive role; her main function is to be instrumental to the Beast's metamorphosis (by offering herself as the object of his love more than by loving him), with little for her to be gained in this pseudo-therapeutic process of "conversion". I deliberately use a term with religious connotations, in syntony with Andreas Rost's suggestion about the Christian undertones of the story, culminating in "a supernatural heavenly sphere into which the couple finally ascends" (this volume, p. 141). A feature of the film, this is, that Rost and others (myself included) find problematic. But perhaps we should just give in to Cocteau's recommendation to the viewers, delivered in his own voice-over in the opening sequence, to suspend our (dis)belief, and to regress to a childhood condition: for children, he says, "believe what they are told and doubt it not" (Cocteau, 1946, p. 4).

* * *

It seems significant that, for Beauty, the gift of the rose (a kind of poisoned chalice) should come from her beloved father. Such a mediation implies that, in order to bloom from her girlhood condition into a sexually mature woman, Beauty needs first to resolve her Oedipal complex, that is, to separate from her papa (to Avenant who had proposed to her, she had simply answered: "I want to stay unmarried and live with my father" (Cocteau, 1946, p. 36). For Thomas Mintz, "Beauty wants the father to give her an acknowledgement of her now-blossoming sexual desires. Perhaps she wants him to respond to her sexual desires, or perhaps she merely wishes to let him know that she is growing up" (1969–1970, p. 617).

The mother being absent from the story, "the third" in the equation is represented, not unambiguously, by the Beast. Its/his competitor, the suitor whom we have met in the early part of the film and who re-emerges in its concluding scenes, would be the fourth pole in this rather strange triangle. However, he turns out to be the Beast's own alter ego morphed into a prince—not surprisingly, also considering that it is the same actor, Jean Marais, who plays these different roles.[6] As Christina Wieland clarifies, "The story portrays vividly the split in the father into an idealised father figure and a Beast, and how this split is repeated in the daughter's perception of him … Beauty can now be either with the Beast or with father but not with both of them at the same time. She can now go on worshipping the father's idealised image from a distance while she lives with the Beast" (1991, pp. 138–139). The father as the object of Beauty's tender feelings and the Beast as the object of her sexual desires are presented then as two sides of the same Oedipal coin.

The Beast is introduced to us as a cruel monster, intent on punishing Beauty's father with death and then on keeping her imprisoned in his castle. But the miracle of love at first sight makes the Beast more and more dependent upon Beauty, moving from being her master to becoming her loyal servant. This is something which, despite his beastly yet anthropomorphic appearance (a "look" which we could locate somewhere between King Kong, the Cowardly Lion from THE WIZARD OF OZ, and the ELEPHANT MAN), she cannot resist.

For Dennis DeNitto, LA BELLE ET LA BÊTE "is a story of a young woman's initiation into sexual womanhood by turning away from the sterile, taboo relationship with her father and accepting the reality of man as both romantic lover and sexual husband. The Beast is emotionally the romantic lover, but his appearance is a reminder of the existence of male sexuality. When Beauty ceases to reject the latter, the dual dimensions of the suitor become combined in a prince whose virility is part of his attractiveness" (1976, p. 130). Or perhaps Beauty lets herself be seduced by what Marina Warner describes as his "irresistible synthesis of repulsiveness and attractiveness" (2008, p. 1) because, in Dante's words, *"amor ch'a nullo amato amar perdona"* ("Love that exempts no one loved from loving in return") (*Inferno*, Canto 5, p. 103, in Alighieri, 1300).

Ah, the redemptive power of love! "Love", claims the Prince, "can make a man become a beast. Love can also make an ugly man handsome" (Cocteau, 1946, p. 374, footnote 130). There is a long tradition of monsters who have been blessed with it: from cursed ghostly sailors like the Wagnerian *Der fliegende Holländer* to such a small beast as the Frog in the Brothers Grimm's story.

One may then be tempted to dispose of LA BELLE ET LA BÊTE in the comfortable "love story", or even romcom cinematic pigeonhole—and not without some valid reasons for it: an impoverished good girl meets a rich aristocrat (still hiding underneath a beast's costume), they fall for each other and, having overcome a few inevitable obstacles, fly off, among clouds and puffs of smoke, to a happy-ever-after life together ... Where else could such a narrative belong? Yet, despite its shortcomings (from Georges Auric's self-indulgent music score to the mediocre acting of most members of the cast), Cocteau's "fairy tale with no fairies" is so stylish in its absurd and yet masterful handling of the story, if not in the otherwise predictable story itself, as to fit no category at all. It stands alone as a unique instance of what cinema can offer us: a wonderful, albeit slightly withered, hypnotically scented, black-and-white … ROSE.

Notes

1. The story of Beauty and the Beast has been retold in different versions, including by Angela Carter under the title of "The Courtship of Mr Lyon" (1979).
2. A film which "unfolds to a perfectly poised slow tempo in surreal settings" (Warner, 2008, p. 4).
3. The rose in *La Belle et la bête* seems to have a similar function as that of the McGuffin in many Hitchcock's films: an object important to the protagonist, but ultimately irrelevant to the overall plot.
4. Beauty gives an impressive demonstration of her love for him when she cries diamond tears to rescue him from poverty, in contrast with her sisters' fake tears, induced by the smell of onions and intended to steal the key to a treasure.
5. DeNitto writes: "Mirrors and mirror images in art often serve as bridges between what we too frequently view as the separate worlds of reality and illusion, the mundane and the magical, the conscious and the unconscious" (1976, p. 133).
6. His name, Avenant, in French means "attractive", a description fitting his own appearance but wholly unsuited to the beastly looks of his *Doppelgänger*.

References

Alighieri, D. (1300). La Divina Commedia, *Inferno*, Canto 5 (p. 103). In: *Dante. Tutte le opere*. Florence, Italy: Sansoni, 1965.

Carter, A. (1979). The courtship of Mr. Lyon. In: *Burning Your Boats. Collected Stories* (pp. 144–153). London: Vintage, 1995.

Cocteau, J. (1946). *Beauty and the Beast*. French and English edition. Scenario and dialogues by Jean Cocteau. R. M. Hammond (Ed.). New York: New York University Press, 1970.

De Malherbe, F. (1598). *Consolation à M Du Périer*. In: *Oeuvres complètes, Vol. 1*. Paris: Hachette, 1862.

DeNitto, D. (1976). Jean Cocteau's *Beauty and the Beast*. *American Imago, 33*: 123–154.

Freud, S. (1916a). On transience. *S. E., 14*. London: Hogarth.

Leprince de Beaumont, J. -M. (1756). La Belle et la Bête. In: *Contes moraux pour l'instruction de la jeunesse* (pp. 1–32). Paris: Barba, 1806.

Mintz, T. (1969–1970). The meaning of the rose in "Beauty and the Beast". *Psychoanalytic Review, 56*: 615–620.

Mulvey, L. (1975). Visual pleasure and narrative cinema. *Screen, 16*(3): 6–18.

Stein, G. (1913). Sacred Emily. In: *Geography and Plays*. Boston, MA: The Four Seas Company, 1922.

Warner, M. (2008). Cocteau's fairytale for grown-ups. In the booklet accompanying the DVD of LA BELLE ET LA BÊTE (pp. 1–5). London: British Film Institute.

Wieland, C. (1991). Beauty and the Beast: The father's unconscious and the riddle of femininity. *British Journal of Psychotherapy, 8*: 131–143.

CHAPTER FIVE

"You can't say no to the Beauty and the Beast ..."* Or: an ending and no beautiful beast

Christine Kirchhoff†

When I saw the film LA BELLE ET LA BÊTE for the first time in preparation for this paper, I thought it was the longest, slowest, and most boring film I had ever seen in my whole life. At the same time I worried that it would be completely impossible to glean something resembling a presentable interpretation from the tangled mass of meanings presented and the diversity of scenes in which each shot and every detail seemed overdetermined. And I felt I had fallen among teenagers: the whole time it's about sex, and in a rather distorted way. And I began to cringe inwardly when, yet again, something in the film started to smoulder and smoke. But I'll get to that later. I felt pinioned, time dragged, and when the film did finally come to a close, I was dreadfully disappointed by the ending.

Now, one could quickly interpret my boredom, the feeling of being constrained, the feeling that time is slowing down and coming to a standstill, as being "a countertransference towards the film" (cf. Hamburger, 2006; Hamburger & Leube, 2014; Reiche, 2001, p. 27) and thus begin to conjecture what is happening in the film, with what

*David Bowie, "Heroes", 1977.
†Translated by Shivaun Conroy.

affects or emotional states I've reacted to the film, and what this means from a psychoanalytical perspective. But first I would like to take a step back and look at the conditions under which I watched the film: the first thing to be noted is that I had to see it; after all I wanted to—and was supposed to—give a talk about it. This could explain in part my feeling "Oh dear, I can't get away from this": simply switching off the film and postponing it indefinitely—a possibility, had I chosen the film myself—was not an available option. The fact of the matter was that I could not get away from it.

To complicate matters, the film's narrative tempo and particularly the length of the shots did not suit my viewing habits.[1] Having grown up with MTV, I now regularly watch American "quality" TV, that is, series. Despite all their differing characteristics, what is common to these formats (music videos as shown on MTV non-stop in the early days and series, such as THE WIRE, 24, or SIX FEET UNDER) is the pace—quick cuts between scenes and narrative threads, rapidly changing camera shots—non-linearity in development and narration, and the interweaving of multiple narrative threads with several different characters. Although I certainly have seen quite a few films with a different tempo and narrative style—slower and more linear, as an everyday consumer of films and series I am used to the features listed above. So I reacted to the slowness in cut and camera work of LA BELLE ET LA BÊTE with a confusion which turned to boredom, caused not so much by psychological but rather aesthetic factors and my subjective attitude to them. Evidently I required a process of acculturation to the unaccustomed style of the film, all the more so due to radical developments in digital technology today that make it possible to present film fantasies with no apparent inconsistencies or artificial scenery that might irritate the viewer. One has to be aware and remind oneself while viewing them that today's films are fabricated on the computer. If you take them at face value, nothing much will strike you. With LA BELLE ET LA BÊTE, notwithstanding all the impressive artistry, it is evident at first sight that we're dealing with a masquerade, with, for instance, a human disguised as an animal. You see that—and how—the Beast has been made into a beast; you immediately register that the set is artificial. On the whole, the film is slow-paced; there is very little build-up of suspense in the plot, perhaps because it is already familiar.

The starting point for the following considerations is my own affective reaction to the film, dominated by boredom, the sense of being overwhelmed, pinioned, embarrassed, and bitterly disappointed at the end. In addition to the causes previously mentioned, I regard my boredom as a defence—a defence against the sense of being overwhelmed and drawn into something undifferentiated and uncanny, being confronted with a plethora of strange objects. When I did begin to let the film affect me, to see how it functions formally and what this could mean beyond the story it ostensibly tells, I was drawn to it and at the same time repelled; I felt sucked in and spewed out over and again. Inwardly taking a step back, I was fascinated by what I believed to see on the surface it presented. The longer I engaged with the film, the more the positive impression gained the upper hand, possibly also a result of my having achieved more of a distance to the film in the sense of a triangulation: film—me—interpretation.

Initially the film seems to present a typical "Cinderella-happily-ever-after" narrative. Modest Belle—devoted to her father, bullied by her vain sisters, diligently doing the housework, and instead of jewels wishing merely for a simple rose—proves not only courageous in sacrificing herself for her father and going to live with the Beast; she also succeeds in seeing the inner beauty of the monster, in liberating him, and finally floating up to heaven with him. The disconcerting element of the narrative seems to derive from the ending, since somehow something doesn't seem quite right with that last scene—but what is it?

On method

In *Mutterseelenallein* (All Alone) and continuing in *Mutterseelenallein 2*, Reimut Reiche (2001, 2011) strongly criticises psychoanalytical cultural interpretations. In the following, I engage with Reiche and thereby elucidate my own methodical approach in the interpretation of LA BELLE ET LA BÊTE.[2]

In his critique of "systematical utilisation of the so-called countertransference of the observer" (2001, p. 29), Reiche pleads for "abandoning the deep hermeneutical formula *What is the text doing to me?* and to separate the residue into two formulas: What is the text doing? And: What am I doing with the text?" (ibid., pp. 31 f.) This strikes at the core of psychoanalytical interpretation since it is precisely this question—*What is the text doing to me?*—which characterises the psychoanalytical approach of including one's own affects and fantasies in an interpretation. Reiche concludes that neither deep hermeneutical interpretations nor psychoanalytical interpretations deriving from the author's psyche will be able to generate new insights (ibid., p. 32). The problem underlying this diagnosis is expressed by the formula "as psychoanalysts we know that $a = x$" (ibid., p. 25). A procedure taken from clinical practice—linking the comments of the analysand (Reiche's *a*) with a concept *X-1* in order to reach an interpretation *X-2* which the analyst in turn then links to *a* (ibid.)—is, he claims, transferred unquestioningly to a non-clinical application of psychoanalysis. Thereby, according to my understanding of Reiche, it is methodically overlooked that temporarily forgetting pre-knowledge is extremely important for clinical work—expressed by Bion as the ideal of "no memory, no desire" (1967b) and by Deserno as "priority of method over knowledge" (1990). In "subsuming a under x" (ibid.) what is found will be precisely what one expected to find on the basis of conceptual presuppositions.[3] Moreover, what makes art art—the form—is neglected.[4]

This doesn't mean, as one might quickly conclude, that one should ignore the countertransference; at another point Reiche, referring to Adorno's insistence on the "priority of the object", stipulates that the observer, in order to perceive the form, must "'add' their own condition and mental state" to the work, and is therefore compelled to work with the countertransference. The countertransference must, however, make itself available "to be consumed and extinguished by the work" (ibid., p. 27).

Of necessity, the observer interpreting the work (picture, installation, film, etc.) must engage with it in order "to transform the picture, exploiting all its idiosyncrasies of form, into a narrative and to consolidate this narrative into a diagnosis on affective mental states, on affective and cognitive horizons of the epoch" (ibid., p. 10). In *Mutterseelenallein 2* Reiche (2011) elaborates his method: every interpretation must "take the reconstructive path of describing the work" (p. 75), keeping in mind that one is always analysing the "protocol of the picture", never the picture itself (ibid.) and that one can only grasp one's own affective response in a mediated manner (ibid., p. 78). The "unconscious in art" is not to be found in the depths, but can only be accessed via the surface:

> As soon as we have apprehended an element of meaning or significance in an artwork, we have made this element "visible" to ourselves. Making it visible means that we have brought it to the surface

> *in a figurative sense*. Each work consists only of such surfaces—to be grasped anew over and again. (ibid.; emphasis added)

It is precisely here that the "so-called countertransference is latently implied" (ibid.). If the description is successful, the countertransference dissolves into it (ibid., p. 79). On this basis, Reiche concludes that it is not necessary to fall back on "psychoanalytical professionalized pronouncements on our affective reactions to the work of art" (ibid., pp. 78 f). Before attempting to reply on this point—that it may not be necessary, but in fact possible and even advisable—I would like take up one more aspect of Reiche's methodological approach. He sees methodology as producing a "structural homology" between the analysis of the "dreamt dream" and the "painted picture" (ibid., p. 80). The emphasis on the production of the homology qua method is in my opinion important inasmuch as it serves as a clarifying reminder that a work of art is not a dream—and the method, as Freud once said, should arise from the object—while, nonetheless, indicating that the interpretative approach can proceed analogously to the method of dream interpretation. In interpreting a picture, instead of latent dream thoughts, one approaches the "latent meaningful structure" in the "unconscious structural principles of the picture" (ibid., pp. 80 f.). Interpretation of both dreams and works of art remains inconclusive (ibid., p. 84).

Now with regard to affective reactions, why shouldn't we draw on what Reiche polemically refers to as "psychoanalytical professionalized pronouncements", meaning, psychoanalytical concepts? In the process of visualisation described by Reiche, something is brought up, "in a figurative sense", to the surface. And this is doubly true: first, because an image is borrowed from another context in order to understand and be capable of reflecting upon this process (lifting to the surface). Second, because transference takes place here. I'd like to suggest that recourse to psychoanalytical concepts—where available—occurs at some point in any case; the important point is to be aware that these concepts already figure in visualisation, arising as soon as desire and memory come back into play. As Horkheimer and Adorno said, "In a certain sense all perception is projection" (1947, p. 187), only "the absence from it of reflection" can be seen as "pathic" (ibid., p. 189). In terms of the interpretation of a picture, text, or film based on psychoanalytical concepts, this means that these concepts can help to raise something to the surface, making something visible that otherwise would not have been found; it would simply have been overlooked or its retrieval not considered worthwhile. That is not to say that it was deposited there by the method and its concepts, nor does it mean that it (of itself) had always been there in the precise form in which it is subsequently described.

Freud, too, was aware that there can be no non-categorical perceptions, that categories (in this case, psychoanalytical concepts) are not just involved in the interpretation and explanation of a phenomenon, but rather are already constitutive in determining what is possible or how it is perceived. In his clear manner, Freud expresses this as follows:

> We need not feel greatly disturbed in judging our speculation upon the life and death instincts by the fact that so many *bewildering* and *obscure* processes occur in it—such as one instinct being driven out by another or an instinct turning from the ego to an object, and so on. This is merely due to our being *obliged* to operate with the scientific terms, that is to say with the figurative language, peculiar to psychology (or, more precisely, to depth psychology). We could not otherwise *describe* the processes in question at all, and indeed we could not have *become aware* of them. (1920g, p. 60; emphasis added)

Thus one must avail oneself of a particular language in order to perceive and describe anything. So Freud knew about the role of language, and thus also of concepts, in constituting perception, without confusing this with "constituting reality". Applied to film interpretation, this means that the knowledge of psychoanalytical concepts allows one to perceive the staging of unconscious content and also to be able to describe it more fittingly than would be possible if one were limited to verbalising the relevant affect ("It feels kind of strange", "Makes me uneasy", "I'm getting tired", etc.).[5]

Naturally, such an interpretation cannot be more than an *offering* of an interpretation. The possibility of at least a belated acceptance[6] of this offer—as it occurs within the analytical setting (an interpretation is or isn't effective, was too early or too late)—is not, for the most part, an option here, or if it does actually occur, it is at another level, namely when the audience accepts or rejects the interpretative offer. But here, too, caution is warranted since this "accepting" could also be the result of a temptation to identify, to participate in "knowing that x = a", an effect familiar from group formation; just as "rejecting" it could indicate a communally shared defence.

This leads to the question of whom or what we can make statements about in the first place. Who is actually the object of the interpretation? I'd like to suggest that what is being interpreted here with the aid of psychoanalytic concepts is the potential of the work (in this case, the film) to stage unconscious emotional dynamics, to bring them to public attention and allow them potency. The interpretation arrived at relates to the process taking place between the recipient and the film and needs to be seen in terms of its own limitations: we are most certainly, also from a psychoanalytical perspective, dealing with a selection and are neither aiming to nor would we be able to grasp the full range of the film's aesthetic qualities. In setting the focus of my interpretation on the events in the castle and the relationship between Belle and the Beast, I have made a selection that excludes other emphases. Moreover, I concentrate on the theme of sexuality, which means that other aspects are neglected or that my findings would be given different accents if described in another theoretical framework. Thus, the interpretation I present here is not one of the entire film, but rather of that which can be rendered visible in the scenes I have chosen. And here, too, the methodological approach is also a conceptual one: without the knowledge of the concepts invoked, I would perhaps not even have noticed what I attempt to describe in the following, or if I had, I would not have understood it in this way. I describe the scenes I have selected and this necessarily means distorting them to some extent: subjectivity and method already influence the description (Reiche, 2001, p. 37; 2011, pp. 77 ff.).

In analogy to Freud's procedure in *The Interpretation of Dreams*,[7] I try to translate formal attributes into latent dream ideas, formulating a narrative which incorporates formal-aesthetic aspects of the film (to the extent that I can perceive them): in my verbal rendition of the scenes from the film, the interpretation already plays a role. I do not explicitly examine the historical situation in which the film was developed, or the person of Cocteau as its director.

In the castle

"Screened Women", the title of the panel for which this contribution originated as a lecture, is quite appropriate to the film in its ambiguity: to "screen" meaning both to shield and to present. The film does both, which relates to the question posed at the beginning of these reflections: where are the women in LA BELLE ET LA BÊTE? Running through the personnel line-up of the film, it is not easy to identify an adult woman. The mother is absent and the three sisters—daddy's sweetie and two wannabe princesses—are portrayed as girls and behave accordingly. Traces of womanly attributes are to be found, if anywhere, in the Beast—his clothing and demeanour are at least partly ambiguous.

Or is this supposed to be the story of how the girl Belle becomes a woman? From this perspective we would be dealing with a coming-of-age film: girl with Oedipal attachment to father encounters the wild beast "sexuality". This dangerous temptation appears first in the form of Avenant, who makes advances, embracing her and trying to kiss her: "I'll snatch you by force from this stupid existence" (Cocteau, 1946, p. 36).

At any rate, the topic seems to be that of sexuality; what becomes of the girl is another question. What particularly strikes the viewer is that things are constantly smouldering in the film. The Beast, especially, is literally steamy. The situations in which he begins exuding smoke suggest the demonical, wild, uncontrollable aspect of sexuality: the Beast is not quite stable. Even when Belle's father enters the castle, smoke wafts towards him (ibid., pp. 78 f.). As he sits at the table, smoke billows from the mouths of the candelabra men (ibid., p. 82), a scene which is repeated when Belle sits in despair at the same table having just seen her very sick father in the mirror (ibid., p. 134).

Concerning the fumes or smoke Cocteau suggests another interpretation. At the beginning of the film, where he calls upon the spectators to take on a childlike perspective, we read: "They [the children] *believe* that the hands of a human beast that kills begin to smoke and that this beast is ashamed when a maiden dwells in his house" (ibid., p. 4). I'd like to suggest that Cocteau's proffered interpretation be understood in analogy to the dream interpretation as an obfuscation: the theme is sexuality, aggression, and shame. It is not when he kills, but rather when he is desirous that the Beast's hands smoke, and for this he must feel shame.[8]

The notably absent adult woman is present in fantasies of the early mother, which the film stages opulently: from the moment that Belle enters the Beast's castle, it all revolves around her. Everything concerning Belle happens automatically; the whole castle seems to welcome her and draw close to her. The camera pans to her lower abdomen. The candelabras stretch up towards her when she approaches them;

she is lifted onto a carpet which then carries her along, the doors open automatically, the blanket on her bed folds back. When she sits down at the dinner table, everything is already prepared and she is waited on (ibid., pp. 144 ff.) This is reminiscent of the omnipotent fantasies of babies as described by Winnicott—illusionary ideas which must, according to Winnicott (1953), first have been a reality for the baby in order for him to be able to give them up.[9] Moreover, on the castle premises, outside and inside spaces do not appear to be clearly distinguished. In Belle's room the vegetation grows rampantly just as it does outside. There are several portals or archways which lead, so to speak, from the inside to the inside or from the outside to the outside; they look like passages of transition, but on the far side everything looks exactly the same.[10]

Doors and windows, halls and corridors, billowing curtains, candle holders protruding from the wall, erect—the latter impressing as potent objects, but dismembered and fixed to the wall: all this could be an indication that what's being presented here are partial objects; likewise the male heads in the columns following every movement with their eyes and the movements and encounters of Belle and the Beast. Everything occurring in and around the castle is ambiguous, obscure, adding up to an overall impression of uncanniness.

What stands out in this pre-Oedipal confusion and perhaps leads us further is the question of what exactly is happening between Beauty and the Beast; what is being negotiated. On the manifest level, nothing much occurs, but there is a sequence of scenes which clearly allude to a sexual quality, suggesting orgiastic excitement.

Belle enters the castle for the first time (Cocteau, 1946, pp. 124 ff.): the tempo is almost slow-motion. Drawn along, floating lightly as if being pulled by a current—which at one point, at the door, she tries to withstand—Belle enters the castle. The candle holders stand out erect from the walls. She floats onwards, the camera pans to her lower abdomen. She shrinks back from the candle holders at the door, but then enters, surrounded by smoke. All around her there are plants, inside and outside. She sees the mirror, which at a later point will show her the beast, and sits agitated, agonising in front of it. The mirror says: "I am your mirror. Reflect for me and I will reflect for you." The mirror shows the father. The next shot shows the bed with the blanket sliding onto the floor of its own accord. Belle is frightened and runs away, out of the castle, down the grand perron; everywhere there are rampantly growing plants. The Beast appears, he roars. She faints.

It continues: the Beast lifts her up and carries her away, up the stairs. The music goes boom-boom-boom; she lies turned outwards at an awkward angle in his arms. The candle holders jut out from the wall. The Beast lays Belle upon her bed, the music turns ecstatic, the Beast leans over her—she wakes up and is shocked. The Beast is totally exhausted. As he turns away, he promises not to do anything, other than appearing for dinner at seven. And he stumbles out, not without warning Belle: "You must not look me in the eyes" (ibid., p. 144, footnote).

In the next shot the men in the columns to the left and right of the fireplace stare out of the wall. It is seven o'clock and Belle is about to dine. The Beast enters the room. Belle, sitting at the table, reacts physically to the appearance of the Beast; she first slumps down and then draws herself up stiffly, is barely able to maintain her posture; she grips the arms of the chair, closes her eyes, breathes heavily. When the Beast says that everything in the castle belongs to her and that she should tell him her wishes, it begins to get smoky again. And when she answers the Beast's question of whether she would be his wife with "No" and the Beast leaves, moving backwards towards the entrance, she slumps back into the chair. Where there is smoke there's a fire, says the proverb. The choreography of excitement, tension, relaxation or, respectively, powerlessness intimates the sexual act, staged here as a massive failure.

It is against this background that the transformation of the Beast into a Prince is to be seen, the most obvious transition the film addresses on the manifest level. The ending packs a punch. It is excessive in almost every respect and nonetheless—or for this very reason—disappointing. It is foreshadowed in an earlier scene. Belle and the Beast are walking in the garden (ibid., pp. 169 f.). The Beast sniffs, scenting a doe. It leaves him speechless. He wants to run into the forest, he growls. The doe flees. Is the fleeing doe an image of the girl withdrawing? The Beast's ears prick up. There is aggression in the air. Then all at once it appears to have vanished, and Belle and the Beast, stiltedly and ceremonially, are descending the stairs together, moving away from the great cloud of smoke in the background.

A little later, after the Beast has drunk from Belle's hands, he asks if it doesn't disgust her. Belle answers "No, Beast, I like to. I would never wish to cause you the least hurt" (ibid., p. 172). She is depicted in such soft contours that it is almost painful. A case of splitting?

In the next scene it is night-time (ibid., pp. 174 ff.). In the corridor in front of Belle's room we see two statues, a boy and a girl. Smoke billows forth from the boy. Both follow the Beast's every move. The Beast appears, he is dishevelled and bloody, stares down at his smoking hands; the look in his eyes is wild, almost deranged.[11] He scratches at the door to Belle's room. She opens it: the Beast stands at the threshold, more animalistic than ever before and asks Belle to forgive him for being a beast. Belle, dressed in flowing white, answers that he must not say such a thing, stamps her foot and says, "Clean yourself up!" (Get rid of the dirt, the sexuality?) When she then tells the Beast to go to bed, a growl escapes him. Belle draws back and the Beast urges her to close the door: "Your eyes are burning me. I can't bear your eyes." The Beast staggers out backwards, touching the breast of the female statue with its paw.

Here it seems we are dealing with something that is so dangerous that the only possible response is to close the door. As in the previous scene, there is a splitting here: the pure, white, flowing Beauty and the wild, bleeding, dirty Beast. Just as the two characters fail to come together, so also desire, which can only emerge as a split projection within the Beast, is then suppressed once again (when the Beast says that Belle's eyes are burning him). A possible integration miscarries.

A disappointing ending

The final scene takes up this theme once more. In its incredible plasticity and intensity it calls to mind Freud's finding on "screen memories", namely that the "sensory intensity" (1899a, p. 322), the impression that the images are "exaggerated in an almost hallucinatory fashion" (ibid., p. 312), is to be seen as an indication that at this point memory is distorted, condensed, and displaced.

"The greatest intensity is shown by those elements of a dream on whose formation the greatest amount of condensation has been expended" (Freud, 1900a, pp. 330 f.).

The Beast is transformed into a handsome prince, who takes Belle to his heavenly kingdom without the hint of a puff of smoke. I think the end is disappointing, because everything that could have been achieved in the course of the film fails on several levels.

If we take the Oedipal/adolescent level[12] into consideration,[13] the film addresses Belle's attempt to leave her father and family and to find a new object. This is also elucidated by the mirror which first shows the sick father in need of help (ibid., p. 134) and later the sobbing Beast (ibid., p. 336) for whom Belle—who had in the meantime returned home—leaves her family again. However, they later await her in the heavenly kingdom of the prince, with the prince's heavenly kingdom becoming the new version of the old family, although under different terms: her father will be there, the prince promises little Belle, and her sisters will be her servants (ibid.). So in the end there is no integration or new object, but rather the realisation, piece by piece, of a childish fantasy, crowned with victory in the sisters' rivalry over their father. No happy ending.

What the film also recounts in this scene and what lends the ending its oppressive quality, totally unbefitting for a triumphal happy ending, is the struggle for integration, shown here in the realm of sexuality. On the level of character development, Belle's sexuality, which initially confronts her from without as something foreign, could potentially become her own desire. In other words, a beautiful beast could actually emerge from Beauty and the Beast if the transition from splitting and projection (either/or, black/white) to a successfully integrated object were completed. The great disappointment of the final scene is that once the Beast is transformed into a kitschy fairy-tale prince, integration is arrested—for Belle too: tenderness and sensuality,[14] purity and dirt are not to be mixed. Thus the film ends with a scene that is, at face value, almost too happy an ending—the couple actually ascend to heaven (Cocteau, 1946, pp. 378 ff.)—but is in fact not happy at all because the essential developmental step goes awry. This gives the end its oppressive quality, oppressive precisely because it has been purged of the Beast. The prince sees Belle as "a funny little girl" (ibid., p. 376). That's why, asked whether she is happy now, Belle can only reply that she will have to get used to it (ibid., p. 376).

All the opportunities that arose during the film are blanketed over; the promise of development remains unrealised. No mingling of desires takes place; no integration or toleration of ambivalence is achieved, no relationship to a whole object established. Instead, what Belle demanded of the Beast in an earlier scene comes to pass. He is cleansed or—in the sense of a screen memory—screened.

Notes

1. However, in discussions with older participants of the workshop, I was told several times that "new films" are simply too fast-paced and that this results in certain difficulties.

2. In fact these ideas only occurred to me having already sketched out the rough outline of my interpretation.
3. As a striking example, Reiche cites a work by André Green on Leonardo da Vinci (2001, p. 16).
4. In this context, I cannot go further into Reiche's critique of the "systematic abuse [...] of the psychoanalytical method" in the "practical application of deep hermeneutics", which always occurs when the "so-called countertransference" is taken as a starting point and a work is subsumed under the psychoanalytic concept of choice (2001, p. 30). But I would like to note the following: Reiche's exhortation to examine the surface of the artwork—since it is here that unconscious material is to be found, or, as one could also say, stages itself—refers directly to Argelander's (1970) and Lorenzer's (1970) understanding of mutual enactment, which is actually intended to form the core of a deep hermeneutical interpretation (even if this is often not the case). As I've understood and acquired this method, it is precisely about understanding the scene of which one is oneself a part—the surface of events, what goes on—as an enactment of unconscious fantasies, conflicts, or deficits. One factor involved is the transference/countertransference as a means of integrating the issue of how it feels to be a part of this scene. For discussion of Reiche's critique see also Hamburger (2013).
5. If the subject here were the presentation of gender relationships in "Beauty and the Beast" from a sociological perspective, then the relevant sociological theories would be primarily consulted.
6. In the sense of the Freudian "Nachträglichkeit".
7. "The form of the dream or dreaming is represented with astonishing frequency to represent the concealed content" (Freud, 1900a, p. 332).
8. Avenant and Ludovic also smoke (ibid., pp. 62, 282).
9 "The mother, at the beginning, by an almost 100 per cent adaptation affords the infant the opportunity for the *illusion* that her breast is part of the infant. It is, as it were, under the baby's magical control. The same can be said in terms of infant care in general, in the quiet time between excitements. Omnipotence is nearly a fact of experience. The mother's eventual task is gradually to disillusion the infant, but she has no hope of success unless at first she has been able to give sufficient opportunity for illusion" (Winnicott, 1953, pp. 6 f.).
10. This can be seen in all the shots taken in Belle's room in the Beast's castle. In Cocteau's book (1946) the vegetation in the description of the room and its environs is not mentioned.
11. In the film there is a lot of smoke in this scene, which is not mentioned in the script (see ibid., pp. 178 ff.).
12. "The fact that the onset of sexual development in human beings occurs in two phases," according to Freud "one of the necessary conditions

of the aptitude of men for developing a higher civilization, but also of their tendency to neurosis" (1905d, p. 135), means that in adolescence, sexual development, interrupted by a period of latency, is continued. The infantile, remodelled, is put to new effect; thus the Oedipal is also staged anew.

13. As for instance the interpretations of Bettelheim (1954) and Henderson (1967), criticised by Burton (1978), which interpret the film at the Oedipal level from Freudian and Jungian perspectives.
14. For Freud, the task of puberty, in accordance with his own assumption of the double onset of sexual development, was the "convergence of the affectionate current and the sensual current" (1905d, p. 207).

References

Argelander, H. (1970). *Das Erstinterview in der Psychotherapie*. Darmstadt, Germany: Wissenschaftliche Buchgesellschaft.

Bettelheim, B. (1954). *Symbolic Wounds; Puberty Rites and the Envious Male*. Glencoe, IL.: Free Press.

Bion, W. R. (1967). Notes on memory and desire. In: E. Bott Spillius (Ed.), *Melanie Klein Today Vol. 2 Mainly Practice*. London: Routledge, 1988.

Burton, A. (1978). Beauty and the Beast: A critique of psychoanalytic approaches to the fairy tale. *Psychocultural Review: Interpretations in the Psychology of Art, Literature and Society*, 2: 241–258.

Cocteau, J. (1946). The Beauty and the Beast. R. M. Hammond (Ed.). New York: New York University Press, 1970.

Deserno, H. (1990). *Die Analyse und das Arbeitsbündnis. Eine Kritik des Arbeitsbündniskonzepts*. Munich, Germany: Verlag Internationale Psychoanalyse.

Freud, S. (1899a). Screen memories. *S. E., 3*. London: Hogarth.

Freud, S. (1900a). *The Interpretation of Dreams. S. E., 4–5*. London: Hogarth.

Freud, S. (1905d). *Three Essays on the Theory of Sexuality. S. E., 7*. London: Hogarth.

Freud, S. (1920g). *Beyond the Pleasure Principle*. In: *S. E., 18*. London: Hogarth.

Hamburger, A. (2006).Traum und Zeit. Traumerzählungen als Elemente der Spannungsdramaturgie. *Forum Der Psychoanalyse*, 22: 23–43.

Hamburger, A. (2013). Arbeit in der Tiefe. Vorüberlegungen zu einer skeptischen Kulturanalyse. In: H. Hierdeis (Ed.), *Psychoanalytische Skepsis* (pp. 123–183). Göttingen, Germany: Vandenhoeck & Ruprecht.

Hamburger, A., & Leube, K. (2014). Wie im Kino. Zur Filmanalyse in der Gruppe. Methodologie der psychoanalytischen Filminterpretation anhand von Lars von Triers "Melancholia". In: R. Zwiebel & D. Blothner (Eds.), *Melancholia—Wege zur psychoanalytischen Interpretation des Films* (pp. 72–109). Göttingen, Germany: Vandenhoeck & Ruprecht.

Henderson, J. L. (1967). *Thresholds of Initiation*. Middleton, CT: Wesleyan University Press.

Horkheimer, M., & Adorno, T. W. (1947). *Dialectic of Enlightenment*. J. Cumming (Trans.). New York: Continuum, 1993.

Lorenzer, A. (1970). *Sprachzerstörung und Rekonstruktion*. Frankfurt, Germany: Suhrkamp.

Reiche, R. (2001). *Mutterseelenallein. Kunst, Form und Psychoanalyse*. Frankfurt, Germany: Stroemfeld.

Reiche, R. (2011). *Mutterseelenallein 2. Das Tabu der Schönheit in Kunst und Psychoanalyse*. Frankfurt, Germany: Stroemfeld.

Winnicott, D. W. (1953). Transitional objects and transitional phenomena. [Reprinted in: D. W. Winnicott, *Playing and Reality*. London: Tavistock/ Routledge, 1999.]

PART III

THE BEASTS

In the second dialogue on LA BELLE ET LA BÊTE and its gender constructions, "monsters", "animals", "beasts", or "*bêtes*" are at the centre of interest—and the "losses in translation" already indicate that there is much more than mere animal nature to the many-layered figure of La Bête, originally presented in the baroque novel by Barbot de Villeneuve published in 1740. In the French, "*bête*" alludes to the (more or less advanced) level of education and refinement in matters of morality and sensibility—and Barbot plays on this double meaning when she has La Bête regretting his own lack of sensibility and Belle parrying with, "You have enough sense to want to assure yourself of it" (cited in Chapter Seven, this volume).

Marianne Leuzinger-Bohleber interprets the construction of masculinity against the historical foil of the year in which LA BELLE ET LA BÊTE was filmed. The provocation of presenting, one year after the end of the Holocaust, a poetic fairy tale in which the antipodes of good and evil are postulated and simultaneously blurred offers the film's audience, as a means of repairing damaged identity, the possibility of taking recourse to early patterns for the formation of object representations. The central issues are adolescence as a process of disengagement from one's actual parents and the establishment of internalised, positive parental figures. The fairy tale of LA BELLE ET LA BÊTE emerges in this light as a "survival attempt".

Andreas Rost responds with a history of the movie monster from the perspective of the cinema scholar. La Bête's ugliness, which has always been a pivotal factor in the story, is asserted by Cocteau but not actually demonstrated, since he rather adheres to a Cartesian conception of the soul: trapped inside the animal, there is a noble and generous spirit. La Bête thus stands in diametrical opposition to other monsters of film history, whose bestiality is staged as being attractive, both to female protagonists and in the eyes of female viewers.

CHAPTER SIX

Once upon a time—Beauty and the Beast—a surrealistic survival attempt in the year 1946?

*Marianne Leuzinger-Bohleber**

When I watched Jean Cocteau's classic of cinema history again, I was well able to imagine that it evoked highly ambivalent feelings among critics and the audience in 1946. The divisions it dealt with—between "good and evil", the authentic and the fraudulent, the loyal and the traitors—must have been very far away from everyday reality directly after the greatest catastrophe of human civilisation, the Holocaust and the unimaginable destruction in Europe.

Against this foil, the protagonists of LA BELLE ET LA BÊTE appear in stark contrast to the inwardly and outwardly annihilated men and women so impressively portrayed in such works as Rainer Werner Fassbinder's trilogy DIE EHE DER MARIA BRAUN (THE MARRIAGE OF MARIA BRAUN) (D 1979), LOLA (D 1981), and DIE SEHNSUCHT DER VERONIKA VOSS (VERONIKA VOSS) (D 1982), but also in one of his last films, LILI MARLEEN (D 1981) (Felix, 1998). As Andreas Rost (Chapter Seven, this volume) illustrates, in comparison to the many brutal monsters of cinema history, Cocteau's Beast seems almost quaint, more like a figure from a cabinet of curiosities.

---

* Translated by Susan Jones.

Nevertheless, even today the film still has a tremendous power to fascinate us. It begins with an association that relates to school, education, and enlightenment: the opening titles are written in chalk on a blackboard and are erased again and again. In the face of a world in rubble, the collapse of all values and ideals, the confrontation with the unimaginable suffering humans can inflict on other humans, and the despairing question of "education after Auschwitz" (Adorno, 1970), the suggestion is: "school learning" has to be obliterated. Instead, the surrealist and poet Cocteau invites the viewer to be captivated by the world of fairy tales: "*Once upon a time …*" "Symbolically speaking, the story of the monster reflects a civilisation that was laid low in occupied France, distorted by a curse …" (Kuwert, 1998, p. 142).

Do traumatised[1] adults need fairy tales?

Do adults, too, need fairy tales (like children, see Bettelheim, 1975)—a journey into the unconscious initiated in this instance by the poetry of film? Viewers of LA BELLE ET LA BÊTE are spirited away into intermediate spaces (Winnicott, 1971) where they are magically confronted with catastrophic experiences, death anxieties, unconscious fantasies, drive impulses, and aspects of self that have been split off. Does this confrontation with traumatic horrors and split-off, unconscious aspects of the personality offer opportunities for emotional transformation?

The costumes by Christian Bérard and the interiors, the landscape, the light are all reminiscent of the Flemish painters Jan Vermeer and Pieter de Hoogh; the depiction of the "monster's" castle with fabulously enlivened columns and chandeliers that are human arms brings to mind the engravings of Gustave Doré. Memories of earlier centuries in Europe are called up, they too characterised by war and destruction, for example during the Thirty Years' War when—due to crimes, famines, and epidemics—entire regions of Europe were razed and immeasurable human suffering resulted.

But Cocteau was not inviting the viewer to flee into denial of what had just occurred or to relativise it by looking further back into human history, nor was he advocating that all be forgotten in the manner that was widespread in the 1950s and designated by the Mitscherlichs as the "inability to mourn" (1967). Instead, he conveys a "forced irrealism" (Kuwert, 1998, p. 142): confrontation with an archaic world of childhood fantasies and conflicts stored away in the unconscious, but coloured by a longing for development and for redemption from the horrors of the recent past. An emotional survival strategy for people everywhere—in France, Germany, Russia, England?

"Once upon a time ..."

As we know, the impact of fairy tales in widely diverse cultures is founded on the fact that, more or less independent of the actual historical situation in which they are told, they are appealing because they give symbolic contours to unconscious fantasies and conflicts, condensing them into images and narratives that are universal inasmuch as they frame embodied memories[2] from early childhood and infancy that are deposited in the unconscious of each of us. Snow White is poisoned by her Oedipal rival, the evil mother-in-law consumed with envy, who must be killed before Snow White can marry her prince. Hansel and Gretel push the witch into the stove in order to find their way out of the oral state of childhood dependency and fantasies and, in an adolescent process of disengagement, to discover their own way through a forest full of dangers. "If our fear of being devoured takes the tangible form of a witch, it can be gotten rid of by burning her in the oven!" (Bettelheim, 1975, p. 120). In this way, fairy tales give shape to the pre-ambivalent, magical-egocentric thinking of the child at the age of about four to six years, and contribute to emotional orientation: heroes and rascals, witches and fairies are clearly distinguished from one another. Moreover, the child's basic sense of trust is reinforced, since the good ones always win ...

With LA BELLE ET LA BÊTE Cocteau leads the viewer, in a time of societal collapse, into the sphere of the primal process, where all opposites are blurred. Belle and Bête intermingle: in the sense of a projective identification, Belle even sees the monster in her own mirror image. Looking into the mirror is disturbing: Belle not only sees herself, but also her dying father, and later the dying Beast whom she is only able to save because she had already, earlier on, been willing to surrender to him and die in her father's stead. Did looking into a mirror trigger, for many people after the collapse of National Socialism, a longing for death, for fusion with a redeeming primal object as the final relief from unbearable guilt and shame, loss and despair? All over Europe, there were many in the first years after the war who saw suicide as the only way out (poignantly depicted, for example, in Wolfgang Borchert's *Draußen vor der Tür* (*The Man Outside*) (1947), in the double suicide of DIE SÜNDERIN

(The Sinner) (D 1951) by Willi Forst with Hildegard Knef, or in that of Veronika Voss in the Fassbinder trilogy already mentioned).

In the course of individual development, it is essential that pre-ambivalent orientations and emotional functionalities be differentiated, that equivocalness be discovered and emotionally tolerated. In (individual and collective) extreme situations, however, the archaic system of orientation takes on an essential function for survival. In the outward reality of concentration camps, for example, being able to distinguish reliably between perpetrators and victims was a matter of life and death. It was fatal for the inner world as well, as Henry Krystal (1968) has shown us, if the clear distinction was lost between good and evil—the inner connection to a "good internal object", the "principle of hope" (Ernst Bloch, 1954). Even after the capitulation, when full measure had to be taken of the breach of civilisation and the extent of the destruction that so many had participated in, it was absolutely necessary for the individual in order to survive to have a clear inward and outward orientation. Was Cocteau intuitively aware of these emotional survival strategies when, in 1946, he reached out with a poetic fairy tale to an audience still reeling from the catastrophic blow to civilisation? An artistic attempt at therapy to counteract ubiquitous thoughts of suicide?

Fairy tales, poetry, and dreams

Like fairy tales, poetry and dreams open a central path to the unconscious. With the poetry of his film, Cocteau uses the camera as a medium "that allows everyone to dream the same dream together—not a dream in their sleep, but rather a waking dream that the audience dreams in a kind of collective hypnosis" (Kuwert, 1998, p. 41). The first encounter between Belle and the Beast—in which she faints, overcome by horror, and the Beast carefully takes her into his arms and carries her into the castle—is in this respect reminiscent of the famous painting "The Nightmare" by Henry Fuseli (Johann Heinrich Füssli) (1790).

In fairy tales—and in dreams—existential human conflicts are enacted symbolically, as if in a primal process: conflicts relating to love and hate, jealousy, resentment and envy, magic and omnipotence, development and regression, paradise and hell, death and life. Both of the film's protagonists, the Beast and Beauty, are in the midst of a dream-like process of development and individuation guided by the unconscious, taking them from a childlike to a more mature capacity for love.

Illusionary idealisations of themselves and others have to be put aside successively; instinctual drives integrated into their own set of values; projections of ugliness, evil, and brutality within themselves need to be acknowledged and integrated into their self-image. Furthermore, in our "hot" cultures (Lévi-Strauss, 1962), adolescent development of identity requires disengagement from one's primary objects: it connects to the passionate pre-Oedipal relationships of early childhood, at the same time—by way of new, often irritating, feelings of disgust or loathing towards the primary object—serving to reinforce the incest taboo for the adolescents and to direct their desires towards new objects.

From today's point of view influenced by attachment theory, developmental studies, and neurobiological research, it is interesting to note that despite her intensive Oedipal relationship to the father, it is Belle's secure attachment to him and to the deceased mother that enables her (as opposed to her siblings) to complete the adolescent process of transformation—an aspect often underestimated in classical psychoanalytic theory of adolescence. In this respect, Belle seems to be less involved than her siblings in a pathological process of mourning for the dead mother. While the two sisters and in his own way the brother persist in maintaining a childish, parasitic posture that appears narcissistic (they expect to be taken care of), in everyday matters Belle assumes the caring role of the mother towards them and her father, in an identification with the dead object. She is the only one of the siblings to face reality (poverty, everyday tasks in and about the home). The fact that she doesn't wish for expensive presents, but simply for a rose, does however indicate her Oedipal relationship to the father, which will necessarily lead to existential conflicts and will have to be resolved in the course of the development unfolding in the fairy tale (see Chapter Four, this volume).

Additional symbols are also of interest, for instance the key entrusted to Belle by the Beast as the means of access to treasures and riches, which was stolen from her by the sisters and then used to break into the temple containing the family treasure in the castle garden. The riches deposited there—gold, jewelry, and gems—symbolise the transgenerational legacies and gifts that the Beast shares with his bride and that they together will take possession of, in the present, as a couple. The existence of the young couple thus rests on the foundation of earlier generations, on a gift that must be handled with great care. Avenant, who wants to usurp this legacy illegally and greedily, pays for this transgression with his life.

From a psychoanalytical point of view, this narrative could be a symbolic depiction of the adolescent challenge: in the process of disengagement and defining identity, the decisive issue is whether the inner relationship to the parental primary objects can be maintained without obliterating their representations as "good objects" due to the aggression necessary for disengagement. In other words, if the parental murder can be carried out symbolically without the inner emotional bond being destroyed and a viable relationship to the primary objects thus becoming unthinkable, then from today's point of view one of the unconscious prerequisites for successful formation of identity is fulfilled (see among others Bohleber & Leuzinger-Bohleber, 2014). If, on the other hand, the relationship to these primary objects is too heavily burdened with aggressive-destructive fantasies due to traumatic experiences (such as infantile, parasitical fixations), laden with need and the inability to lay aside the instinctive urges of childhood, or—as a result of traumatisation—with extreme feelings of powerlessness and helplessness, dissociative states and an unconscious collapse of basic trust in a helping, empathetic object and an active self: then murderous impulses towards the self and the object take the upper hand, as we see in severe adolescent crises or in many male (and female) monsters in the history of the cinema. We see, for instance, Norman Bates in Hitchcock's famous film PSYCHO (USA 1960) refusing to give up his incestuous attachment to the maternal primary object. In his pathological jealousy, he murders his mother and preserves her as a mummy in the cellar. Instead of turning to new love objects and developing an adult male identity, he flees into perversion: he slips into his mother's clothing and, as Janine Chasseguet-Smirgel (1980) has postulated, denies the differences between genders and generations in an omnipotent unconscious fantasy of an anal phallus.

By contrast, LA BELLE ET LA BÊTE stimulates in the viewer a longing for successful individuation and formation of identity, for the discovery of a way out of the archaic world of blood and thunder, destruction and suicidal insanity—a longing for an integration of passion and tenderness, which is impressively portrayed in many key scenes of the film.

The development within the film demonstrates that not until both the Beast and Beauty admit to their own vulnerabilities and passive wishes, to their existential dependence on one another as husband and wife, not until both can allow narcissistic (infantile) omnipotence to die within themselves—not until then is the Beast transformed into the Prince. It is psychologically profound that the sudden transformation into an "ideal prince" evokes ambivalent feelings in Belle: she senses that maintaining the pre-ambivalent split between "black and white", "winner and loser", "libido and aggression" would mean abandoning passionate instincts and drives (the "beast"). Into her inner representation of a mature love object, she has to integrate the Prince and the Beast, Avenant and her father, at the same time integrating the madonna and the whore into her own self-representation. "Like a frightened and unwilling bride, Beauty matures from a girl to a woman through the integration and sublimation of her sexual (hunger) and aggressive (anger) drives" (Wu, 1997, p. 377). Wieland (1991) describes another aspect of this process in terms of overcoming the split in the representation of the father, which she characterises as decisive for the formation of feminine identity:

> The story portrays vividly the split in the father into an idealised father figure and a Beast, and how this split is repeated in the daughter's perception of him. Beauty, in order to keep the idealised father alive, has to split him off and keep him separated from the Beast [...] It is also important to realise that the healing of the split comes about by lessening of both idealisation and persecution, i.e. by the father being ill and the Beast dying of a broken heart. At that moment Beauty realises the vulnerability in both the father and the Beast and perceives the humanness in both. The extremes of idealisation and persecution collapse. Beauty is now ready to love a man by seeing the vulnerability of the Beast. And the Beast can turn into a man only through Beauty's love and through giving up his own beastly power. (p. 138)

On the basis of psychoanalytic clinical practice, as well as many modern films and novels (from Elfriede Jelinek to Karl Ove Knausgaard or television series such as BORGEN, which currently has high audience ratings in Denmark), we know that despite emancipatory movements, such gender-specific conflicts, integration processes, and issues of identity formation have lost none of their urgency for women and men: in fact, the opposite may be true. It has indeed become more acceptable that a woman let out her "beast" in business, sexuality, and the family, or that a man be a sensitive and empathic lover, partner, and father. But the emotional integration of active and passive roles—of passion and tenderness, phallic dominance and submissiveness, autonomy and dependency, narcissism and generativity—is a developmental process that remains highly susceptible to disturbances. And as current discussions on intersubjectivity and embodiment in modern psychoanalysis show, this process can never be negotiated by a single individual, in a monadic capsule, but rather must always be accompanied by societal discourse—perhaps also by new fairy tales and myths.[3]

Gender and gender conflicts

In closing, a short psychoanalytical illustration of such contemporary gender conflicts and my associations to this topic evoked by Cocteau's film:[4]

> In the condition of Mr. M., I had a kaleidoscopic view on many of the gender-specific fantasies and conflicts just described. Well over six feet tall, with a striking tousled head of curly hair and startling light-blue eyes in an immobile, pale face, he struck me as similar to the Beast in Cocteau's film. It all didn't fit together: his conspicuously masculine body with wide shoulders and a muscular chest; his feminine, fairy-like clothing and gentle way of moving. He seemed to waft his way up the stairs to my consulting room. His vacuous glance and a facial expression seemingly frozen in shock were entirely incongruous with the grand gesture in which, without any invitation, he sat down on *my* chair and opened the interview with the words, "I am a narcissistic-exhibitionistic transvestite." Then he handed me a thirty-page handwritten manuscript: "Please study this, it's my life history; in it, I come to the conclusion that I need psychoanalysis ..." Every bit as striking and unforgettable was my own reaction with an immediate and in my own experience very unusual countertransference. The thought that flashed through my head was: "Wait a minute, young man, after all, transvestism is a perversion. I should rather send you off into behavioural therapy!" I was dismayed by this strongly emotional defence reaction, since it obviously contained sadistic fantasies and a pronounced wish to gain some distance.[5]
>
> Only in the course of a long and intensive psychoanalysis did we finally understand that in this bizarre behaviour of Mr. M. in this first encounter, "embodied memories" of his severe early childhood traumatisation were contained. It emerged that his mother,

in deep post-partum depression, had been unable to overcome her disappointment that M. was a boy and not the girl child she had longed for; she was unable to accept him in his masculine body and adequately to perceive or mirror (Stern, 1985) his "emerging self". When M. was two years old, a brother was born and died shortly after. Again, the mother sank into deep depression. In his fourth year, she photographed M. several times in girls' dresses. She prevented him from receiving attention from his father or from boys in his peer group.

We can apply the insight of trauma research: as a survival strategy, M. tried to transform what he was passively exposed to into something he himself could actively afflict (cf. among others Bohleber, 2010). Locked in his mother's bedroom after a serious accident (contusion, complex fracture of the leg) and a long, traumatic hospital stay, he discovered at the age of four that he was less lonely and not as over-flooded by unbearable negative feelings when he put on his mother's underwear. He felt sexually stimulated in an exciting way. The transvestite symptom allowed him to deny his separation from the traumatising primary object and at the same time made him independent of it: he didn't need the object any more! During adolescence, after further severe traumatisations, this pathological attempt at resolution developed even further: Mr. M. masturbated in women's clothing, pushing his penis between his thighs, rubbing it through the panties, and ejaculating. Symbolically, this represented having coitus with himself: he didn't need women any more! As became visible in the enactment of the assessment interview with me, he had taken total control of his objects.

But just as in a fairy tale, or in Cocteau's film, he was only able to find a way out of his narcissistic capsule—his extreme isolation or "social death"—by managing to accept his dependency on the Other. Together with the analyst, in an extremely painful process of insight, he ultimately realised how radically he had denied his dependency on his own body (the sense of being damned to live in the "wrong", rejected body), on the love object, and on reality: unconsciously, he was convinced that he could be both a woman and a man, mother and child, analyst and analysand, dependent on no one, in possession of a grandiose self and inseparably melded with an omnipotent parental imago (Kohut, 1971). Like a leaden seal, the transvestite perversion protected the fragile self from fragmentation and disintegration (Morgenthaler, 1974).

Consequently, the struggle to acknowledge dependencies, separation, and emotional differentiation ran through the analysis like a continuous thread, and with it the revitalisation of multiple severe traumatisations in the transference. Just one example: during the second year, Mr. M. took me by surprise with the information that he was to undergo a gender correction operation the following week. This completely unexpected announcement confronted me in the countertransference with extreme feelings of helplessness, powerlessless, and dependency on him as an object not under my control. Seen in retrospect, in the transference he was enacting his early traumatisations, among other things: could he himself determine his gender, or did his love object (his analyst) have the power of definition?

As discussed above and elsewhere, it emerges as indispensable for a process of sustained emotional transformation that traumatic experiences be relived in the transference to the analyst so that they can be understood in detail, in some approximation of the idiosyncratic "historical truth", and be worked through in a supportive, containing relationship (Bohleber & Leuzinger-Bohleber, 2014; Leuzinger-Bohleber, 2014a). In this process, dreams still prove to be the *via regia* because, as in the analysis of Mr. M., they often contain the key to unconscious worlds of fantasy and conflict (cf. among others Leuzinger-Bohleber, 2006). For instance, during the fourth year of analysis he related the following dream: "I was walking around in the mountains with a pram, and two or four bears fell out of it. Then my mother came along, and I gave her two clumps …"

With "two or four", he associated "two sons and one stillborn and one girl", revealing that he—in the magical thinking of the two year old—apparently had experienced his dead brother as both a boy and a girl, and that he had attempted to give the mother a substitute with anal gifts ("clumps"). The unconscious connection of gender, birth, and death thus became accessible for analytic work: a process of inner differentiation and of separation from the inner, maternal object set in, and along with it the first cautious steps towards reconciliation with the traumatised and traumatising primary object. Gradually, Mr. M. was able to do without his transvestite protective wall and to begin, in the reliable and empathetic analytic relationship, a painful process of grieving and of de-idealisation: he became more able to bear the fact that he possessed "only" a male body and that he felt dependent on his drives and his desires for a love object—the analyst.

A surrealistic survival attempt?

It requires a long, cautious, and painful approach to gain access to what was previously unrepresented, to traumatic material—not only for the individual (cf. Leuzinger-Bohleber, 2014a and 2015, Levine, Reed, & Scarfone, 2013). On the societal level as well, collective traumatisations, particularly due to man-made disasters, cast their shadow onto the first, the second, and even the third generation. On the societal level, outward capitulation frequently is followed by inner capitulation, and tragically, more often among victims and bystanders than among extreme perpetrators, who tend to deny and split off any feelings of guilt or shame and to seek relief in a new, "false" identity—as analysed in exact and accurate detail by Costa-Gavras in his film MUSIC BOX (USA 1989). In 1946, many victims couldn't bear to go on living after their extreme traumatisation. They took recourse to suicide or lived in a restricted, sometimes seemingly bizarre dissociative state—also masterfully illustrated in film, for instance by Helen Mirren as Emerence in Istvan Szabó's impressive THE DOOR (H 2012) (cf. Leuzinger-Bohleber, 2007, 2014b).

It therefore seems entirely possible to me that with his poetic film LA BELLE ET LA BÊTE, a fairy tale, Cocteau was unconsciously calling attention to ubiquitous, timeless fantasies of heaven and hell, death and life, love and hate—as his own contribution to a surrealistic survival attempt in the year 1946.

Notes

1. Here, I am applying a narrow definition of trauma, in accord with Bohleber (2010). As a result of trauma—a sudden, unforeseen, extreme experience usually characterised by a threat to one's life and by death anxiety, natural protection against stimuli is breached. The ego is exposed to a feeling of extreme powerlessness and to its own inability to exert control over the situation and to cope with it. The ego is flooded with panic and extreme physiological reactions. This experience leads to an emotional and physiological state of shock. Moreover, the traumatic experience breaks down the protective shield of empathy

provided by the internalised primary object and destroys trust in the continual availability of good objects and in the expectation of human empathy. In trauma, the internalised good object as an empathetic mediator between self and environment falls silent.

2. The ubiquity of this archaic world of fantasies is related to bodily factors: it is firmly established that the human infant is "psychophysiologically premature" and only survives—all over the world—when able to mobilise his caregivers to provide the attention and affection necessary for survival. As a result, the experience of dependency, helplessness, and powerlessness is present in the unconscious of every human being and through "embodied memories" (together with further existential experiences in early years) significantly affects later thought, behaviour, and feelings (e.g., Leuzinger-Bohleber, 2015; Leuzinger-Bohleber, Emde, & Pfeifer, 2013).
3. An article in the online periodical *Cultural Zeitgeist* ("Beauty and the Beast/LA BELLE ET LA BÊTE: Between Novel and Film") reflects on the changing role assumptions among couples: "The novel, *LA BELLE ET LA BÊTE* (1756), contains the look of love, which is patriarchal and therefore conforms to the conventions of active male and passive female. La Bête is a symbol of monstrosity and cannot be looked upon, which makes him active and Belle is seen in terms of masculine desire, which renders her passive. As a consequence, the spectator is the subject of the gaze and is culturally male, placing the female in an exhibitionistic role. On the other hand, in [the film] *LA BELLE ET LA BÊTE* (1946), the gaze and the expression of sexuality do not conform to the patriarchal and Western tradition. The cinematography constructs the female character Belle as impassive, providing her with a sense of agency and power. The male characters, such as Prince Charming and at times Avenant, are viewed as objects of the gaze and as passive. La Bête has conflicting gender issues and is controlled by the females, rendering him also as passive. The gaze is therefore seen as homoerotic and shows that the "*phallus is not a mark of construction of subjectivity*" ... allowing the female spectator to appropriate the gaze (p. 5).
4. In this volume, I make reference to a case that we discussed at length in an interdisciplinary colloquium (supported by the Köhler Foundation, Darmstadt) on the dialogue between psychoanalysis and neuroscience. In his notable contribution "Solo mit Dame. Traumgeschichten einer Psychoanalyse" ("Solo with Lady. Dream Stories from a Psychoanalysis") Andreas Hamburger (1998) has argued persuasively in favour of drawing analogies between the dream (fairy tale, film) and the psychoanalytical process of transformation, as I also do in the present chapter. Moreover, a catamnesis twenty-five years after the end of this analysand's psychoanalysis reveals a sustained transformation

of his gender identity, indicating that—at least in this case—the psychodynamic hypotheses developed here were corroborated in the clinical context (see also Leuzinger-Bohleber, 2015).

5. At the time, I was mentoring a student thesis on the unmistakably sadistic overtones in the established techniques of "classical behavioural therapy" for treating perverse patients.

References

Adorno, T. W. (1970). Erziehung nach Auschwitz. In: *Erziehung zur Mündigkeit, Vorträge und Gespräche mit Hellmuth Becker 1959–1969* (pp. 92–109). G. Kadelbach (Ed.). Frankfurt, Germany: Suhrkamp.

Bettelheim, B. (1975). *The Uses of Enchantment: The Meaning and Importance of Fairy Tales*. New York: Vintage, 1989.

Bloch, E. (1954). *The Principle of Hope*. N. Plaice, S. Plaice, & P. Knight (Trans.). Cambridge, MA: MIT Press, 1986.

Bohleber, W. (2010). *Was Psychoanalyse heute bietet*. Stuttgart, Germany: Klett-Cotta.

Bohleber, W., & Leuzinger-Bohleber, M. (2014). Pubertierende ticken anders. Ein Forschungsüberblick zu Psyche und Gehirn in der Adoleszenz. *Sonderheft Pubertät* (pp. 14–18). Stuttgart, Germany: Thieme.

Borchert, W. (1947). *Draußen vor der Tür*. Reinbek: Rowohlt 2008.

Chasseguet-Smirgel, J. (1980). Réflexions sur la perte de la realite dans la perversion (avec particuliere de référence au fétichisme). Unpublished lecture, held in the training centre of SGP, Zurich on 19 September.

Cultural Zeitgeist (2012). Beauty and the Beast/La Belle et La Bête: Between novel and film. Reflections on films and waves of art house cinema, 14 November. http://culturalzeitgeist.wordpress.com/2012/11/14/beauty-and-the-beast-la-belle-et-la-bete-between-novel-and-film/ (last retrieved on September 3, 2015).

Felix, J. (1998). Rainer Werner Fassbinder: In: T. Koebner (Ed.), *Filmregisseure. Biographien, Werkbeschreibungen, Filmographien* (pp. 221–227). Stuttgart, Germany: Reclam.

Hamburger, A. (1998). Solo mit Dame. Traumgeschichten einer Psychoanalyse. In: M. Leuzinger-Bohleber, M. Koukkou, & W. Mertens (Eds.), *Erinnerung von Wirklichkeiten. Psychoanalyse und Neurowissenschaften im Dialog, Vol 2, Folgerungen für die psychoanalytische Praxis* (pp. 96–118). Stuttgart, Germany: VIP.

Kohut, H. (1971). *Narzißmus. Eine Theorie der psychoanalytischen Behandlung narzißtischer Persönlichkeitsstörungen*. Frankfurt /M.: Suhrkamp.

Krystal, H. (1968). *Massive Psychic Trauma*. New York: International Universities Press.

Kuwert, B. (1998). Jean Cocteau. In: T. Koebner (Ed.), *Filmregisseure. Biographien, Werkbeschreibungen, Filmographien* (pp. 140–143). Stuttgart, Germany: Reclam.

Leuzinger-Bohleber, M. (2006). Psychodynamic and biographical roots of a transvestite development: clinical and extra-clinical findings from a psychoanalysis. In: P. Fonagy, R. Krause, & M. Leuzinger-Bohleber (Eds.), *Identity, Gender and Sexuality. 150 years after Freud*. Controversies in psychoanalysis series, 1 (pp. 43–73). London: International Psychoanalytical Association.

Leuzinger-Bohleber, M. (2007). Überlegungen zu Constantin Costa-Gavras' "Music Box". In: R. Zwiebel, & A. Mahler-Bungers (Eds.), *Projektion und Wirklichkeit. Die unbewusste Botschaft des Films*. Schriften des Sigmund-Freud-Instituts, Reihe 2: Psychoanalyse im interdisziplinären Dialog, Vol. 5 (pp. 128–148). Göttingen, Germany: Vandenhoeck & Ruprecht.

Leuzinger-Bohleber, M. (2014a). Den Körper in der Seele entdecken—Embodiment und die Annäherung an das Nicht-Repräsentierte. *Psyche—Zeitschrift für Psychoanalyse und ihre Anwendungen, 68*: 922–950.

Leuzinger-Bohleber, M. (2014b). "Ich spüre immer, wenn der Tod kommt . . ." Hinter der Tür. In: S. Doering & H. Moeller (Eds.), *Mon Amour trifft Pretty Woman. Liebespaare im Film* (pp. 249–262). Heidelberg, Germany: Springer.

Leuzinger-Bohleber, M. (2015). *Finding the Body in the Mind: Embodied Memories, Trauma, and Depression*. London: Karnac Books.

Leuzinger-Bohleber, M., Emde, R. N., & Pfeifer, R. (Eds.) (2013). *Embodiment—ein innovatives Konzept für Entwicklungsforschung und Psychoanalyse*. Schriften des Sigmund-Freud-Instituts. Reihe 2: Psychoanalyse im interdisziplinären Dialog, Vol. 17. Göttingen, Germany: Vandenhoeck & Ruprecht.

Lévi-Strauss, C. (1962). *Das wilde Denken*. Frankfurt, Germany: Suhrkamp, 1973.

Levine, H. B., Reed, G. S., & Scarfone, D. (Eds.) (2013). *Unrepresented States and the Construction of Meaning*. London: Karnac.

Mitscherlich, A., & Mitscherlich, M. (1967). *The Inability to Mourn: Principles of Collective Behaviour*. London: Grove, 1975.

Morgenthaler, F. (1974). Zur Theorie und Therapie von Perversionen. *Psyche—Zeitschrift für Psychoanalyse und ihre Anwendungen, 28*: 1077–1099.

Stern, D. (1985). *Die Lebenserfahrung des Säuglings*. Stuttgart, Germany: Klett-Cotta, 1992.

Wieland, C. (1991). Beauty and the Beast: The father´s unconscious and the riddle of femininity. *British Journal of Psychotherapy, 8*: 131–143.

Winnicott, D. W. (1971). *Playing and Reality*. London: Tavistock.

Wu, J. (1997). Beauty and the Beast: A myth of sadness, madness, and hope in anaclitic depression. *Psychoanalytic Review, 84*: 365–380.

CHAPTER SEVEN

Coming over to the wild side: women's yearning for beastly encounters in the course of film history

*Andreas Rost**

In the wider framework of our topic, "beasts" or "beastly creatures"—be they animals or humans or a mixture of both—are regarded as a construction of screen masculinity. This contribution will try to show diversifications and differences between Cocteau's film and its literary source and will draw comparisons with other cinematic creations of beastly male images in film history.

In my understanding the core of Cocteau's screen plot is—to a very large extent—indebted to the moralistic tale (*conte*) published by Mme Leprince de Beaumont (1711–1780) in 1756 under the title of *La Belle et La Bête*.[1] Although Cocteau omits fairies or witches from his narrative, his prologue to the film invites the spectator to reactivate a childlike naivety as an adequate mode of reception, since the plot of his film also relies heavily on magic. Confronted with the beastly and ugly appearance of the hairy inhabitant of a mysterious residence, La Belle is asked to make a *virtuous* decision,[2] that is, to marry this creature despite its appalling appearance. This decision ultimately becomes possible due to her enormous achievement in terms of perception and abstraction:

*Translated by Harriet Schlosshauer, Hans Jokel, & Susan Jones.

La Belle's perception goes beyond the appalling appearance and sees, within the animal-like body, a human and virtuous soul that can only be liberated from its ghastly spell by her love and her loving glance.

Within the fable as well as the film, we can discern a Cartesian heritage: both film and tale postulate a dichotomy between an animal-like appearance and a hidden human essence. In his *Discours de la Méthode*,[3] René Descartes insisted on the clear separation of body and soul[4]—a logical necessity for him, who believed that the soul lived eternally after the mortal body died.

Thus the animal appearance of the character known as La Bête is merely incidental and not essential. It conceals his true essence rather than revealing it.[5] The mask hiding the actor Jean Marais is thus misleading if understood as a clue to his character. Traditionally, masks hint at certain inner characteristics of the bearer (cf. Belting, 2013, p. 150), outwardly signifying the emotional processes within a figure,[6] and inducing the spectator to develop projections. By the same token, film critics are justified in applying psychoanalytical approaches to interpretation.

Despite Descartes and his distinction between body and soul, we nonetheless have to admit that La Bête's body—for all his

Figure 1. Wearing a virginal crown, backlighted and filmed in soft focus, La Belle opposes her father's objections to her marrying La Bête and insists on the monster's goodness. She lifts her eyes upwards towards heaven, which promptly rewards her noble posture by turning La Belle's tears into diamonds (LA BELLE ET LA BÊTE 01:02:03).

courteous and civilised demeanour, his dignified clothing and refined speech—accommodates at least two souls, since he does not refrain from hunting and devouring deer and thus causing bloodshed on his estate, to the dismay of La Belle. She rebukes him severely when he appears in bloodied clothing indicating that he has been catering to his untamed and animalistic nature. After postulating a sovereign and pure Cartesian human soul, we now have to acknowledge that the latter must surrender some of its territory to animalistic impulses. These amount to much more than what Descartes would call "*les esprits animaux*" (1637, pp. 118–120), which he also situates within the human body, responsible for mechanical or cybernetic processes like muscular movement etc.

There is another Cartesian reference as well, when the beast admits his lack of brains, a deficiency which can already be derived from the French word *bête*. When used as an adjective it also means "dumb" or "stupid", and in the derivative noun "bêtise" simply signifies "stupidity". In the tale and the film alike, the animal concedes his *manque d´esprit*:

> "Outre que je suis laid, je n'ai point d'esprit," he says in shot no. 169 (in the numeration by Hammond, 1992) ["Aside from being ugly, I have no mind."] And La Belle replies that in order to recognize this lack of intellect, one has to have at least some, because an idiot would not even notice his own deficit: "On n'est pas bête, reprit La Belle, quand on croît n'avoir point d'esprit: un sot n'a jamais su cela."

The argumentation here follows the scheme of Descartes' "*Cogito ergo sum/Je pense, donc je suis*"—Descartes overcomes his doubts about his own existence by the logical conclusion that one must exist in order to be able to have doubts about it. So once again La Belle succeeds in socialising with the animal by discovering traces of intellect behind the Beast's effort to negate it.

The great mental effort invested by La Belle to cope with the repugnant fact of having to deal with an ugly monster is revealed shortly, when she speaks abstractly about his frightening appearance: "Je vous avoue que je suis bien contente de votre bon coeur; quand j'y *pense*, vous me paraissez plus si laid" ("I admit that I'm quite satisfied with your good heart; *thinking* about it, you don´t seem quite so ugly to me any more"). To which the beast answers by emphasising the contradiction his existence rests upon: "Oh! dame oui! J'ai le cœur bon, mais je suis un monstre" ("Oh yes, madam, I have a good heart but I am a monster all the same").

The lasting contradiction between the inner goodness and the frightening features of the monster, which make La Belle tremble, is resolved within the tale and the film by the *power of thought* which transcends the ephemeral body in favour of the substantial good heart within. Surprisingly, one must add, because the Beast fulfils the definition of a monster given by the philosopher Noël Carroll: "For on my account, horror is signaled by the presence of monsters who *cannot* be accommodated naturalistically by science" (1990, p. 145).

Leprince says next to nothing about the monster's appearance, except "une bête si horrible" (Hammond, 1992, p. 262) or "cette horrible figure" (p. 264), not enough to guide our imagination in any particular direction. Even closer description would, in literature, always remain sketchy compared to the concretisation required of a film director and his crew. The literary tale gave Cocteau *carte blanche* to create a horrible creature of his own imagination. What he came up with, however, was a peculiar mixture of Puss in Boots and *roi du soleil* (Louis XIV) that appears rather tame to viewers today.[7] His mild manner and refined speech further reduce the fright he might cause at first sight. Even more winning is the competition between La Belle and La Bête over who will be more obedient and subservient to the other—in the end La Belle takes the prize for submissiveness.

This *gesture of succumbing* is already insinuated in the poster advertising the film LA BELLE ET LA BÊTE (F 1946). In its composition of figures, it echoes the motif used for L'ETERNEL RETOUR (F 1943)—the film that made Marais a star. In a clever marketing strategy of the distributor, both posters show the male protagonist standing upright above a woman who is bent over backwards. He is the "conqueror", the one who gets the girls, the person in charge—and this is recognisable even though he is wearing an animal mask in the second case.[8] The name Marais on the poster serves as a confirmation. In the first poster, in 1943, Marais's glance rests on the woman's eyes, but in 1946 more on her mouth, emphasising even more strongly the sensual force of the encounter (suggested also by the proximity of their faces). At the same time, the enhanced contrast between the woman's bright face and the dark rendering of the man's features creates an opposition between a *highly* lit *female* beauty and a *low*-lit *male* counterpart: in the L'ETERNEL RETOUR poster, a low-key version of the standard Marais image—clean-shaven,

Figure 2. For the posters advertising L'ETERNEL RETOUR and LA BELLE ET LA BÊTE, the photo composition was almost identical in terms of depicting the relationship between man and woman, extending the hype over Marais (at whose feet the ladies swooned) to the later film even though it disguised him as a beast.

Apollonian—but for LA BÊTE obviously Dionysian,[9] his unkempt fur in stark contrast to Josette Day's smooth skin and fragile beauty.

Delicate white women and dark hairy beasts

This light-dark contrast in the presentation of the couple on the poster and in the film draws on a visual scheme that had already proven successful in Merian C. Cooper's and Ernest B. Schoedsack's film KING KONG (USA 1933), where the contrast is heightened by the monstrous difference in size between the huge *dark* hairy ape and the tiny *white* woman (offered to him during a rite of sacrifice). The German edition of the film added a racial component with its title KING KONG UND DIE WEISSE FRAU (KING KONG AND THE WHITE WOMAN). Since the white dress, like a bridal gown, culturally connotes virginity, the image immediately suggests rape (and in 1933, perhaps also racist assumptions) as a motivation for the behaviour of the over-dimensioned ape.

Again we see the image of submission, which will reoccur in many films to come, with the female subject being *subjected* in the literal sense to the male ruler of the pictorial space: she succumbs and is "overlorded". While at the outset of KING KONG the woman is held

Figure 3. The white woman on board the expedition vessel has been abducted by dark-skinned natives in masks. They later offer her, tied to poles, as a human sacrifice and as a gift of appeasement to the giant ape who—in this final image—gladly accepts this living toy (KING KONG 00:32:58-00:41:40).

prisoner, later on the ape is the captive in chains, on display for a huge crowd in New York. At the sight of the white woman in the audience he breaks loose, abducts her and takes refuge on the Empire State Building, the highest phallic symbol in New York in 1933.[10]

In the following examples, we will see a metamorphosis of men into beasts evoked by a chain of associations that link *animals* with *nakedness* and thus with *sexuality*. This linkage is not yet explicit in Jacques Tourneur's film CAT PEOPLE (USA 1942), but the remake by Paul Schrader under the same title (USA 1982) leaves no doubt that Irena Gallier (played by Nastassja Kinski) and her brother Paul (Malcolm McDowell) are transformed into black panthers when their sexual desire is aroused.

The same metamorphosis has Count Dracula, in Francis Ford Coppola's version of BRAM STOKER'S DRACULA (USA 1992), alternating between human being, ape, and wolf[11] when he lures Lucy (dressed in red) out into the labyrinth of the garden to copulate with her, anxiously observed by Mina (dressed in white) whose facial expression oscillates between shock and fascination at the unabashed sexual pleasure Lucy experiences.

Compared with Friedrich Wilhelm Murnau's early version of NOSFERATU (D 1922), Coppola has shifted the focus: he depicts female

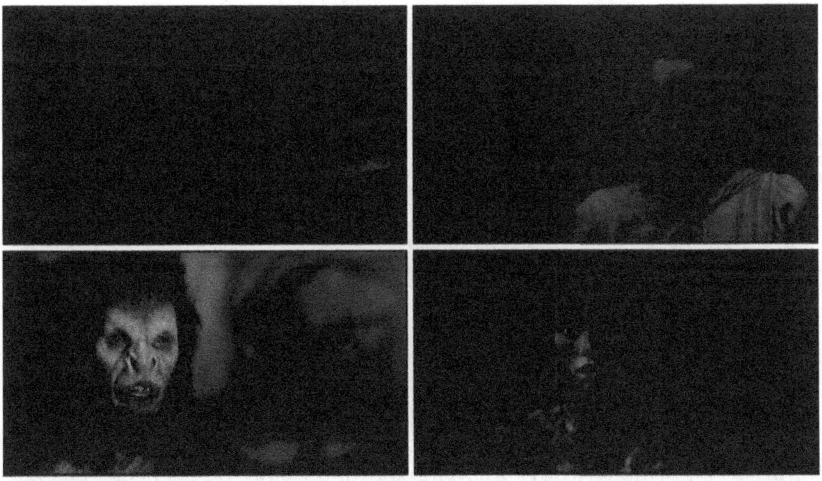

Figure 4. While Lucy is enticed by Dracula's lure into the garden labyrinth where she lustfully submits to the count's assault and he transforms into an animal, Mina at first tries to hold Lucy back, then is torn between horror and attraction as she watches them. In the shot showing Mina's reaction, with her face flickering in changing colours of light, she seems to be looking directly into the camera, that is, at the cinema spectator (DRACULA 00:40:39–00:40:59).

sexual lust projected onto the beastly Dracula. This reframing of the old story is documented by Michael Ballhaus in his autobiography:

> The story as Coppola told it (...) was less a story about the savage vampire and his final destruction. It was rather the story of women who are yearning for the sensuousness of the vampire, for a surrender that transcends death. (Ballhaus & Seidl, 2014, p. 225)

Ballhaus adds another important remark about the casting and function of Winona Ryder starring in the role of Mina because she, more than any other actress, was the "face" of her generation. She offered female spectators an ideal projection surface:

> Winona Ryder was the face of the moment, the female star, in whom young women of the same age saw themselves mirrored. She gave each film she starred in a contemporary significance—no

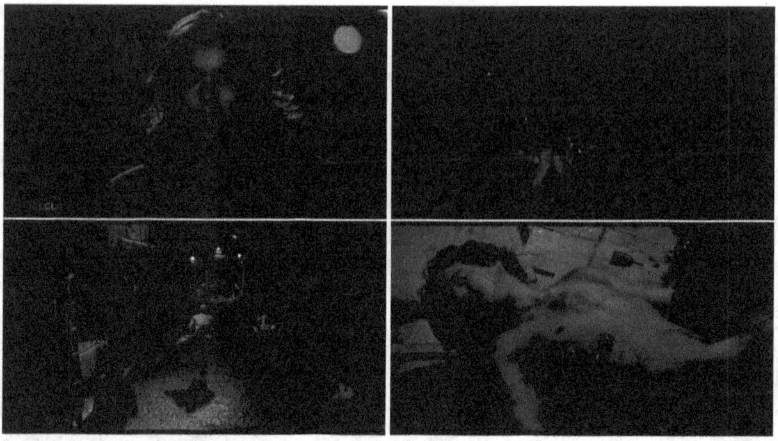

Figure 5. Uttering words of love, the woman fearlessly approaches David in his metamorphosis as a werewolf. The animal prepares to leap at her, but due to the police bullets, we will never know whether his leap was meant to be a lustful conquest or a lethal attack (AN AMERICAN WEREWOLF IN LONDON 01:27:25—01:27:46).

> matter if the film was set in the early nineties, or in London and Transylvania a hundred years earlier. (ibid., p. 226)

The chain of associations reaching from animality through nakedness to sexuality also figures in John Landis's film AN AMERICAN WEREWOLF IN LONDON (USA/GB 1981) when the female protagonist, under police protection, approaches the werewolf in a cul-de-sac, pledging her love[12] for the beast, who is her boyfriend temporarily transformed into a wolf. Before leaping onto the woman the wolf, however, is struck down by police bullets. In dying, he changes back into the figure of a naked handsome young man, his body now pierced by bullet holes. The gloomy and sordid alley with garbage cans and litter under the man's body tell us that this scene of sexuality is offered refuge only in the darkest and most inhospitable corner of the city.

So far we have dealt with film examples showing the breakthrough of a beast out of a male body under the pressure of sexual impulses. In DRACULA as well as in the drama of the WEREWOLF we witness a female protagonist who is fascinated despite—or because of—these apparently frightening features, or spellbound as Mina was between horror and lust. In the following examples, however, the beast will not need to take on the shape of an animal when a sexual encounter between a man and woman begins. The guise of a male human body with a somewhat sleazy look can also suffice.

Our first example is the ex-convict Max Cady (played by Robert De Niro) in Martin Scorsese's CAPE FEAR (USA 1991).[13] Against a backdrop of fireworks, Cady appears as a spooky figure projecting sexual energy, a projective foil[14] for the unfilled desire of a frustrated wife, Leigh Bowden (played by Jessica Lange). She sees him sitting on a stone wall at the edge of her (ostensibly) peaceful property.

The sequence had begun with a sex scene between Sam Bowden (Nick Nolte) and his wife Leigh in a remarkable cinematic depiction shifting from colour into black and white, then into negative while showing the couple's clutched hands as if in an X-ray. With a close-up of Leigh's closed eyes, the colour is restored and fades out into yellow. We see Leigh rising from the bed, unnoticed by her sleeping husband, and settling down in front of the mirror at her dressing table. She is confronted by her own reflection, a cinematic convention which introduces the motive of a *Doppelgänger* or split personality representing a repressed aspect of the woman. Leigh tries to connect with it by closing her eyes and rubbing her temples as if to relieve a headache. Scorsese inserts a fade-out into saturated red at this point, suggesting that Leigh is drifting off into a realm of sensual thoughts or desires within herself. The next shot, a zoom to Leigh putting on red lipstick as if preparing for a rendezvous in the middle of the night, confirms our impression that she is seeking a way out of a stagnant and sterile marriage. She takes a look through the closed blinds into the garden. Here another fade-out into red signals once again that she may in fact be looking to the inside—towards wishful images of a different, more exciting life. What she sees through the blinds is Max Cady sitting casually on the garden wall in front of the house, as if expecting her for a date. His persona seems to be the more exciting male alternative to her dull husband: Cady is set into profile not only by the acoustic and visual crescendo of the fireworks behind him but is also exaggerated in height and might by a camera slanted up towards him from below the wall. Thus he is enhanced as an almost heavenly figure, the sky behind him alight with bursting red rockets visually linking back to Leigh's lipstick and the red fade-outs we have already seen.

Similarly, Cady offers a focal point for the efforts of the teenage daughter Danielle (Juliette Lewis) to break out of her overprotected and restrictive home situation. She is in puberty and her parents, who

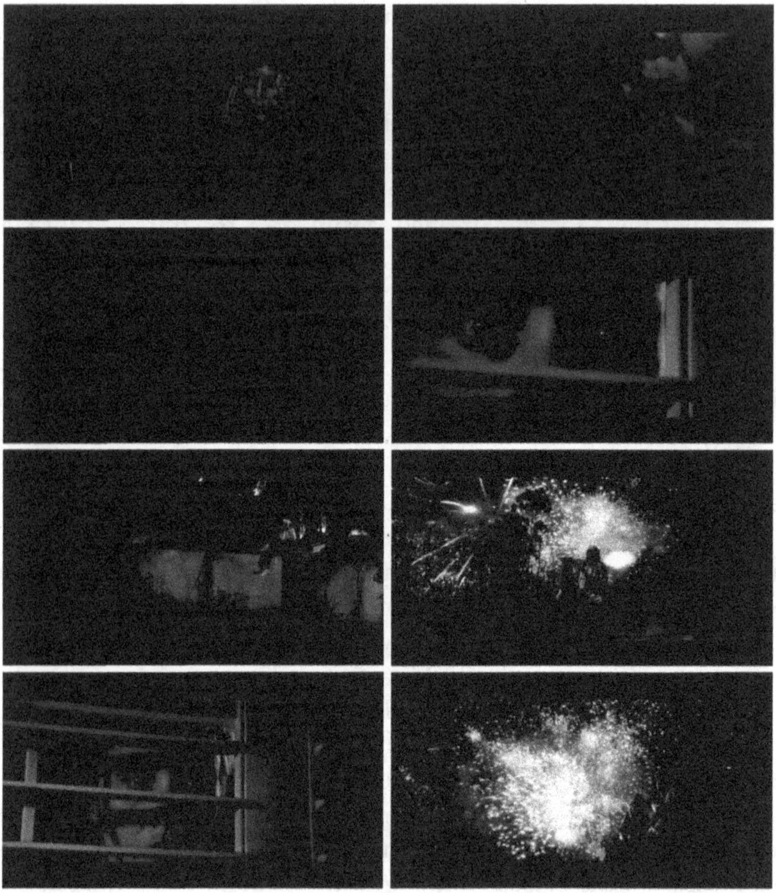

Figure 6. Her lipstick freshened up, Leigh peeks through the blinds and discovers Max Cady sitting on the garden wall, as if waiting for her to show up. When she wakes up her husband to show him the intruder, Cady has vanished—which is consistent with the idea that he is primarily her vision of a desirable male figure (CAPE FEAR 00:14:06–00:14:41).

are constantly at odds with one another, don't understand her wish to get away. Remembering Danielle's appearance at the beginning of the movie (she speaks directly into the camera to inform us that what has happened and is going to be shown on screen is *her reminiscence* and recollection of the events around Cape Fear), we see Cady playing the role of a catalyst in the process of her coming of age. In this respect her narrative functions in the manner described by Marianne

Leuzinger-Bohleber in the preceding chapter: that her "longing for development" can be expressed by a "confrontation with an archaic world of childhood fantasies and conflicts stored away in the unconscious" (Chapter Six, p. 132).

Cady pretends to be a drama teacher so that he can lure Danielle to an appointment with him on the stage of the school auditorium. This was arranged in a phone call during which Cady was hanging head-down from an exercise bar. This top-down position distorts his features diabolically. Hard lighting exaggerates his wrinkles and enhances the contrast to the youthful Danielle who is smirking childishly. His face appears entirely churlish and unnaturally distorted when the camera revolves 180 degrees around its lens axis, thereby turning Cady's face right side up and the surroundings upside down.

Through a dark cellar corridor, Danielle reaches the auditorium where Cady is awaiting her, smoking grass and sitting on the stage in a small "witch's"-hut lit from within. To break the ice and establish confidence he offers her a few tokes from the joint. When he speaks to Danielle, who begins to doubt his identity as a drama teacher, he focuses on the painful conflicts with her parents who don't want her to grow up and explore her sexuality. "It's all about self-discovery, the inner voyage. […] You can't escape your demons by just leaving home." Characterising himself as a "big bad wolf" out of the "Black Forest", he quotes Henry Miller describing an erection as "a piece of lead with wings on it". Cady offers Danielle an *amuse-gueule* of this kind of hard-on by putting his thumb into her mouth and having her suck it. He concludes this first initiation into sexual arousal by giving her an extended kiss on the mouth.

Cady, a beast or a monster in a human skin, presents the antithesis of the puritanical "American way of life" in a small town, whose hypocrisy he exposes by talking about facts of life that proper members of society consider dirty, to be kept under cover.[15] Against this backdrop of a twisted double standard, the honourable lawyer Sam Bowden is having a raucous affair with Lori (Illeana Douglas), his squash partner, and he even is stirred by the erotic charm of his daughter Danielle, rebuking her for being too scantily dressed around the house in his presence ("not a child any more"). As an adolescent she tries to run away from her parents who, estranged as they are, want her to remain a child as the last link connecting them. "Your parents don't want you to achieve adulthood," Cady points out to her. Despite

Figure 7. At their meeting on the stage of the school auditorium, Cady and Danielle gradually get closer to each other. While at first red-and-white-striped poles form a divider (no accident that they're the colour of police cordons), this border later disappears from the spectators' view and Danielle finds herself on dangerous ground or in troubled water, since for no apparent reason a rescue ring (also red-and-white) is hanging on the hut and serves as a premonition of what awaits her later on in the houseboat on the river (Cape Fear 00:55:34–01:05:00).

his uncanniness, which greatly disturbs her parents' peace of mind, she feels attracted to him because of his understanding for her teenage problems and due to his permissiveness.

In *Dreadful Pleasures—An Anatomy of Modern Horror*, James Twitchell argues that teenagers are so fond of horror films because they provide first aid on pressing issues of sexual excitability—or "the usage of lust", as Michel Foucault would have put it:

> Like fairy tales that prepare the child for the anxieties of separation, modern horror myths prepare the teenager for the anxieties of reproduction. They are fantastic, ludicrous, crude and important distortions of real life situations, not in the service of repression (though they have certainly that temporary effect) but of instruction. These fever dreams do more than make us shiver; they are fables of sexual identity. Horror myths establish social patterns not of escape, but entry. (1985, p. 7)

Though CAPE FEAR cannot be reckoned within the horror film genre in Carroll's definition, it seems consistent with Twitchell's that Scorsese stages Danielle's seduction by the "big bad wolf" within a fairy-tale set on a theatre stage down in a cellar, with its gloomy atmosphere. He thus anchors this *rite de passage* not only within the thriller genre but also alludes to the fairy tale. Stephen Heath emphasises the importance of the *cinematographic space* in relation to the events occurring there: "it is precise that 'events *take place*'" (1981, p. 19). The setting is not a neutral location for events but an important component and mediator within the drama of emotions foreboded by the atmosphere the set design evokes.

Seen in this perspective, CAPE FEAR and LA BELLE ET LA BÊTE show some affinity in spirit as far as the establishment of an adequate *environment for the action* is concerned, with the development of the female protagonist being initiated in a magical and fairy-tale-like surrounding.[16] Just as Scorsese chose the theatre stage as a meeting and starting point for violating rules (smoking grass and initiating erotic foreplay between a minor and a grown-up who calls himself a "big bad wolf"), Cocteau created an exceptional location with the mysterious castle behind a dense curtain of trees, where the rules of everyday life are suspended by surreal occurrences and the scenic framework is given for Belle's process of detachment from her family of origin.

Of special significance is the room into which the *unconscious* Belle, who has fainted at the sight of La Bête, is "transported" by him, that is, carried in a *horizontal* position, and *crosses the threshold* in a prominent arrangement of shots: first the camera shows La Belle in the arms of La Bête from behind while he is carrying her upstairs to the bedroom; then laterally when he passes by a statue of a woman with one naked breast. After that the camera rushes ahead to "penetrate" the room and show Belle floating in feet first, and around her legs we see her dress being transformed into a glittering white gown as she is carried over the threshold. Suddenly the camera "jumps" back into the hallway, where Belle's torso is still clothed in her modest everyday dress, and not until the camera has re-entered the room does it present the entire sumptuous gown worked with pearls, the bridal gown in which she is placed on the bed. This accomplished, La Bête seems mesmerised by Belle's beauty and, at close distance, turns his desiring glance to her body. His gaze awakens her, and she is shocked by the threat of his longing. Drawing away, la Bête forbids Belle to look straight into his eyes, as they betray his lust.

In *Thrills and Regressions*, Michael Balint has explained "*Angstlust*" ("lustful anxiety") in the context of "primary love", a state of being in which neither the world nor anyone in it has "demands, of his or her own" and there is even a "rejoicing of the environment on being destroyed by the individual" (1959, p. 22). He diagnoses quite early infantile needs and joyful satisfaction associated with destructive rage or losing the sense of being grounded in reality. He speaks of an "un-earthing" suspension with a thrilling quality that explains the popularity, later in life, of fairground attractions like roller-coaster rides that toss us around so that we lose control of the body. This argumentation can be extended to the pleasures of cinema audiences who rejoice in the orgies of destruction on screen when watching films like Michael Bay's The Rock (USA 1996) or Transformers movies (so far four sequels from 2007 to 2014 have been released), or find themselves being propelled through space though sitting in a cinema chair. This happens in 2-D or, even better, 3-D movies like James Cameron's Avatar (USA 2009) with travelling shots or computer generated images (CGIs), which don't require cumbersome camera equipment.

Counting on these primordial thrills and regressions, dizziness and loss of balance, it seems consistent that Scorsese stages the final showdown in Cape Fear on a swirling and rocking boat tossed around by a thunderstorm on a swollen river, thus "un-earthing" his protagonists who will later even be deprived of their boat, which is split apart by a rock in the stream. This loss of firm ground is redoubled mentally

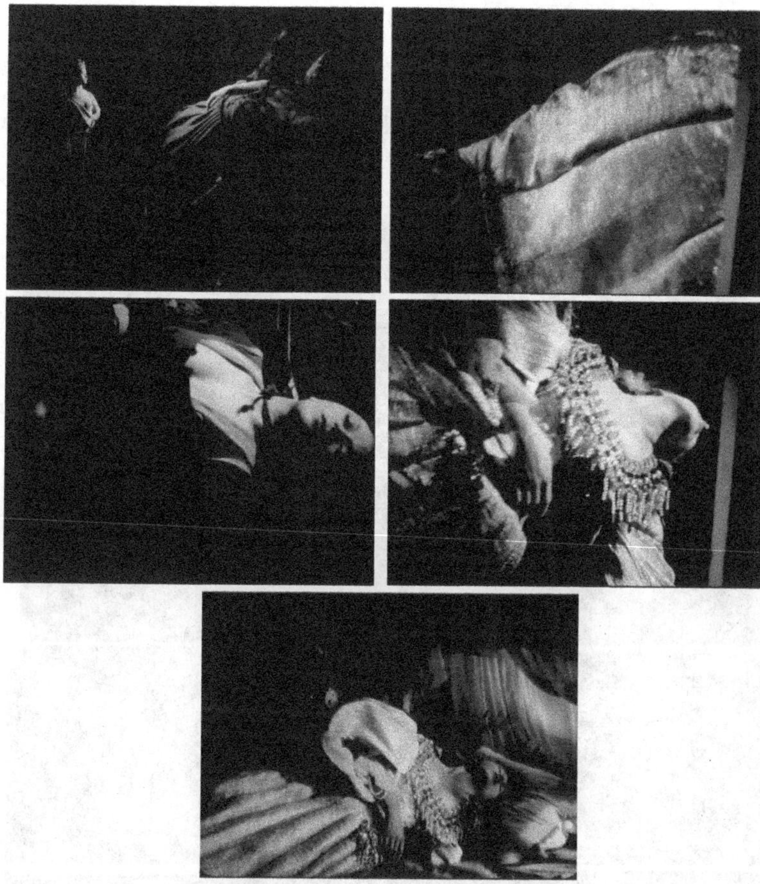

Figure 8. La Bête takes advantage of unconscious La Belle, carrying her to up to bed while her dress is transformed into a bridal gown as they cross the threshold. What he has in mind is elegantly hinted at by the statue displaying one bare breast (LA BELLE ET LA BÊTE 00:33:27—00:34:23).

by the shambles that Leigh's marriage has been reduced to. And so it seems unsurprising when—the keyword is "loss"—she connects with the beast Max Cady, who has tied up her husband on the deck and is kicking him as this night of realignment of all values takes its course. Trying to protect her daughter from being raped, Leigh offers herself instead in an act of appeasement that may, however, be a covert yielding to a strange desire within herself—considering her projection upon Cady's first appearance amid fireworks, now called to mind by the phallic torch in Cady's hand.

Departing from an aesthetics of depiction or representation (*Darstellungsästhetik*), the structural linkage of fireworks to Cady in two

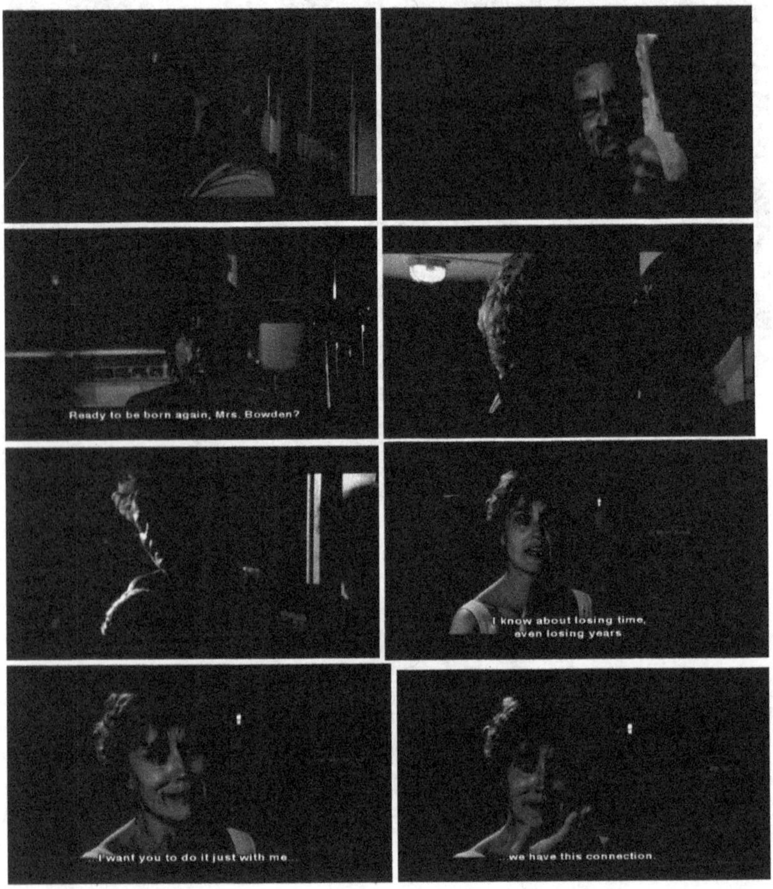

Figure 9. During the final showdown, Leigh Bowden connects mentally with Cady due to the experience of "loss" that she shares with him when she thinks of the years of her marriage compared to his years in prison. Primarily, she wants to distract him from raping her daughter, but the burning pyrotechnical phallic torch in his hand reminds us (and Leigh?) of Cady's lascivious posture on the garden wall and the desire it kindled in her (CAPE FEAR 1:43:46–1:47:43).

instances points towards a different aesthetic approach to this film—in the strict sense of *aisthesis* (= sensation, feeling). It is rather a *projective* one relating to the reception of images (*Rezeptionsästhetik*) on the part of women, treating *the beasts* in film history as *projections of a female sexual fantasy*.[17] For me as a male spectator, however, it would be presumptuous to venture too far in this direction, assuming the role of a female recipient. Therefore, I maintain my previous line of argumentation in terms of representational aesthetics, in the awareness that the seemingly firm ground of audio-visual "facts" can be shaken by connotations and associations emerging during the process of perception. The following film example demonstrates this in the realm of scents and odours, whereby the imagination of the spectators plays a decisive role.

David Lynch is said to have created "a road movie into the abyss of the soul"[18] when he came up with WILD AT HEART (USA 1990), which indeed rattled many critics in Germany at the time[19] with its provocative depictions of distasteful events. In a shabby motel room, for example, slimy Bobby Peru (Willem Dafoe), by sly and beastly designs, succeeds in breaking the resistance of Lula (Laura Dern), who is pregnant, and lures her into a state of sexual submission.

The degree of disgust already established at the beginning of this scene, with a close-up of Lula's vomit and the flies buzzing around, is heightened when Bobby Peru enters the room on the pretext that he has to use the toilet. In the spectator's imagination, the stench of the vomit mixes with the smell of urine, accentuated by Peru bragging that his (audibly) horse-like stream of piss proves his potent masculinity. Thus having marked his domain or hunting ground, he takes advantage of the absence of Lula's boyfriend Sailor (Nicholas Cage) and starts his bodily assault on the girl by approaching her face extremely closely with his ugly mouth filled with foul protruding teeth, softly uttering the words "Fuck me!" and pressuring Lula to repeat these words. With its upward tilt onto Peru´s fish-like mouth, the camera highlights his ugliness that surely can engender nothing but loathing on an empathetic level with Lula, the protagonist, since the cinema audience—male or female—feels sympathy for her from the outset. It seems to be out of the question that Lula could ever agree to sexual intercourse with this filthy creature. Bobby Peru—captured in an up-slanting camera angle—seems the very opposite of the theophanic "figure of light" that Scorcese made out of Cady sitting under the fireworks. But against all expectations, Lula yields to Peru's wooing—or at least her vagina does in expectation of Bobby's cock. Checking out the moisture between her thighs, Peru can rejoice in his triumph at having won over Sailor's girl. But instead of enjoying his conquest he humiliates her twice: first by making her submit and then by frustrating her when he says abruptly that he has to go and might come back to her "some other time".

With the filthiness of Lula's motel accommodation, we once again have entered a sleazy location as a backdrop for sexual arousal. In this case there is no metamorphosis into an animal-like creature untouched by civilisation, but the setting is nevertheless a rather uncivilised atmosphere contaminated by strong odours[20] of vomit and urine, the stench of sweaty clothes and foul teeth, which together with the scent of Lula's yearning vagina makes for quite an olfactory cocktail. By means

Figure 10. When Bobby Peru grabs Lula in the motel room, at first there is only physical violence holding their bodies close together. But Peru's suggestive repetition of "Fuck me!" makes Lula gradually give in to his demand, which—considering the outset of the scene—comes as a complete surprise to an empathetic spectator (WILD AT HEART 1:20:55–1:21:46).

of synaesthetics Lynch's film tries to break open the incrustations of civilisation and lead us back to some dog-like state where smells are not offensive, but rather diverse and fascinating.

In this respect the achievement of such a film seems to correspond to the effect that Roland Barthes described under the notion of "punctum", pertaining to certain photographs whose reception he believed produced a state of natural wildness stripped of any cultural indoctrination: "Je suis un sauvage, un enfant—ou un maniaque; je congédie tout savoir, toute culture, je m'abstiens d'hériter d'un autre regard" (1980, p. 82). Or in my own translation: "I am a savage, a child—or a maniac; I renounce all of science, all of culture, I refuse to adopt any other perspective."

Oscar Roehler, the German director, paid homage to David Lynch's WILD AT HEART with his film LULU UND JIMI (D 2009). The latter considerably reduces the aspects of disgust and loathing by opting for a stylistic transformation into a colourful, idyllic, and fairy-tale-like teenage romance unfolding in a 1950s setting and by relying, like Lynch, on an evil witch-like mother figure, a collaborating doctor and psychiatrist, and a hired killer, but adding the new topic "racism in Germany", since Lulu's lover is a coloured guy.

A tendency in remakes towards increased susceptibility for the "Beast"

What conclusion can be drawn from this short selection of examples from cinema history? Would it be going too far to discern a tendency to cater to female longing for the beast as the vanishing point of sexual desire? At least two of my examples, compared with former versions of the same story, reveal an intensified gender focus in the plot, in favour of a female perspective on beastly male seducers. This becomes apparent in the comparison between Murnau's NOSFERATU (D 1922) and Coppola's version of BRAM STOKER'S DRACULA (1992), as Michael Ballhaus has pointed out; and again in the case of J. Lee Thompson's CAPE FEAR (1962) and the Scorsese version of 1991. Although Robert Mitchum is seen to take off his shirt in the earlier version, for the benefit of female fans (has there ever been a Mitchum film where he kept his shirt on?), Robert De Niro as Cady is much more of a womaniser on many emotional and physical levels and with different types of women: Sam Bowden's girlfriend, his wife, and his daughter. Cady's sexual potency is aesthetically underlined by the mise en scène with the crackling fireworks, in Leigh's case, or the "big bad wolf" scene in which Danielle sucks his thumb.

Furthermore it is remarkable—and it brings us back to LA BELLE ET LA BÊTE—that *recourse to fairy-tale worlds* is taken in other films, as well, to set in motion the disengagement of girls or young women from their parents: Danielle's seduction by Cady begins on a fairy-tale stage set with a gingerbread house and *Little Red Riding Hood* allusions made by the "big bad wolf"; Lula's escape from home is accompanied by quotes from Victor Fleming's THE WIZARD OF OZ (USA 1939). In Oz, the dwarf-empire with a seemingly omnipotent wizard is a projection of anxieties felt by Dorothy (Judy Garland) on the brink of puberty, when she seeks refuge in a fantasy world for the last time.[21]

Recently, Christophe Gans directed a new version of LA BELLE ET LA BÊTE (D/F 2014),[22] a fairy-tale scenario shot mainly in the Babelsberg Studios near Berlin and taking full advantage of their extensive production design facilities combined with CGIs. Thus it boosts the fairy-tale narrative into the *fantasy genre* as a grand spectacle, while retaining the thematic focus on a *girl's passage into womanhood*. In fact this theme is staged prominently from the outset when we first see the heroine (played by Léa Seydoux) confiding to the statue on her mother's grave that she is entering a new phase in her life: "Here, Mother, a new life begins that I believe I am ready for." As the youngest and prettiest of her father's three daughters, his favourite, she is envied by her foolish sisters, but is not cast in the Cinderella role that Cocteau had emphasised. After her father's (André Dussollier) bankruptcy and the move to the countryside, La Belle enjoys growing vegetables and even gets her sisters to lend her a hand.

Another difference: sacrificing herself to the Beast in lieu of her father is not the result of virtuous obedience, but of an act of revolt. In an impulse of stubbornness, she declares that if she has already caused her mother's death at her birth, she doesn't want to be guilty of her father's death as well. In contrast to Cocteau's version, her becoming prey to the Beast is not so much the result of an arrangement between him and her father, but more of a decision she makes herself in a state of anger.

Just like Belle's father, lost in the nocturnal snowstorm and plunging down a slope with his horse into a white-out, then coming to in the castle, Belle herself on her wild ride through the forest is struck as if by a magic bolt, falls into a dream state, and awakens in La Bête's empire. Coming from that white night, they find themselves in a bright summer landscape topped by the enchanted castle on a hill, overgrown with jungle-like foliage. The harsh contrast makes this new world seem as unreal as the Empire of Oz—a *realm of the imagination* where wishes are fulfilled (food ready at the table, the horse attended to, flowers blooming everywhere) "along the short path of regression" (Freud, 1900a, p. 572) as if in a daydream. On the other hand, this new sphere is not restricted to an "identity of perception", as would be the case in a dream, since spectacular items can be exported: coming from the castle, Belle appears in her father's modest home wearing a splendid dress.

Under the premise of a dream-like, imagined world—as in THE WIZARD OF OZ—of course terrifying creatures must be reckoned with; but in the case of the Gans remake, the digital surprises and visceral sound design with subwoofer effects are so overdone as to overwhelm the spectator with their volume, or the sheer size and supernatural power of the giants at the command of the leonine Beast. On the empirical level (judging by my own goosebumps at that moment), here the monster really functions as a spooky terrifying creature and the viewer experiences an echo of the feelings reflected in the horrified expressions of the protagonists.

In contrast to Cocteau's heroes, who outdo one another in politeness, here such concepts as "virtue" and "goodness" needn't be sought behind a terrifying façade: in Gans's version, La Belle and La Bête act on different premises. La Belle finds La Bête disgusting and tells him so quite bluntly. Not until she tries to escape across a frozen lake does this change. La Bête catches up with her and thrusts his massive body onto her so that the ice cracks beneath her back and—as if baptised[23] or reborn—she is pulled out of the water by La Bête and from this moment on behaves towards him like a docile and loving woman.

Another difference from Cocteau's version is worth mention: an explicit backstory is woven into the plot, dreamt by La Belle in episodes during her nights in the castle. It tells of La Bête's past and why he was transformed into a terrifying monster. As a Prince (played by Vincent Cassel), a rather rough, feisty fellow who enjoys the Dionysian side of life, he hunts down the golden hind, whom his Princess (Yvonne Catterfeld) had begged him to leave unharmed. After the lethal blow, a naked woman emerges from the animal—comparable to the naked man appearing in the London-werewolf film after the wolf is killed—and reveals herself as the "Nymph of the Woods" (1:11:00), a daughter

Figure 11. La Bête (Vincent Cassel) as the prince with a crossbow and La Belle (Léa Seydoux), here in three variations, have been described by critics almost unanimously as an incongruous couple whose mutual attraction is hard to explain. (The stills are in various formats and without time references from the press package of Concorde Film, distributor of the new Gans version of LA BELLE ET LA BÊTE, D/F 2014).

of nature gods, who had at times taken on human form to get to know human love. As a punishment for inflicting death on the hind, the Prince is put under the spell of becoming a beast himself. This backstory brings an animistic conception of nature, ruled by gods, into the foreground,[24] in contrast to Cocteau's more or less Christian idea of a supernatural heavenly sphere into which the couple finally ascends, into an *unio mystica*. Instead, Gans's ending has the former Prince with his feet firmly on the ground, tending to bucolic chores.

Gans's insertion of the backstory has other consequences, as well. The bed La Belle is brought to rest on not only has the connotation of coitus, as in Cocteau, but also denotes the wish once expressed by the former Prince in this very bed: that his Princess would bear him a son. This wish is not made explicit later on towards La Belle but it lingers on nonetheless as an unfulfilled desire known to us from the backstory. What makes La Belle, who openly pronounces her disgust towards La Bête, yield to his desire in the end? Surely it is not his "good heart" since La Belle knows from her dreams about the Prince's past ribaldry and the golden hind. The attraction rather seems to result from the untamed force and wildness that she eventually gets used to and no longer finds appalling. Compared to Cocteau's Belle, Gans's figure has the advantage of knowing both facets of La Bête thanks to her dream visions: the monstrously distorted one under the spell, and the Dionysian human one, the combination of the two forming a mixed or composite creature, a "Mischwesen",[25] as familiar to us from dreams.

For spectators who have seen LA VIE D´ADÈLE (F 2013) by Abdellatif Kechiche, starring Léa Seydoux in a very daring exposure, Belle may also appear to be a "Mischwesen". They will remember her naked, lusty body in the role of the lesbian Emma, which left a lasting sensual impression. By this standard, the *chaste* sensuousness displayed by Josette Day as La Belle in Cocteau's movie is supra-sensual—not about to burst any textiles, and perfectly suited for the heavenly realm she then enters.

There were hardly any reviews that found Gans's film excellent or satisfying. Especially the personae and their interpretation by the cast were said to give no inkling whatsoever of why La Belle felt attracted to the frightening Beast. My attempt at an explanation would go back to the analysis of the sublime in Immanuel Kant's *Kritik der Urteilskraft* (Critique of Judgement) (1795). In chapter Twenty Three dedicated to the "Analytic of the Sublime" he distinguishes the Sublime, in its immeasurable greatness and freedom from form, and the Beautiful, which is bound into a delimited form.[26] Whereas the Beautiful "directly brings with it a feeling of the furtherance of life" ("*directe ein Gefühl der Beförderung des Lebens bei sich führt*"), the Sublime is marked by "a negative pleasure" ("*negativ Lust*"):

> ... a pleasure that arises only indirectly; viz. it is produced by the feeling of a momentary checking of the vital powers and a consequent stronger outflow of them, so that it seems to be regarded as emotion—not play, but earnest in the exercise of the Imagination. [*... eine Lust ..., welche nur indirecte entspringt, nämlich so, daß sie durch das Gefühl einer augenblicklichen Hemmung der Lebenskräfte und der darauf sogleich folgenden desto stärkeren Ergießung derselben erzeugt wird, mithin als Rührung kein Spiel, sondern Ernst in der Beschäftigung der Einbildungskraft zu sein scheint*]. (ibid., p. 88)

Kant goes on to emphasise that "... the mind is not merely attracted by the object but is ever being alternately repelled, the satisfaction in the sublime does not so much involve a positive pleasure as admiration or respect," in this way calling for supplementary thought: "... for no sensible form can contain the sublime properly so-called. This concerns only Ideas of the Reason, which, although no adequate presentation is possible for them, by this inadequacy that admits of sensible presentation, are aroused and summoned into the mind" (ibid.). Kant gives the example of the storm-ridden ocean—"its aspect is horrible"—and tries to explain the turning point of negative lust into "Ideas that involve higher purposiveness" (ibid.), whereby one departs from the sensual realm and "arouses in us the feeling of this supersensible destination" (ibid., Chapter Twenty Seven).

This effort at philosophical explanation transports us into higher spheres and perhaps brings us closer to the psychological explanations laid out by Freud in *Jenseits des Lustprinzips* (*Beyond the Pleasure Principle*) (1920g) and Balint in *Thrills and Regressions*.[27]

Notes

1. Discussed in greater detail, particularly with reference to Barbot (1740) and Apuleius, in Chapter Three, this volume.
2. The last sentence of Leprince de Beaumont's tale, after the Beast has been changed into a prince, reads: "Ses sujets le virent avec joie et il [le prince] épousa la Belle, qui vécut avec lui fort longtemps et dans un bonheur parfait, parce qu'il était fondé sur la vertu." My translation (AR): "His subjects saw this with joy, and he married the Beauty who with him lived a long life of perfect happiness, as it was based on virtue."
3. Written near Ulm in 1619, during the Thirty Years' War, *Discours de la Méthode* was first published in French in 1637 in Amsterdam. I cite this treatise according to the edition of La Librairie Vrin, Paris, 1971.
4. "[L]'âme par laquelle je suis ce que je suis, est entièrement distinct du corps" (Descartes, 1637, p. 91). See also "[L]a nôtre [l'âme] est d'une nature entièrement indépendente du corps et, par conséquent, qu'elle n'est point sujette à mourir avec lui" (ibid., p. 125).
5. Realised similarly—albeit in reverse—in such films as Ridley Scott's ALIEN (USA 1979) or John Carpenter's THE THING (USA 1982), with a beast-like alien capable of startling mutations emerging from a human body.
6. For "Peter Hall, […] founder of the Royal Shakespeare Company, […] the mask reveals the 'quintessence of emotions'. It served as a medium of expression by overstepping the limits of nature and by transmuting life into art. 'By hiding we reveal.' As Hall saw it, the Greeks introduced the mask in order to separate theatre and life. Due to its extremely

controlled expression, a single facial expression, the mask had more authority than an *uncontrolled* face and became a foil for projections (*tool of the imagination*) as long as the play lasted" (Belting, 2013, p. 65).

7. Cocteau's art director Christian Bérard tells us that illustrations by Gustave Doré "pour les contes de Perrault" (Hammond, 1992, p. 19) provided inspiration for the film.
8. As a concession to Marais's female fans, Cocteau had to cast him twice, that is, also unmasked in the role of Avenant. Otherwise, seeing Marais almost exclusively as a pair of eyes behind an animal mask would have been just too much for the fans (cf. Azoury & Lalanne, 2003, pp. 48 f.).
9. Dionysus is the "god of intoxication, of sexual arousal and ecstasy" and also "lord of the celebrating mob, which includes wild animals and all kinds of primal creatures" (Abenstein, 2005, p. 100).
10. It's generally known what Freud wrote about ascending stairs and climbing up to heights in dreams as a symbolic representation of orgasm. Noteworthy in this context are also Luis Buñuel's TRISTANA (F 1970) or Hitchcock's VERTIGO (USA 1958).
11. Bram Stoker's novel of 1897, as David Rogers (2000) points out in his "Introduction" to this text, provides "an almost infinite number of shapes, most familiarly those of wolves and bats and dogs" (p. x) for Dracula's shifting appearance, a wide spectrum of metamorphoses for modern digital filmmaking to feast on and perfect. Dracula's transformation correspondents to Lucy's "into a Darwinian one, a figure whose 'heartless cruelty' and 'voluptuous wantonness' [Stoker, 1897, p. 175] connote the brutal promiscuity of the world depicted by nineteenth-century natural history" (ibid., p. xii), while Mina tries to maintain the alternative model of chastity and self-control, more in the vein of F. W. Murnau's NOSFERATU (D 1922).
12. "David, please let me help you," and "I love you, David," she says to calm the aggressive wolf, who nonetheless attacks.
13. This is a remake of J. Lee Thomas's version of CAPE FEAR (USA 1962), distributed in German under the title EIN KÖDER FÜR DIE BESTIE (BAIT FOR THE BEAST). The original film is based on John D. MacDonald's novel *The Executioners*, published in the USA in 1957.
14. Edgar Morin's film theory (1956) assumes that spectators experience screen figures as crystallisations or incarnations of their own emotional states which are enacted and defused in a process of projective identification—and this applies particularly to emotions otherwise unacceptable for cultural reasons. Conversely, Morin sees films as introjecting or embodying behavioural patterns that conform to societal conventions and therefore contribute to maintaining social coherence.

15. The *Süddeutsche Zeitung* (December 12, 2013) reported on a six-year-old pupil in Colorado who was suspended from school because he kissed a girl, a friend, on her hand. The school staff regarded this as a case of sexual harassment, because he had already kissed the girl on her cheek. Now his file in school lists him as a sexual molester. His mother is trying to revoke this decision: she is now in a spot since her son is asking what sex means.
16. I pointed out before that the film begins as an account of Danielle's reminiscence; at the verge of adulthood, she is deeply affected by what she has gone through.
17. James Twitchell argues in this vein when he writes: "Monstrous doubles do terrible things on purpose—the question is, whose purpose? They may not have a mind of their own, but that is only because they have the desires of the dreamer" (1985, p. 79).
18. This phrase was coined by Professor Klaus Schreyer (then heading the Documentary Dept. of Munich's Film School—now called the University of Film Munich)—in a discussion on Lynch's WILD AT HEART and BLUE VELVET (USA 1986).
19. For example, Hans Günther Pflaum, "Der Triumph des Effekt-Haschers. Kritische Anmerkungen zu Lynchs BLUE VELVET" (Rost, 1994, p. 93).
20. Of all the senses, the olfactory is the least civilised and most insistent, resisting our attempts to ignore it. We can close our eyes, ears, mouth, and refrain from bodily contact, but breathing can hardly be avoided.
21. David Bordwell and Kristin Thompson see the implicit meaning of this film in Dorothy's quest for refuge in a childlike fantasy world to fend off the metamorphoses setting in with puberty (1993, p. 50). Obviously, at sixteen Judy Garland (born in 1922) was too old for the main role. But this incongruence between the actress and her role has fostered a great fascination with Garland's performance, particularly in the gay community, welcoming the fact of an overt gender construction in Garland´s performances (cf. Cohan, 2005).

    In Germany, Katrin Oltmann has argued in a similar vein. Her explicit aim in film interpretation is "to disclose (film) identity as an effect of performances and identification strategies, and at the same time to expose how violently the societal machinery of role definition proceeds in assigning gender to individuals" (2008, p. 42). In general, however, gender critique is based on structural premises assuming that there are natural contingencies on which societal allocations of significance are based. The incongruence between biological sex and gender thus serves as a starting point for postulating (in partial accord with Judith Butler) the "cultural fabrication of sex"—well illustrated in Monika Treut's film GENDERNAUTS (D 1999). Gender critique focuses on examining films, particularly from the classical era of Hollywood studio productions, to uncover standards and deviations in sexual orientation and behaviour and to discern how the performances suggest subtext relating to alternative "queer" lifestyles: a means of discovering, in ostensibly "straight" stories, variations on homosexuality, gayness, or queerness.

22. According to the press booklet, Christophe Gans did not have a remake of Cocteau's film in mind, but rather a new adaptation of the French folk tale as originally set down by Gabrielle-Suzanne de Villeneuve in 1740, which—in contrast to the later edition by Mme Le Prince de Beaumont in 1756—is more strongly inspired by ancient mythology.
23. Baptism is a symbolic death, as we know from the Christian cult. Submerging the whole body vests even more symbolic meaning in the ritual than the few drops of water used in its refined version.
24. In an interview, Gans explains his shift in emphasis when drawing on the Villeneuve tale: "Villeneuve's story was inspired mostly by Greek and Roman mythology, particularly by Ovid's *Metamorphoses*. There, the gods are crafty characters who change themselves into animals so that they can intermingle with and seduce mortals. I wanted to integrate this aspect into the film: the divine sanctuary that enables contact between human beings and the forces of nature. Something similar is to be found in the films of Hayao Miyazaki, which are rooted in the ancient animistic religion of Japan" (Gans, 2014, p. 8).
25. "Die Herstellung von Sammel—und Mischpersonen ist eines der Hauptarbeitsmittel der Traumverdichtung" ("The construction of collective and composite figures is one of the chief methods by which condensation operates in dreams") (Freud, 1900a, p. 292).
26. Kant's text also says, in chapter Twenty Three: "The Beautiful in Nature refers to the form of the object, consisting in its delineation (*Begrenzung*); the Sublime, however, can also be found in a formless object inasmuch as it is characterized by limitlessness (*Unbegrenztheit*)" (p. 87).
27. The English version of my essay, originally in German, was corrected by Harriet Schlosshauer, Hans Jokel, and Susan Jones, to whom I express my deepest gratitude and thanks for their effort to get my text into the present shape.

References

Abenstein, R. (2005). *Griechische Mythologie*. Paderborn, Germany: Schöningh/UTB.

Azoury, P., & Lalanne, J. -M. (2003). *Cocteau et le Cinéma. Désordres*. Paris: Cahiers du Cinéma et Centre Pompidou.

Balint, M. (1959). *Thrills and Regressions*. London: Hogarth.

Ballhaus, M., & Seidl, C. (2014). *Bilder im Kopf. Die Geschichte meines Lebens*. Munich, Germany: Deutsche Verlagsanstalt.

Barthes, R. (1980). *La chambre claire. Note sur la photographie*. Paris: Cahiers du Cinéma, Gallimard, Seuil.

Belting, H. (2013). *Faces. Eine Geschichte des Gesichts*. Munich, Germany: C. H. Beck.

Bordwell, D., & Thompson, K. (1993). *Film Art. An Introduction (4th edition)*. New York: McGraw-Hill.

Carroll, N. (1990). *The Philosophy of Horror or Paradoxes of the Heart*. New York: Routledge.

Cohan, S. (2005). *Incongruous Entertainment. Camp, Cultural Value, and the MGM Musical*. Durham, UK: Duke University Press.

Descartes, R. (1637). *Discours de la Méthode*. Paris: Librairie Vrin, 1971.

Freud, S. (1900a). *The Interpretation of Dreams. S. E., 18*: ix–627. London: Hogarth.

Freud, S. (1920g). *Beyond the Pleasure Principle. S. E., 18*. London: Hogarth.

Gans, C. (2014). *Die Schöne und das Biest*. [Press kit from the German distributor Concorde Filmverleih, delivered as pdf-file.] Munich, Germany.

Hammond, R. (Ed.) (1992). *Jean Cocteau, La Belle et la Bête*. Paris: Éditions du collectionneur.

Heath, S. (1981). Narrative space. In: *Questions of Cinema* (pp. 19–75). London: Macmillan.

Kant, I. (1795). *Critique of Judgement (2nd ed. revised)*. Translated with introduction and notes by J. H. Bernard. London: Macmillan, 1914. (*Kritik der Urteilskraft*. Hamburg, Germany: Felix Meier Verlag, 1974 (reprint of the edition from 1924)).

MacDonald, J. D. (1957). *The Executioners*. New York: Simon & Schuster.

Morin, E. (1956). *Le Cinéma ou l'Homme imaginaire*. Paris: Les Editions de Minuit.

Oltmann, K. (2008). *Premake/Remake. Hollywoods romantische Komödie und ihre Gender-Diskurse*, 1930–1960. Bielefeld, Germany: Transcript.

Rost, A. (Ed.) (1994). *Bilder der Gewalt*. Frankfurt, Germany: Verlag der Autoren.

Stoker, B. (1897). *Dracula*. Ware, UK: Wordsworth Classics, 2000, with an introduction by David Rogers.

Twitchell, J. (1985). *Dreadful Pleasures. An Anatomy of Modern Horror*. New York: Oxford University Press.

INDEX

Abject 68, 70
Absolutism 50
Adolescence 6, 10, 51–52, 78, 104, 106, 118, 121, 124, 129, 133, 135–136, 139, 155
Adorno, T. W. 82, 89, 114–115, 125, 132, 143
Aeschylus 10–11
Aesthetics 9, 19–21, 24–25, 27, 29–30, 32, 36–37, 62, 87, 103–104, 112, 117, 160–161
Aggression 78, 88, 99, 118, 120, 136–137, 169
Alland, W. 85
Allegory 23
Amor 7, 47, 49–52, 58–59, 62, 64, 68, 70, 74, 92–93
Amor and Psyche 7, 47, 49, 51, 58–59, 62, 66, 74, 93
An American Werewolf in London (USA, GB 1981) 152
Analysand 20, 33–34, 39, 43, 102, 114, 139, 142
Animal bridegroom 47–49, 51–52, 60, 62, 85
Anti-Semitism 82, 88
Antonioni, M. 24–25, 29
Anxiety 6, 18, 75–76, 141, 158
Ape, monkey 75, 88, 103, 149–150
Apollinaire, G. 80
Apuleius 7, 47–50, 53, 58, 62–64, 66–67, 69, 72, 74–76, 88–89, 93, 168
Aramis see Magical horse Magnifique
Argelander, H. 22, 123–124
Aristophanes 10, 12, 74
Arlow, J. 24, 29, 40
Arrow 49, 63, 74, 76, 78
Art, work of art 3, 9, 25, 43–45, 48, 60, 79–80, 82, 99, 103, 109, 114–115, 123, 143, 168–169

Artist 27, 33, 37, 61, 79–80, 82, 102
Ascension 77, 106–107, 113, 121–122, 141, 166–167
Attachment 63, 99, 106, 118, 135–136
Audience 3, 6, 8, 16, 31, 39, 43–44, 62, 72–73, 77–79, 82, 85, 116, 129, 131, 134, 137, 150, 161
Author 3, 44, 46, 57, 77–79, 82, 89, 91, 114
AVATAR (USA 2009) 158
Avenant 63–65, 72–73, 75–78, 81, 84–85, 107, 109, 118, 123, 135, 137, 142, 169

Backstory 63, 165–166
Baker, R. L. 51, 89
Balint, M. 158, 168, 172
Ballhaus, M. 151, 163, 172
Barbot Gallon de Villeneuve, G. -S. 47, 50, 52–55, 57–58, 62–64, 66–67, 69, 72, 75, 88–89, 129, 168, 171
Barchilon, J. 52, 89
Baroque 50, 56–57, 67, 70, 72, 129
Barthes, R. 44, 79, 89, 163, 172
BARTON FINK (USA, GB 1991) 30
Baudry, J. L. 20–21, 40
Bauks, M. 47, 89
Bay, M. 158
Beauty (see also Belle) 53, 56–58, 77, 83–84, 89–94, 100–104, 106–111, 119, 121–124, 131, 134, 136–137, 143–144, 168
Beauty (see Belle) 137
BEAUTY AND THE BEAST (USA 1991) 83
Belle 7, 9–10, 43–58, 61–65, 67–93, 99, 101–102, 104–106, 108–113, 117–123, 129, 131–137, 143, 145–149, 157–159, 164–168, 172
Belting, H. 146, 169, 172
Benton, R. 18, 40
Bérard, Ch. 102, 132, 169
Berberi, T. & V. 83, 89
Bergman, I. 21
Bergstrom, J. 4, 12
Berman, E. 35, 40, 82, 90
Bertolucci, B. 21, 25
Bête 53, 56–57, 62, 76, 83–84, 89–94, 100–102, 104, 106–113, 117–124, 131–138, 143–144, 147–148, 158, 163–169
BETIPUL (ISRAEL, 2005–2008) 16
Bettelheim, B. 6, 12, 47, 90, 124, 132–133, 143
Biography 27, 33–34, 36–37, 82
Bion, W. 114, 124
Bloch, E. 134, 143
Block, M. 4, 12
Blothner, D. 41, 92, 94, 124
BLOW-UP (GB 1966) 24–25, 29
BLUE VELVET (USA 1986) 170
Blüher, H. 6, 12
Boccaccio 7, 50, 58
Body 3, 6–8, 20, 32, 49, 66, 74–76, 81, 85–86, 100, 102, 104, 138–139, 141, 146–148, 152–153, 158, 165, 167–168, 171
Bohleber, W. 51, 90–91, 136, 139–141, 143
Böhme, H. & G. 62, 90
Bolden, J. 83, 90
Bollas, Ch. 38, 40
Bollmann, S. 5, 12
Boorman, J. 28
Borchert, W. 133, 143
Bordwell, D. 170, 172
BORGEN (DK 2010–2013) 137
Bottigheimer, R. B. 47, 51–52, 56–57, 90
Bourgeoisie 8, 15, 56
BRAM STOKER'S DRACULA (USA 1992) 150, 163

Brandes, H. 5, 12, 42
Braun, Ch. von 25, 40, 131
Breker, A. 81
Breuer, J. 16
BRINGING UP BABY (USA 1938) 62
Broumas, O. 84, 90–91
Broyles, K. E. 21, 41
Brunotte, U. 6, 12
Buñuel, L. 80, 101, 169
Burton, A. 47, 90, 124
Butler, J. 5, 12, 87, 90, 170

Cage, N. 161
Cameo 46
Camera 4–5, 21, 25, 28–30, 32, 41, 46, 63, 70, 77, 112, 118–119, 134, 151, 153–155, 158, 161
Cameron, J. 158
Campion, J. 18, 24, 28, 31–32, 35
Canova, A. 59–60
CAPE FEAR (USA 1991) 153–158, 160, 163, 169
Carroll, N. 148, 157, 172
Carter, A. 109
Cassel, V. 165–166
Castle 49, 53–57, 63–64, 66–67, 69, 72–76, 88, 100, 102, 106, 108, 117–120, 123, 132, 134–135, 157, 164–165
CAT PEOPLE (USA 1942) 150
Chaplin, Ch. 102
Chasseguet-Smirgel, J. 15, 25, 27, 40, 136, 143
Child 5, 18, 20, 24, 32, 49, 58, 68, 70, 133, 139, 155, 157, 163
Childhood, child 5, 17, 26, 31–32, 37, 46, 102, 107, 132–133, 135–136, 138, 155
Cicero 74, 90
Cinderella 103, 113, 164
Cinema 3, 5, 8–10, 13, 15–16, 19–20, 29, 31–32, 35–37, 41, 43, 46, 54, 58, 85, 101–102, 105, 109–110, 130–131, 136, 143, 151, 158, 161, 163
CITY LIGHTS (USA 1937) 102
Civilté 60
Clothing 75, 118, 136, 138–139, 147
Co-construction 35
Cocteau, J. 9, 43–47, 51, 56, 61–68, 70, 72–91, 94–95, 101, 103–110, 117–119, 122–124, 130–134, 138–139, 141, 144–145, 148, 157, 164–167, 169, 171–172
Coen, E. & J. 30–31
Cohan, S. 5, 12, 94, 170, 172
Connell, R. 7, 12
Consciousness 18, 20–21, 29–30, 34, 37–38, 82
Construction 5, 8–10, 46–47, 63, 78–79, 84, 87, 99, 104, 129, 142, 145, 170–171
Cooper, G. 31
Cooper, M. C. 149
Coppola, F. F. 150–151, 163
Cotten, J. 3
Countertransference 22–23, 25, 34–36, 38, 111, 113–115, 123, 138, 140
Courten, A. von 58
Cro (Rapper) 81
Cupid and Psyche 8, 57, 90
Cutback 29

da Vinci, L. 37, 88, 123
Dafoe, W. 161
Damon, M. 83
Dante Aligheri 108–109
Daxelmüller, C. 48, 90
Day, J. 45, 104, 149, 167
De Niro, R. 153, 163
De Nitto, D. 63, 77, 91
De Vries, L. 49, 91

Death 24, 37, 44, 49–50, 55, 59, 78, 80, 108, 116, 132–134, 140–141, 151, 164, 166, 171
Deleuze, G. 22, 40
DELIVERANCE (USA 1972) 28
DeNitto, D. 108–109
Dern, L. 161
Derrida, J. 46, 91
Descartes, R. 130, 146–147, 168, 172
Deserno, H. 21, 40, 114, 124
Dettmering, P. 15, 40
Development (psychology) 28, 67, 77, 83, 85, 106, 122–124, 133–135, 138, 144, 155, 157
Diaghilev, S. 80
Diamond, D. 16, 27, 40
Diana (goddess) 74–76, 78
Dickens, Ch. 105
DIE EHE DER MARIA BRAUN (D 1979) 131
DIE SEHNSUCHT DER VERONIKA VOSS (D 1982) 131
DIE SÜNDERIN (D 1951) 133
Dieckmann, H. 47, 91
Dieterle, W. 62
Dinges, M. 8, 12–14
Dinner 54, 57, 68–69, 119–120
Dionysus 169
DiPaolo, M. 84, 91
Director 20, 23, 26–27, 31–32, 34–35, 38–39, 46, 117, 148, 163, 169
Disney, W. 70, 83–84, 86, 89–92, 95
Doane, M. A. 4, 12
Douglas, I. 155
Dream 18–21, 26, 30, 32, 37, 54–55, 58, 64, 69, 115, 117–118, 121, 123, 134, 140, 142, 157, 164–169, 171
Dressler, M. C. 4, 12
du Luis, C. 83
DUEL IN THE SUN (USA 1946) 3, 13
Dussollier, A. 164

E. T. THE EXTRA-TERRESTRIAL (USA 1982) 85
Education 86, 129, 132
Eighteenth century 5, 47, 60, 62, 101
ELEPHANT MAN (GB 1980) 108
Elias, N. 7, 12
Embodiment 87, 101, 133, 138, 142
Emotion 8, 29, 32, 34, 36, 38–39, 106, 112, 114–115, 117, 132–138, 140–141, 146, 163, 169
Empathy 17, 29, 34, 38, 85, 141–142
Enactment 20, 43, 123, 139
Enlightenment 7, 51–52, 62, 125, 132
Envy 6, 58, 133–134
Erdheim, M. 51, 91
Erhart, R. 57, 62, 83, 88, 91
Euripides 10, 12
Evers, S. 83

Fairy tale 7, 45–47, 49–52, 54–56, 58, 62, 67, 77–78, 80, 83–84, 87–90, 101–102, 104, 106, 108, 122, 124, 129–130, 132–135, 138–139, 141–142, 146, 157, 163–164
Fantasy 10, 24, 29–30, 34–36, 38, 52, 55, 112–113, 118–119, 123, 132–133, 136, 138, 141–142, 155
Fassbinder, R. W. 131, 134, 143
Father 4, 17–18, 28, 48, 53–58, 63–68, 72, 74–75, 88, 99, 102–108, 110, 113, 118–122, 133, 135, 137, 139, 144, 146, 164–165
Felix, J. 93, 131, 143, 172
Fellini, F. 21, 26, 40
Femininity, female 4–10, 12, 17–19, 34, 46–47, 51–53, 58, 62–64, 74–79, 81–82, 86–87, 99–100, 102, 108, 110, 121, 130, 136, 142, 144, 148–153, 157, 161, 163–164, 169

Feminism 4–5, 9, 13, 19, 25, 33, 35, 91, 105
Fetishism 36, 102
FIGHT CLUB (USA, D 1999) 33
Film effects 31, 36–37, 65, 165
Film interpretation 15–16, 19–20, 22–24, 34, 36–37, 40, 78, 113, 116–117, 170
Film theory 4–5, 13, 92, 169
Fincher, D. 33
Fischlin, D. 65, 81–82, 91
Flashback 29–30
Foreshadowing 28
Forest 18, 50, 65–67, 74, 120, 133, 164
Form, formal means 16, 29–30, 33, 36, 65, 67, 70, 76, 112, 132, 149, 153, 155, 160
Forst, W. 134
Foucault, M. 44, 79, 91, 157
French Revolution 8
Frenzel, E. 87, 91
Freud, S. 16, 18–21, 23, 30, 37–38, 40–41, 44, 91, 103, 109, 115–117, 121, 123–124, 144, 165, 168–169, 171–172
FROM HERE TO ETERNITY (USA 1953) 31
Fuseli, H (Füssli, J. H.) 134

Gabbard, G. 18, 21, 30, 40–41
Gaines, J. 5, 13
Gans, Ch. 164–167, 171–172
Garland, J. 164, 170
Gavras, C. 141, 144
Gaze 3–6, 9, 13, 22, 78, 105, 142, 158
Gender 5–9, 13, 25, 35, 46, 50–52, 59, 60, 79, 86–87, 105, 123, 129, 136–138, 140, 142–143, 163, 170
GENDERNAUTS (D 1999) 170
Gennep, A. v. 5, 13
Gide, A. 80, 91
Gilmore, D. D. 6, 13
Gonsalvus, P. 60–61
Goodness 104, 146, 148, 165
Götzl, S. F. 84, 91
Greek tragedy 6, 18
Grimminger, R. 8, 13
Guattari, F. 22, 40

Hains, M. 83, 91
Hamburger, A. 3, 8–9, 13, 38, 41, 43–44, 46, 51, 82, 86, 91–92, 105, 111, 123–124, 142–143
Hammond, R. 90, 109, 124, 147–148, 169, 172
Hark, I. R. 5, 12, 94
Harris, A. 82, 92
Hartmann, E. 30, 41
Hay, S. H. 84, 91–92
Hearne, B. 50, 53, 58, 62, 83, 91–92
Heath, S. 89, 157, 172
Hegemonic masculinity 7–9, 87
Henderson, J. -L. 84, 91, 124–125
Hesiod 74
Heterosexuality 77, 80, 84, 87, 105
HIGH NOON (USA 1952) 31
HIROSHIMA MON AMOUR (F, J 1959) 29, 31
History 5, 7, 9–10, 13, 16–17, 22, 33, 35, 44, 46–47, 49, 51–53, 58, 62, 68, 83, 85–86, 91, 102, 130–132, 136, 138, 145, 161, 163, 169
Hitchcock, A. 23, 26, 30–31, 35, 40, 109, 136, 169
Hitler, A. 81
Holm, C. 59, 92
Homosexuality 6, 80–82, 84, 105, 171
Horkheimer, M. 115, 125
Huston, A. 83
Hyperconnectivity 38

Iconography 58, 88
Identification 4, 18–19, 34, 38, 105, 116, 118, 133, 135, 169–170
Identity 5–8, 10, 17–18, 36, 38, 46, 52, 62, 80, 83–86, 129, 135–137, 141, 143, 155, 157, 165, 170
Image 3, 5, 10, 18–21, 24, 28–34, 37–38, 58, 65, 67–68, 109, 121, 133, 145, 153, 158, 161
In Treatment (USA, 2007–2010) 16
Infancy, infant, infantile 106, 124, 133, 136, 158
Initiation 5–6, 108, 155
Intention 21, 37, 68, 76–77, 79

Jean Cocteau fait du cinéma (F 1925) 80
Jeffords, S. 70, 92
Jelinek, E. 137
Jephthah's daughter 47–49, 52, 66
Jokel, H. 145, 171
Jones, J. 3, 131
Jones, S. 15, 43, 145, 171

Kant, I. 167–168, 171–172
Katrinaki, M. 74, 92
Kechiche, A. 167
King Kong (USA 1933) 62, 85, 108, 149–150
Kinski, K. 83
Kinski, N. 150
Kirchhoff, Ch. 10, 66, 88, 99, 106, 111
Kirley, J. P. 25, 41
Knausgaard, K. O. 137
Knef, H. 134
Koch, G. 21, 32, 41
Kohut, H. 139, 143
Körner, J. 22, 41
Kracauer, S. 31
Kristeva, J. 68, 93
Krützen, M. 86, 93
Krystal, H. 134, 143
Kuhn, M. 44, 93
Kurosawa, A. 21
Kuwert, B. 132, 134, 144
Kwiatkowski, C. 21, 41

L'Age d'or (F 1930) 80
L'Espoir (E, F 1945) 45
L'Eternel retour (F 1943) 81, 148–149
La Belle et la Bête (Film by Cocteau) (F 1946) 7, 9–10, 43–49, 51–53, 58, 61–67, 69–74, 77–87, 90, 99, 105, 108, 110–113, 118, 129–133, 136, 141–142, 146, 148–149, 157, 159, 164, 166, 172
La Belle et la Bête (literary fairy tale) 46–47, 50–52, 56, 62, 68, 73, 83, 88, 93, 101, 110, 142, 145
La Vie d´Adèle (F 2013) 167
Lacan, J. 18
Lafontaine, J. de 50, 93
Lamott, F. 4–5, 13
Landis, J. 152
Lange, J. 153
Langer, S. K. 31, 41
Language 15, 18, 20, 28, 32, 34, 38, 44, 57, 116
Last Tango in Paris (I, F 1972) 25
Last Year at Marienbad (F, I 1961) 15
Laszig, P. 16, 41, 94
Latent meaning 20–21, 27, 31–35, 37–38, 114, 170–171
Lauzon, J. -C. 26, 29, 31
Le Piacevoli Notti 51
Le sang d'un poete (F 1932) 80
Léolo (F, CDN 1992) 26, 29, 31
Leprince de Beaumont, J. -M. 47, 51, 56–58, 62–64, 66–68, 72, 75, 88, 93, 101, 110, 145, 148, 168, 171

Les amours de Psyché *et de* Cupidon 50, 93
Les Parents terribles (F 1948) 89
Leube-Sonnleitner, K. 38, 41, 43, 51, 92, 111, 124
Leuzinger-Bohleber, M. 10, 51, 87, 95, 106, 129, 131, 136, 140–144, 155
Levine, H. B. 141, 144
Lévi-Strauss, C. 135, 144
Lewin, B. 21, 41
Lewis, J. 153
Lili Marleen (D 1981) 131
Liminality 6
Lippert, R. 19, 41
Liptay, F. 62, 93
Literature 5, 8, 15, 18–19, 27, 44, 60, 62–63, 105, 148
Lola (D 1981) 131
Lorenzer, A. 22, 43–44, 51, 93, 123, 125
Love 7, 23–24, 31, 49–56, 59, 62, 65, 70, 74–77, 80, 84–86, 99, 107–109, 134, 137, 140–142, 146, 152, 158, 166, 169
Ludovic 64–65, 72, 76–77, 81, 105, 123, 135, 139–140
Lugosi, B. 83
Lulu & Jimi (D 2009) 163
Lumière brothers 16
Lynch, D. 161, 163, 170

MacDonald, J. D. 169, 172
Magic 46, 49–51, 53, 55, 57–58, 65–68, 70, 74–75, 85, 100, 102, 104, 109, 123, 133–134, 140, 145, 157, 164
Magical glove 74–76, 102
Magical golden key 74–76, 102
Magical horse Magnifique 54, 74–75, 79, 102, 161, 164–165
Magical mirror 6, 33, 57, 68, 70, 74–76, 102, 104, 109, 118–119, 121, 133, 139, 153
Magical Ring 55, 156
Magritte, R. 103
Mahler-Bungers, A. 16, 42, 144
Maier, C. 23, 41
Malherbe, F. de 103, 109
Malraux, A. 45
Marais, J. 45, 72–73, 79, 81–82, 85, 90, 104–105, 107, 146, 148–149, 169
Marriage 7, 49–50, 52, 56–58, 69, 78, 133, 145, 153, 159–160
Masculinity, male 3–10, 19, 25, 34–35, 41, 51–52, 62–66, 72–76, 78–87, 90, 92, 104–106, 108, 118–120, 124, 129, 131, 136–137, 141–142, 145, 148–150, 152–154, 161, 163
Masculinity, male, male 10, 47, 58, 62–63
Masoni, L. 49, 93
McBain, Ed 83, 93
McDowell, M. 150
Medium 8, 19, 22, 24, 27, 32, 36, 44–46, 99, 102, 104, 134, 168
Megas, G. A. 47, 93
Melusine 87
Mercatante, A. S. 88, 93
Mertens, W. 6, 9, 13, 15, 31, 40–41, 43, 51, 91, 93, 143
Metamorphoses 49, 74, 171
Meuser, M. 8, 13
Miller, H. 155
Minghella, A. 17, 31
Mintz, T. 53, 93, 107, 110
Mitchum, R. 163
Mitscherlich, A. & M. 144
Miyazaki, H. 171
Monaco, J. 31, 41
Monster (see also Bête) 10, 49, 53, 57, 76–78, 84–85, 89, 94, 108,

113, 129–133, 136, 146–148, 155, 165
Morgenthaler, F. 140, 144
Morin, E. 169, 172
Mother 4, 6, 18, 20–22, 30, 32, 35, 50–51, 56, 66, 74, 88, 100, 102, 107, 118, 123, 133, 135–136, 138–140, 163–164, 170
Motif 5, 7, 9–10, 23, 43, 46–55, 58, 62, 66–68, 75, 78, 82, 84–90, 148
Mulvey, L. 3–4, 13, 35, 41, 105, 110
Murnau, F. W. 150, 163, 169
Music 31, 38, 45, 86, 108, 112, 120
MUSIC BOX (USA 1989) 141
Myth 52, 58–59, 70, 72, 74, 78, 89, 144

Narcissism 36, 78, 103, 135–136, 138–139
Narrative 13, 17, 20, 22–24, 32–39, 41, 46–47, 49, 52–53, 58, 64, 73–74, 76–78, 87, 102, 108, 110–114, 117, 133, 136, 145, 154, 164
Neumann, E. 14, 42, 47, 92–93
Nineteenth Century 57–58, 60, 82, 87
Nolde, E. 58
Nolte, N. 153
NOSFERATU (D 1922) 83, 150, 163, 169
Noziere, F. 93

Object (inner) 23, 36, 99–100, 103, 116, 119, 122, 129, 134–136, 139–140
Object (of gaze) 3–5, 105, 113, 142
Object (of interpretation) 115, 117
Object (of love) 107–108, 121–122, 136–137, 139–141
Object (partial) 63, 66, 99–100, 102, 119
Object (philosophy) 33, 114, 167, 171
Object (primary) 133, 135–136, 139–140, 142
Oedipus 18, 22, 36, 40, 59, 72, 99–100, 107–108, 118–119, 121, 124, 133, 135
Oedipus Rex 81
Oltmann, K. 170, 172
ORPHÉE (F 1950) 89
Otis-Cour, L. 7, 13
Ovid 74, 93, 171

Pagel, J. F. 21, 41
Parély, M. 79, 81, 90
Pathography 44
Peck, G. 3
PEEPING TOM (GB 1960) 4
Perrault, Ch. 51–52, 62, 88, 93, 169
Pflaum, H. G. 170
Picasso, P. 58
Piegler, T. 16, 41
Plot 23, 26, 28, 50, 55–58, 63, 68, 72, 75, 78, 86–87, 109, 112, 145, 163, 165
Poet, poetry 5, 46, 78–80, 94, 103, 132, 134
Popkin, M. 80, 94
Postmodernism 25, 38
Pouchain, P. 80–81, 94
Powell, M. 4
Primal scene 23–24, 29, 36, 40, 69
Primary process 30
Prince 84, 104, 106, 108, 120–122, 136, 142, 165–166, 171
Proust, M. 80, 94
Psyche 7, 15, 40–41, 48–50, 52, 59, 64, 66, 68, 72, 88–89, 92–93, 95, 143–144
PSYCHO (USA 1960) 16, 136
Psychoanalysis 1, 15–16, 33, 40, 90, 142, 144
Psychoanalyst 27, 33, 43–44, 82, 114, 139–141
Psychoanalytic *see* Psychoanalysis
Psychoanalytic situation 33, 38

Radiguet, R. 80
Raphael 59
Rauschenbach, B. 25, 42
Ray, N. 31
Rear Window (USA 1954) 23
Rebel Without a Cause (USA 1955) 31
Reception theory 9, 21, 33–35, 38–39, 44, 51, 79, 82–83, 86, 145, 161, 163
Reductionism 31, 37
Reed, G. S. 141, 144
Re-enactment 20, 22
Regression 18–19
Reiche, R. 22, 42–44, 82, 94, 111, 113–115, 117, 123, 125
Reinhardt, U. 50, 58, 94
Renaissance 7, 59
Resnais, A. 15, 29, 31
Riou, Y. 80–81, 94
Riquet à la Houppe 51, 62
Rococo 68, 72, 77
Roehler, O. 163
Rogers, D. 169, 172
Rohde-Dachser, Ch. viii, 18, 42
Rosa, H. 26, 42
Rose 10, 50, 52–53, 57, 67, 74, 93, 99, 102–103, 107, 109–110, 113, 135
Rost, A. 10, 88, 107, 130–131, 145, 170, 172
Rousseau, H. 58
Ryder, W. 85, 151

Sabbadini, A. 10, 16, 42, 53, 88, 99, 101
Sacrifice, sacrificial vow 47–48, 52, 54, 67, 149–150
Sadistic 4, 23, 138, 143
Sarandon, S. 83
Scarfone, D. 141, 144
Scene 18, 20, 24, 29–30, 32, 34–35, 38, 65–69, 82, 85, 107, 111–112, 117, 119, 136
Schlosshauer, H. 145, 171
Schmale, W. 7–8, 14
Schneider, G. 16, 41, 43, 94
Schnurrbein, S. von 6, 14
Schnyder, A. 48, 94
Schoedsack, E. B. 149
Scholz, S. 8, 13
Schön, E. 5, 14
School 32, 132, 155–156, 170
Schrader, P. 150
Schreyer, K. 170
Schulz, A. 87, 94
Schulze, G. 26, 42
Schwanitz, D. 6, 14
Scorsese, M. 153, 157–158, 161, 163
Self 5, 7–9, 19, 25, 29–30, 33–34, 37–38, 78–82, 86, 106, 108, 132, 135–137, 139–140, 142, 155, 169
Self-analysis 33
Self-psychology 25
Sexuality 6, 10, 35, 45, 49, 51–52, 56–57, 63, 65, 68–70, 76–77, 82, 84, 88, 100, 104–108, 117–124, 137, 142, 150–153, 155, 157, 161–164, 169–171
Seydoux, L. 164, 166–167
Shakespeare, W. 105
Shojaei Kawan, C. 60, 94
Significance 17–18, 23, 28, 34–37, 53, 86, 114, 151, 170
Sisters 49–51, 53, 55, 57, 63–64, 67–68, 72, 75, 77, 79, 81, 103–106, 109, 113, 118, 122, 135, 164
Sklar, R. 82, 92
Skye, L. 83
Smoke 45, 69, 72, 88, 100, 108, 111, 118–121, 123
Socialisation 15, 51, 84
Sound 10, 31, 38, 46, 75, 165
Space 30–31

Spectatorship 9, 105
Spielberg, S. 85
Spitz, R. 22
Stein, G. 103, 110
Stern, D. 139, 144
Stoker, B. 150, 163, 169, 172
Straparola, G. F. 7, 14, 51–52, 94
Stravinsky, I. 80
Studlar, G. 82, 94
Surrealism 80, 131–132, 141
Suspense 23, 76, 112
Swahn, J. O. 49, 94
Swiderski, R. M. 89, 94
Symbol 15, 18, 24, 31–32, 38, 47, 51, 53, 62–63, 87–88, 103, 133, 135–136, 142, 150, 169, 171
Szabó, I. 141
Szczepaniak, M. 8, 14

Tarkowski, A. 15, 40
Taylor, J. 12, 83
TÊTES (F 1947) 89
THE 400 BLOWS (F 1959) 26
THE DOOR (H 2012) 141
THE ENGLISH PATIENT (USA, UK 1996) 17, 31
The Girl without Hands 48
THE HUNCHBACK OF NOTRE DAME (USA 1939) 62, 93
THE PIANO (AU, NZ, F 1993) 18, 24, 28, 31–32, 35
THE ROCK (USA 1996) 158
THE SILENCE OF THE LAMBS (USA 1991) 17
THE WIZARD OF OZ (USA 1939) 108, 164–165
Thomas, J. L. 14, 24–25, 29, 107, 169
Thompson, K. 87, 94, 163, 170, 172
Tourneur, J. 150
Transference 17, 22–23, 25, 34–35, 90, 115, 123, 140
TRANSFORMERS (USA 2007–2014) 158
Trauma 24, 29, 132, 136, 138–142
Treut, M. 170
Triangulation 29, 36, 72, 79, 107, 113
Truffaut, F. 26
Turner, V. 6, 14
Twentieth Century 6, 9, 16, 19, 58, 62
Twitchell, J. 157, 170, 172

Ugliness, ugly 52, 55, 62, 67, 69, 104, 108, 130, 135, 145, 147, 161
Unconscious 18–24, 26–29, 33, 35, 37–38, 43, 51, 82, 109–110, 114–117, 123, 132–136, 140, 142, 144, 155, 157, 159
Undine 87
Unicorn 58, 88
Uther, H. -J. 47, 50, 87, 94

Vadim, R. 83
Valentino, R. 82, 94
VERTIGO (USA 1958) 30–31, 35–36, 40–41, 169
Vidor, K. 3
Viewer 18–20, 30–35, 38–39, 43–46, 67, 72, 74, 76, 90, 99, 102, 107, 112, 118, 130, 132–133, 136, 148, 165
Viewing experience 4, 21, 32, 34, 37, 39, 111
Virgin 47–49, 53, 74, 78, 105, 149
Virtue 57, 99, 145–146, 164–165, 168
Voice-over 29, 46, 107
Von Hoff, D. 95
Vow 47–48, 50, 66

Wagner, R. 31, 108
Warner, M. 108–110
Warren, S. 83
Wedekind, F. 44, 92
Wieland, C. 107, 110, 137, 144

Wild at Heart (USA 1990) 161–163, 170
Williams, J. S. 80–81, 91, 95
Winnicott, D. W. 119, 123, 125, 132, 144
Wohlrab, S. 16, 42
Woman 3–10, 19, 35, 60, 77, 102, 104–106, 118, 131, 137, 139, 149, 151, 161, 163–164
Wrye, H. 16, 40
Wu, J. 137, 144

Zeul, M. 15–16, 24–25, 35, 41–42
Zinnemann, F. 31
Zipes, J. 84, 95
Zoom 30, 153
Zwiebel, R. 16, 41–42, 92, 94, 124, 144